IERI Monograph Series

Issues and Methodologies in Large-Scale Assessments

VOLUME 3

IERI

October 2010

A joint publication between the International Association for the Evaluation of Educational Achievement (IEA) and Educational Testing Service (ETS)

ISBN 978-886854096-8

Copies of this publication can be obtained from:

IERInstitute
IEA Data Processing and Research Center
Mexikoring 37
22297 Hamburg,
Germany

IERInstitute
Educational Testing Service
Mail Stop 02-R
Princeton, NJ 08541,
United States

By email: ierinstitute@iea-dpc.de
Free downloads: www.ierinstitute.org

Copyeditors: Paula Wagemaker, Editorial Services, Christchurch, New Zealand with David Robitaille, and Jeff Johnson
Design and production by Becky Bliss Design and Production, Wellington, New Zealand

IERI Monograph Series

Issues and Methodologies in Large-Scale Assessments

Volume 3	2010

TABLE OF CONTENTS

Introduction

Dirk Hastedt (Editor)
IEA Data Processing and Research Center

Matthias von Davier (Editor)
Educational Testing Service

We are pleased to present Volume 3 of the *IERI Monograph Series*.

In 2007, the International Association for the Evaluation of Educational Achievement (IEA) and Educational Testing Service (ETS) decided, as part of efforts directed at improving the science of large-scale assessments of educational achievement, to establish the IEA-ETS Research Institute (IERI). IERI undertakes activities focused on three broad areas of work: research studies related to the development and implementation of large-scale assessments, professional development and training, and dissemination of research findings and information gathered through large-scale assessments. Since IERI's establishment, many activities have taken place in pursuit of the institute's mission.

One such activity is the institute's biannual training academies, which typically see 20 to 25 researchers from around the world attending each session. These academies provide researchers with training on the use of international large-scale assessment databases, and on more advanced statistical techniques for analyzing these data. To date, a total of six academies have been held. By the time this volume is distributed, the seventh academy will have taken place.

This third volume of the series "Issues and Methodologies in Large-Scale Assessments" presents a range of research undertaken using large-scale assessment data. Some of the papers address substantive questions of concern to educational policymakers and other stakeholders; other papers address methodological and design issues of large-scale survey assessments.

In the first paper, Nicole Bellin, Oscar Dunge, and Catherine Gunzenhauser, drawing on IEA Progress in International Reading Literacy Study (PIRLS) data from Germany, use a multi-level approach to evaluate differences in student achievement among classes taught with different organizational approaches.

The second research paper, written by Sandip Sinharay, Zhumei Guo, Matthias von Davier, and Bernard P. Veldkamp, is more technical in orientation. Using U.S. National Assessment of Educational Progress (NAEP) data, the authors present an innovative approach to evaluate the fit of latent regression models. The authors assert that this new approach will improve the quality of analytical procedures in large-scale assessments.

The third paper, by Sonia Ilie and Petra Lietz, investigates the Heyneman-Loxley effect. This effect—or, perhaps more appropriately, conjecture—states that school quality has a greater impact on student achievement in countries that are less developed economically than in more economically developed countries. This effect was originally observed in 1982 and is also evident in analyses of the IEA Trends in International Mathematics and Science Study (TIMSS) 2003 data. Interestingly, this effect seems to have vanished in the last 20 years—at least for the data that have been examined. Nevertheless, the Heyneman-Loxley effect appears to interest policymakers today as much as it interested their counterparts more than two decades ago. As an example, several research papers presented at this year's meeting of the American Educational Research Association (AERA) in Denver, Colorado, addressed this topic.

The fourth paper, by Jiahe Qian, again uses U.S. NAEP data, but aims this time to improve the measurement of trends in large-scale assessments. The author applies a mapping technique, originally designed for comparing performance standards from state assessments of public school students, to detect score inflation in certain districts over time.

In the fifth paper, Éva D. Molnár and László Székely use IEA PIRLS data for Hungarian-speaking children from three countries. This paper is a more content-oriented one. The authors analyze the relationship between reading literacy and learning motives and the factors determining motives for learning. They also compare learning motives and reading-literacy achievements across two data-collection time points.

The sixth paper, by Eugenio Gonzalez and Leslie Rutkowski, describes the logic of sparse booklet designs used in national and international large-scale assessments. The authors discuss past applications of matrix designs in educational measurement, outline the rationale for the formal design principles used, and, through examples, show how this important feature of all major educational survey assessments links to the goals of these studies.

The seventh and last paper, written by Enis Dogan and Ruhan Circi, presents an interesting new concept for evaluating invalid moderator effects that can be introduced in national versions of international large-scale assessment instruments. The authors use the Turkish version of the TIMSS 1999 assessment instrument.

We hope this volume provides interesting material and inspiration for your own work using large-scale survey assessment data. Comments may be sent directly to contributing authors, or to IERI: ierinstitute@iea-dpc.de. Information on submitting papers can be found on the last two pages of this volume or online at http://www.ierinstitute.org.

About IEA

The International Association for the Evaluation of Educational Achievement (IEA) is an independent, non-profit, international cooperative of national research institutions and governmental research agencies. Through its comparative research and assessment projects, IEA aims to:

- Provide international benchmarks that can assist policymakers to identify the comparative strengths and weaknesses of their education systems;

- Provide high-quality data that will increase policymakers' understanding of key school-based and non-school-based factors that influence teaching and learning;

- Provide high-quality data that will serve as a resource for identifying areas of concern and action, and for preparing and evaluating educational reforms;

- Develop and improve the capacity of educational systems to engage in national strategies for educational monitoring and improvement; and

- Contribute to development of the worldwide community of researchers in educational evaluation.

Additional information about IEA is available at www.iea.nl and www.iea-dpc.de.

About ETS

ETS is a non-profit institution whose mission is to advance quality and equity in education by providing fair and valid assessments, research, and related services for all people worldwide. In serving individuals, educational institutions, and government agencies around the world, ETS customizes solutions to meet the need for teacher professional development products and services, classroom and end-of-course assessments, and research-based teaching and learning tools. Founded in 1947, ETS today develops, administers, and scores more than 24 million tests annually in more than 180 countries, at over 9,000 locations worldwide.

Additional information about ETS is available at www.ets.org.

The importance of class composition for reading achievement: Migration background, social composition, and instructional practices

An analysis of the German 2006 PIRLS data

Nicole Bellin
Freie Universität Berlin, Berlin, Germany

Oscar Dunge
Swedish National Agency for Education, Stockholm, Sweden

Catherine Gunzenhauser
Albert-Ludwigs-Universität Freiburg, Freiburg, Germany

In this article, we explore the effects of class composition and teachers' instructional practices on reading achievement in German primary schools. We used data from the German data set for PIRLS 2006 to consider effects of class composition in terms of social and linguistic characteristics. Our analysis also focused on process characteristics of instruction, notably whether teacher instruction, when modified to meet the needs of individual students, alleviated the effects of a disadvantageous class composition. Our particular aim with respect to this study was to examine the processes by which these effects may be transmitted. The results of our multilevel analyses indicated the importance of individual resources and also the effects of class composition variables in terms of language and educational resources on students' reading achievement. We found that the effect of the variety of organizational approaches a teacher was using did not relate to reading achievement and did not reduce the effects of a disadvantageous class composition. However, classes with this composition showed a higher variance in their students' achievement scores. Also, teachers in these classes were already using a variety of instructional methods to accommodate the heterogeneous achievement levels. Controlling for the variety of methods might not be a sufficient means of explaining the transmission processes of class composition: teacher and student interactions at the micro level might also be important factors.

INTRODUCTION

In Germany, in recent years, the generally poorer educational performance of students from immigrant families relative to students from nonimmigrant families has become an issue of increasing concern. This matter gained particular prominence with the release of the results of the Organisation for Economic Co-operation and Development's (OECD) first Programme for International Student Assessment (PISA) survey (see, for example, Baumert, Trautwein, & Artelt, 2003; Stanat & Christensen, 2006). This cross-national study of the educational achievement of 15-year-old students made obvious the particularly large performance differences in Germany between immigrant students and nonimmigrant students (Stanat & Christensen, 2006, p. 6). Different achievement patterns between students from these two groupings have also been evident for some time at the elementary level of the German schooling system (Bos, Lankes, & Prenzel, 2004). The iterations of the Progress in International Reading Literacy Study (PIRLS), which is conducted by the International Association for the Evaluation of Educational Achievement (IEA) and surveys children in the fourth grade (nine-year-olds), present a similar picture. In short, studies of educational achievement over the last decade suggest that the German education system has not been able to meet the demands of its changing student population.

Efforts to explain the processes governing the structural integration of immigrants and the educational success of students from immigrant families in Germany focus on different factors (Esser, 2006; Kalter, 2008). Family and individual resources, such as social capital and competence in the German language, play an important role in educational achievement. School and classroom-based characteristics, such as the selectivity of the German education system,[1] also account for inequality in educational attainment (for an overview, see Stanat, 2006; also Esser, 2006).[2]

Among the weaker factors that are associated with ethnic inequality is the social composition of the school or the class a student attends. Research on the effects of class or school composition on achievement and on how these effects are transmitted is still scarce. However, the evidence that is available indicates that class or school composition characteristics do not directly influence achievement but are mediated by peer-based influences or instructional characteristics (Dreeben & Barr, 1988; Hattie, 2002; Wilkinson, 2002). Analyzing the composition of the student body is useful not only because it allows us to add to this body of literature but also, and more importantly, because it gives us a broader perspective on the social conditions and contexts within which educational processes take place, or, to express this statement another way, on the *mechanics* of educational inequality.

---

1   Unlike other European countries, German students leave primary school at the age of 10 and are tracked into different types of secondary school. This tracked system tends to be highly socially selective. The track that a child enters after primary school determines in large part his or her future educational career.

2   For an account of the German education system, see Baumert, Stanat, and Watermann (2006) and Ditton and Krüsken (2006).

The German PIRLS data provided an opportunity to examine the reading achievement of students with immigrant backgrounds in relation to the composition characteristics of the student body and instructional process variables. Our focus was on the elementary level because it is here that achievement differences have a far-reaching impact on decisions regarding German students' subsequent educational trajectories and long-term educational success (Becker & Lauterbach, 2004). More specifically, we address the issue of class composition in relation to instructional processes that aim to mediate heterogeneity and thereby reduce achievement gaps between students from different social and ethnic backgrounds. Using a theoretical framework, we begin by describing how differences in achievement between immigrant and nonimmigrant students emerge and how composition effects exert an influence. We then, in the empirical part of our examination, include, in a multilevel model analysis, the variables that researchers conducting analysis of composition effects considered and then reported with respect to the German PIRLS 2006 data. We end the article with a discussion of our main findings.

ACHIEVEMENT DIFFERENCES IN THE ELEMENTARY SCHOOL SECTOR: THEORETICAL APPROACHES AND EMPIRICAL EVIDENCE

Differences in educational attainment can be attributed to the primary effects of family background characteristics as well as to the secondary effects arising out of the decisions that families make when selecting educational opportunities for their children. These decisions are based on the expected costs and benefits of those opportunities and the likelihood of achieving a chosen goal (Becker & Lauterbach, 2004; Boudon, 1974; Erikson & Jonsson, 1996). Because students from immigrant families tend to have less social and economic capital than students from nonimmigrant families, primary effects tend to be more pronounced. For example, the members of immigrant families in Germany are nine times more likely than the members of non-immigrant families to have received no formal education and they are more than twice as likely to be on welfare support (Statistisches Bundesamt, 2009, p. 29). Also, these families may not be able to use the social and educational capital that they acquired in their countries of origin because of language difficulties, non-acceptance of qualifications, or poor knowledge of education systems in general or the German education system in particular (Diefenbach, 2007, p. 101).

Another important factor governing educational integration, and therefore educational attainment, that has gained increasing attention in the educational literature in recent years is immigrants' knowledge of their new country. The extent of this knowledge depends on opportunities that these people have both before and after immigration to acquire that knowledge. For example, children of immigrant families will likely be impeded from acquiring the language of the immigrant country if they live in a situation where the language of that country is seldom spoken or not spoken at all (Esser, 2006, p. 9).

Whether from immigrant or nonimmigrant families, students with few economic and social resources are disadvantaged from the time they enter elementary school. Any conceptual model of how school processes affect the achievement of students thus needs to consider the clusters of variables associated with different aspects of the education system. The various recent and current theoretical models that aim to explain differences in student learning tend to consider variables associated with either one or more perspectives or "levels" of the education system.

Models of educational effectiveness based on Carroll's (1963) model of time on task consider student learning in terms of student-related variables. These models position learning effectiveness as a function of aptitude, ability to understand instruction, perseverance, opportunity, and the quality of instruction (see, for example, Creemers, Scheerens, & Reynolds, 2000, p. 283).

Creemers (1994), in his model, distinguishes basic student-related variables as well as variables associated with the classroom and with the school. Among the variables at the classroom level that contribute to educational effectiveness are the types of learning resources (books, computers) available, the way the teacher delivers learning content and manages the learning environment (e.g., clear goal setting, provision of homework), and the procedures and practices the teacher uses to group students so that they receive instruction commensurate with their learning needs and abilities. Variables at the school level include the number of daily hours of instruction and the overall quality of teaching across the school (Creemers, 1994, p. 98).

School-level variables also include those that are context specific. Consideration of these variables began appearing in the literature in the 1980s. The variable that gained the most initial attention was the socioeconomic composition of the student body (for an overview, see Teddlie, Stringfield, & Reynolds, 2000, p. 161). Consideration of the ethnic, social, and abilities composition of the school—and individual classes within a school—followed (see, for example, Portes & Hao, 2004; Portes & MacLeod, 1996).

Researchers are also now paying attention to how these various composition characteristics are mediated by the social interaction between students and their teachers. In their conceptual model of influences on student learning achievement and academic self-concept, Baumert et al. (2006, p. 126) identified five composition characteristics—social, cultural, ability, "at-risk" factors (relating to family situation and school-career choice), and the context-specific effects of different curricula—along with four presumed mediation processes. These mediation processes are the normative culture of the student's parents, the normative culture of students, social comparison processes at the student level (i.e., abilities, attitudes, and achievement of peers), and how instruction is organized and delivered.

The processes by which composition effects are transmitted can be categorized under sociological and psychological explanations and according to approaches that focus primarily on instructional processes (Dar & Resh, 1994; Dreeben & Barr, 1988; Hallinan, 1988; Marsh & Hattie, 1996; Pallas, Entwisle, Alexander, & Slutka, 1994). A focus on instructional processes assumes that the composition of the class, or even the perception that the teacher has of the composition of the class, affects instruction-based characteristics such as pace and level of instruction and teacher expectations (Dreeben & Barr, 1988; Oakes, 2005).

As we noted at the beginning of this article, empirical evidence suggests that, especially in the case of Germany, students from immigrant families fare worse educationally than children from nonimmigrant families (Baumert et al., 2003; Bos, Schwippert, & Stubbe, 2007). Although much of this difference in achievement can be explained by considering the socioeconomic resources of the two groups, a significant difference in achievement remains. This gap appears to be a product of specific effects connected to the specific migration context, for example, language use (Heath & Brinbaum, 2007). Research shows that language used at home and proficiency in the language used at school are important factors explaining the achievement difference (e.g., Alba, Handl, & Müller, 1994; Esser, 2006). However, during the last few years, educational researchers have also taken into greater account composition characteristics, positioning them as distal factors that may influence achievement.

Composition Characteristics

Does the school a child attends influence his or her educational achievement? Without necessarily having any scientific evidence to support their viewpoint, parents tend to think that it indeed matters who is teaching the child and with whom he or she is learning. Even in Germany, where public schools have long been the natural choice for everyone, the enrollment numbers in private schools increased by approximately 21% in the first eight years of this century (Statistisches Bundesamt, 2008). The demographic composition of the student body of a school or a class purported to influence achievement differences is known as the "compositional" effect: "Such an effect is often reported when a school-level aggregate of an individual variable makes an independent contribution to the explanation of outcome variance" (Harker & Tymms, 2004, p. 177). This premise implies that any two students who have similar reading scores but are from different schools or classes will differ in their predicted scores because of the composition characteristics of the school or class they attend.[3]

The influence of composition variables on achievement was signaled as early as the 1960s by Coleman (1966). His results showed that composition characteristics in terms of the social structure of a school seemed to be more important than the school's resources or the quality of teaching (1966). Since then, several studies have verified the influences of school and class composition on achievement (e.g., Ammermüller & Pischke, 2006; Opdenakker & Van Damme, 2001; Rumberger & Palardy, 2005). Thus, in addition to variables associated with individual characteristics and family background resources, achievement can be influenced by the mix of social

---

3 In addition to composition effects, there can also be context effects. The term contextual effect is mainly used to describe effects that include differences between school systems (private or public), class size, or grade levels (Teddlie et al., 2000, p. 162). This article is concerned with the effects of student composition as a function of the aggregated individual variable at the school or the class level.

backgrounds represented in the class or the school (e.g., socioeconomic status, percentage of non-native speakers) or students' abilities (e.g., Burns & Mason, 2002; Caldas & Bankston, 1998; Harker & Tymms, 2004).

Through use of a multilevel model, Walter (2008) examined the assumed negative effect of the ethnic composition of the class on students' mathematics, science, and reading achievement with the aim of determining whether this effect was transmitted by the ethno-lingual diversity of the class. After controlling for the different school types in the secondary school system in Germany, Walter found that the social composition of the class had a significant effect on reading achievement only. However, mathematics achievement was significantly affected by the percentage of immigrant students in the class. Compared to classes where less than 5% of the students were from immigrant backgrounds, classes with more than 70% of such students were achieving one year below the normative standard in mathematics. Walter could not trace this effect back to difficulties associated with German as the language of instruction because he found that the language students used at home had no effect on achievement (p. 178). The PISA data for Germany confirmed this pattern, albeit in relation to reading achievement. The data showed that the reading achievement of students in schools with more than 40% of students of Turkish descent was significantly lower than the reading achievement of students in schools where only 5% of the children were from Turkish families. Again, the composition variable of language use at home had no significant effect on achievement (Walter & Stanat, 2008, p. 94).

Composition effects are also discernible in elementary schools in both Germany and internationally (e.g., Cortina, Carlisle, & Zeng, 2008; Rüesch, 1998; Sharp & Croxford, 2003), although the body of evidence is not as large as that for the secondary sector. Cortina et al. (2008), for example, analyzed students' progress from Year 1 to Year 3 in the Michigan Reading First program. They found that the reading gain for students from schools with a high percentage of students deemed economically disadvantaged was 10% lower than the gain for students in schools with a relatively low percentage of economically disadvantaged students. School composition thus had an effect on students' reading achievement additional to the individual effect of few economic resources. Also, but to a lesser extent, learning progress was slower in schools with a high percentage of minority students than it was in schools with a low percentage (Cortina et al., 2008, p. 60). The authors acknowledged not only a lack of data on whether at-risk students receive instruction in reading that is appropriate for their needs (e.g., adaptive teaching methods) but also a need for a closer examination of instructional practices (p. 63).

In Germany, Kristen (2008) used data from the German national extension of PIRLS called *Internationale Grundschul-Lese-Untersuchung* or IGLU-E, which covered reading achievement and mathematics and science, to examine different characteristics assumed to influence ethnic-based inequalities in educational achievement. Kristen's focus was on immigrant students of Turkish descent. Her results showed that, at the level of the individual, students' reading achievement scores depended on whether one or both parents were born in Germany and on the social and cultural resources of the families. Furthermore, if spoken at home, German language had a positive effect on scores. Parental place of birth, social and cultural resources, and German language spoken at home also influenced mathematics achievement. However, Kristen found that the different social and language resources of the students' families did not fully explain the achievement deficit for the Turkish students. At the class level, the mean ability composition of the class influenced reading and mathematical achievement, but did not reduce the negative effects on reading achievement for students from Turkish immigrant families. The language composition of the class did not exert an influence (p. 246). Kristen's findings correspond with those from Walter (2008) and Walter and Stanat (2008).

Overall, research on composition effects is ambiguous in that it is not clear which composition effects influence achievement. Many of the researchers who have published studies associated with this issue do not consider all relevant composition characteristics and do not make clear whether certain composition characteristics are greater for some students than for others (Rumberger & Palardy, 2005, p. 2006). Also, uncertainty remains as to how composition effects on achievement are transmitted. The assumption is that, at the least, they exercise an indirect effect. The literature proposes three possible types of mediation (e.g., Dar & Resh, 1994; Dreeben & Barr, 1988). Explanations focused on the process characteristics of teaching assume a better or worse learning climate and motivated or unmotivated teachers. Sociological approaches consider peer effects as an important factor with respect to generating a positive or a negative learning climate. Psychological explanations argue that teachers may have unreasonably low or high expectations of student achievement in classes with a particular (e.g., homogeneous or heterogeneous) student population. Hanushek, Kain, Markman, & Rivkin (2003), for example, conclude from their consideration of peer influence that

> In general there has been limited attention given to the mechanisms through which peers affect outcomes. The most common perspective is that peers, like families, are sources of motivation, aspiration and direct interactions in learning. Moreover, peers may affect the classroom process—aiding learning[,] ... contributing to the pace of instruction, or hindering learning through disruptive behaviour. (p. 529)

One possible reason for this lack of clarity is the complexity of composition effects and their interactions with so-called school process variables (e.g., class climate or teacher expectancies). This complexity is evident in work done by Opdenakker and Van Damme (2001). They studied the effects on students' mathematics achievement of mean socioeconomic status and mean cognitive capacities, heterogeneity of intellectual capacities, gender composition, and percentage of students using the language spoken at school and at home, as well as the relationships of these variables to several process variables (among them, co-operation between teachers and differences between students). Rumberger and Palardy (2005) grouped schools into three categories based on the prosperity of enrolled students. Having found that these socioeconomic differences influenced student achievement, they went on to explain this effect statistically by considering diverse variables, such as amount of homework and students' perceptions of safety at school.

With respect to the above review, what can be said in summary is that a variety of factors pertaining to the individual, the class, the school, and context (e.g., neighborhood characteristics) influence learning achievement (Helmke et al., 2007, p. 18). For students from immigrant families, educational inequalities also derive not only from the likelihood that these students have fewer economic, social, and cultural resources than students from nonimmigrant backgrounds but also from a disadvantageous composition of the class caused by the composition of the school district. For the individual student, parents' level of educational attainment and their occupation as well as whether the language used at home accords with the language of instruction at school also influence achievement.

At the class level, researchers have examined a variety of composition effects. In the German elementary system, these include the social, ethnic, and linguistic composition of the class. It seems that, here, linguistic composition does not have an effect on achievement and that composition effects do not seem to be transmitted by the opportunities available to use the German language. Overall, though, there is little research on just how these and other composition effects are transmitted. Nonetheless, we can assume that teachers adapt their instruction according to their perception of the ability composition of the class. For example, in classes with a high percentage of at-risk students, teachers may barely use differentiation or adaptive instruction, such as grouping procedures to offer different content, because of the assumed homogeneity of the class. Based on the results of a comprehensive meta-analysis, Hattie (2003) concluded that about 30% of students' achievement variance can be traced back to teacher characteristics. Consideration of instructional variables as well as of composition characteristics therefore seems important.

Although a class may show homogeneity in terms of its social composition, students will still differ in their individual learning capacities. Data for Germany from the 2001 and 2006 iterations of PIRLS (Bos et al., 2004, 2008) showed that instruction in a classroom is, most of the time, teacher oriented and does not take into account the heterogeneity of knowledge held by the individual students in that class. The approaches that teachers do use to meet perceived different achievement levels in class typically involve differentiating learning content and adapting the organizational setting of the classroom: "Adaptive teaching is teaching that arranges environmental conditions to fit learners' individual differences" (Corno & Snow, 1986, p. 621). Any analysis of composition effects should thus also consider the various organizational approaches that teachers use to differentiate their instruction according to student need. It seems reasonable to assume that instruction that is learner oriented is more likely to enhance student learning than instruction that does not take this focus.

STUDY OBJECTIVE AND APPROACH

Our focus when conducting this study rested on a conceptual framework of schooling based on a model of educational effectiveness (Creemers, 1994) and a mediation model of composition characteristics (Baumert et al., 2006). The conceptual model therefore accounted for the input (e.g., student resources), the output (e.g., student achievement in reading), and the various other aspects of the educational process (e.g., teacher characteristics) underpinning the theoretical model of PIRLS (Hornberg, Bos, Buddeberg, Potthoff, & Stubbe, 2007a, p. 22). In an attempt to explain differences in reading achievement between immigrant students and nonimmigrant students, we concentrated our analysis on those aspects of educational inequality that lie beyond the individual level (i.e., composition effects). We also considered the quality of the teacher's instruction within the class. Our aim, in this regard, was to determine whether differentiated learning environments (grouping procedures) may reduce achievement differences.

Although it is obvious that classroom processes rely on complex interactions among many influences—all of which have to be considered—we concentrated on those aspects shown to be relevant in explaining ethnic differences in achievement. We concentrated at the individual level on characteristics of immigration background. One such characteristic is the country in which students' parents were born (research often conceptualizes immigration background in terms of this variable). We also considered the language used at home. To control for the variable of socioeconomic status, we used the variable home educational resources.

At the class level, we considered the influence of class composition in terms of linguistic background, educational resources, and mean reading achievement on the reading accomplishment of 10-year-old students in Grade 4 of the German elementary school system. We also considered, as a process characteristic, a variety of organizational approaches used by teachers.

Our specific research questions were as follows:

1. What proportion of the variance in student reading achievement can be attributed to (i) individual student background characteristics and (ii) the class level?

2. To what extent do specified class composition characteristics influence students' reading achievement?

3. To what extent do teacher instructional characteristics on their own influence students' reading achievement and to what extent do these characteristics have an effect on reducing achievement differences at the level of the individual and at the level of the class?

METHOD

Data and Variables

The reading achievement data that we used for this study came from the German PIRLS 2006 data. The PIRLS iterations use a two-stage process to select participating students. During the first stage, schools are sampled with probability proportional to size. During the second, one or two intact classes of students are sampled. Systematic random sampling is used to select the classes; all classes have an equal probability of being selected (Joncas, 2007). In Germany, during PIRLS 2006, one class per school was sampled, and all students within a sampled class participated (Martin, Mullis, & Kennedy, 2007, p. 241). Of the 8,032 students who were supposed to complete the reading test, 7,899 did so (Hornberg et al., 2007a, p. 39). To account for this cluster design, data analyses were conducted with the appropriate weights (house weight) and multilevel models were used to estimate the coefficients (Bryk & Raudenbush, 1992).

For our analysis, we drew from the German PIRLS 2006 data bank the reading achievement data of 5,464 (in 364 classes) of the participating students. We did not consider data from all 7,899 students who participated because we wanted to include only those students for whom data on all relevant variables were available.[4]

The reading test booklets used in PIRLS 2006 consisted of a literary text and an informational text. Each student received two texts, each with 25 test items (Bos, Valtin, Voss, Hornberg, & Lankes, 2007, p. 86). The tasks that students were asked to complete in relation to these texts tested their understanding and ability to reproduce content as well as comprehension tasks. The reading achievement scores represented five imputed plausible values. The reading achievement scale had 500 as the average and a standard deviation of 100 (Foy & Kennedy, 2008a, p. 5). For our analysis, we considered the overall reading score for the sample of students, and we considered all five plausible values during the estimation process.

In regard to the individual, we also considered *gender* in our model because previous research shows that boys are over-represented on the lower levels of reading competency (Hornberg, Valtin, Potthoff, Schwippert, & Schulz-Zander, 2007b, p. 207). Gender is a dichotomous variable and so has the value of 0 for girls and 1 for boys. In the analysis, we used girls to represent the reference category.

In PIRLS, the immigration background of the students is operationalized by using the variable language used at home. Students participating in the 2006 survey were asked, "How often do you speak the test language at home?" and were directed to check one of the following answers: 1 = always, 2 = sometimes, and 3 = never. Because only 55 of the 5,464 students in our sample reported that they never spoke the test language at home, we recoded this variable as a dichotomous variable by combining the categories "sometimes" and "never." Thus, sometimes and never = 1 and always = 0, thereby representing the reference category.

---

4 Across the individual-level variables, the proportion of missing data ranged from 3% to 20%. At the class level, we had to exclude 40 classes from the analysis because of missing data on the variables for this level.

The country in which parents were born can also be considered an identifier of immigration background. The students participating in PIRLS were asked if their mother or father was born in Germany (1 = yes, 2 = no, 3 = I do not know).[5] The derived variable distinguishes among three categories: students whose parents were both born in Germany, students who had one parent who was born in Germany, and students whose parents were both born in another country. For the analysis, we coded this measure as a stepwise dichotomous variable so that students with both parents born in Germany represented the reference category.

Social and cultural resources are operationalized in PIRLS via the derived variable home educational resources.[6] This index variable consists of the following four items:

1. About how many books are there in your home? (0–10, 11–25, 26–100, 101–200, more than 200);

2. About how many children's books are there in your home? (0–10, 11–25, 26–50, 51–100, more than 100);

3. Do you have any of these things in your home? (computer, study desk/table for own use, books of your very own, daily newspaper);

4. Highest level of education of either parent? (finished university or higher, finished post-secondary education but not university, finished upper-secondary, finished lower-secondary, finished some primary or lower-secondary or did not go to school).

The index variable distinguishes three categories:

- 1 = *high*: student responded "101–200" or "more than 200" to (1) and "yes" to three or more of the variables of (3); parents responded "finished university or higher" to (4) and "26–50", "51–100", or "more than 100" to (2);

- 3 = *low*: student responded "0–10" or "11–25" to (1) and "yes" to two or fewer of the variables of (3); parents responded "finished some primary or lower-secondary or did not go to school" to (4) and "0–10" or "11–25" to (2);

- 2 = *medium*: all other response combinations (Foy & Kennedy, 2008a).

For our analysis, we recoded this variable as a stepwise dichotomous variable so that students with high home educational resources represented the reference group.

At the class level, we considered composition as well as instructional characteristics in the model. We accordingly derived the percentage of students in the class who did not speak the test language before school by aggregating the number of students in relation to the class size to represent the class composition in terms of migration (i.e., linguistic characteristics).

---

5 Three percent of the students did not know where their mother was born, and about four percent did not know where their father was born. Ten percent of the data were missing.

6 This variable was featured in the questionnaire that asked the participating students to answer questions about their home lives and living conditions.

To account for the social composition of the class, we also calculated the percentage of students with low home educational resources. As a process feature accounting for instruction that is responsive to the different learning conditions of the students, we used the variable *teachers use a variety of organizational approaches*. This derived variable consists of six items relating to the question, "When you have reading instruction and/or do reading activities, how often do you organize students in the following ways?" (1 = always; 2 = often, 3 = sometimes; 4 = never):

- I teach reading as a whole-class activity;
- I create same-ability groups;
- I create mixed-ability groups;
- I use individualized instruction for reading;
- Students work independently on an assigned plan or goal;
- Students work independently on a goal they choose themselves.

The derived variable has two values:1 = responded "often" or "always or almost always" to two or more of the options; 2 = responded "often" or "always or almost always" to one or none of the options (Foy & Kennedy, 2008b). We recoded this variable for the analysis into categories 2 = 0 and 1 = 1 so that teachers who used few differentiation techniques represented the reference category (= 0).

Hierarchical Data Structure

Students within schools and classes represent a hierarchical data structure because they are nested within their schools and classes. Students in the same classes tend to be similar in some aspects, due, for example, to selection processes. Therefore, the observations are not completely independent. Disregarding this fact leads to underestimation of the standard errors (Hox, 2002, p. 5). In PIRLS, hierarchical linear modeling (HLM) 6.2 (Raudenbush, Bryk, Cheong, & Congdon, 2004) is therefore used to conduct the data analysis. The Level 1 unit consists of the student variables, and the Level 2 unit represents the composition and instruction characteristics.

For our analysis, we estimated the relevant student variables for Level 1 and then included, as the next step, the corresponding class-level variable. A multilevel model such as this allows us to distinguish different types of group-level variables. The first group of variables (in our case, the use of different organizational approaches) can be measured directly. The second type is generated by aggregating variables from a lower level, that is, the student composition of the class (Stanat & Lüdtke, 2008, p. 326). This approach allowed us to interpret the coefficient of the class composition variable as the direct estimate of the composition effect on reading achievement above the effect of the individual characteristics.

Because of the reciprocal nature of composition effects (a student affects his or her peers and is affected by peers), it is very difficult to separate out causal impacts (Hanushek et al., 2003, p. 530). The most adequate form of analyzing composition effects requires a longitudinal data set (a fact that we considered when interpreting our results); a cross-sectional design does not allow postulation of causal relationships.

Analysis

Descriptive Information

We list the descriptive statistics of the individual-level variables in Tables 1 and 2. The average reading achievement of all students in the sample reached 547, with a minimum of 244 and a maximum of 740 (SD = 67.55). Just over 49% of the students were girls. With respect to migration background, 13% of the students had one parent who was not born in Germany; 15% of the students came from families where both parents were born in other countries. Accordingly, 28% of students never or only sometimes spoke the test language at home. Most of the students (84%) had medium educational home resources.

In nearly every class, a minority of students did not use the test language at home (M = 5.62, SD = 8.59). The class composition ranged from classes with all students speaking the test language at home to classes with 50% of students who did not speak the test language at home. In contrast, on average, one-fifth of the students in every class came from home backgrounds with few educational resources (M = 3.82, SD = 7.33). However, the sample included a broad range of class composition in this respect: there where classes in which 60% of the students came from homes with few educational resources, and there were classes in which no student was deprived in this respect. Teachers usually used a variety of organizational approaches (M = .33, SD = .47), ranging from one scale end (0) to the other (1).

When we analyzed reading achievement, home educational resources, and use of test language at home for the different groups of immigration background, we found that students with both parents born in Germany used the test language at home more often than students with neither parent was born in Germany, but this relationship was not a consistent one (see Table 2).

As a preliminary step, we analyzed the effects of relevant class-level variables on the mean reading achievement of students in every class. Here, we found a significant relationship between the percentage of students who did not speak the test language at home and the class mean reading achievement, thereby explaining 12% of the variance in mean class reading achievement (see Figure 1). As we expected, classes with a higher percentage of students who did not speak the test language at home had lower mean reading scores. However, there was a wide range in mean reading achievement among classes with a low percentage of students who did not speak the test language.

The class mean reading achievement and the percentage of students with few educational resources showed a strong relationship; this variable explained 28% of the variance (see Figure 2). Classes with a high percentage of students with few educational resources tended to have lower mean reading achievement scores. There were, however, some exceptions. Some classes in which most students had few educational resources scored reasonably high in reading, whereas some classes with a high percentage of well-resourced students showed relatively low mean reading achievement.

Table 1: Descriptive statistics

Individual level	
Reading achievement	
M	547.27
SD	67.55
Min	243.87
Max	739.68
Gender	
Boys	49.2%
Girls	50.8%
Migration background	
Both parents born in the country	72.0%
One parent born in the country	13.0%
Neither parent born in the country	15.0%
Language of instruction used at home	
Always	72.0%
Sometimes or never	28.0%
Home educational resources	
High	13.0%
Medium	84.0%
Low	3.0%
Class level	
Percentage of students not speaking test language at home	
M	5.62
SD	8.59
Min	0.00
Max	50.00
Percentage of students with few educational resources	
M	3.82
SD	7.33
Min	0.00
Max	60.00
Teacher uses variety of organizational approaches	
M	0.33
SD	0.47
Min	0.00
Max	1.00

In classes where the mean reading achievement was high, the variance of the achievement score was relatively small, and vice versa. Also, in classes where the percentage of students with low educational resources was high, the variance of the reading achievement increased. This finding implies that, especially in classes such as these, it is important that teachers use a variety of organizational approaches in order to accommodate the individual and different learning needs of their students.

Table 2: Descriptive information: language used at home and immigration background

	Both parents born in Germany	One parent born in Germany	Neither parent born in Germany
Reading achievement	564.67 (58.16)	542.25 (59.42)	515.84 (62.41)
Home educational resources			
High	15%	12%	3%
Medium	84%	86%	91%
Low	1%	2%	6%
Use of test language at home			
Always	87%	54%	18%
Sometimes or never	13%	46%	82%

Figure 1: Relationship between reading achievement and percentage of students who did not speak the test language at home

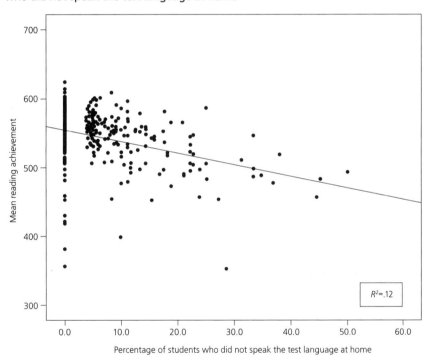

Percentage of students who did not speak the test language at home

Surprisingly, the mean reading achievement did not seem to be linked to teachers' use of a variety of organizational approaches to reading instruction (see Figure 3). However, classes with teachers who used more than two approaches showed a greater variety in mean reading achievement than classes with teachers who used fewer approaches. What this finding tells us is that teachers in classes with a higher variance in achievement scores tend to use more than two organizational approaches.

Figure 2: Relationship between mean reading achievement and percentage of students with low educational resources at home

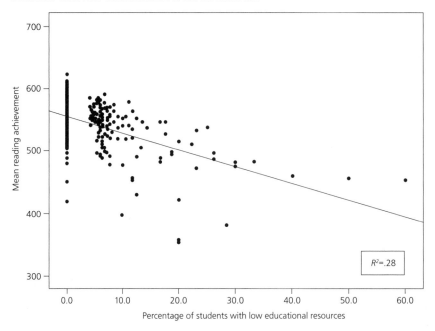

Figure 3: Boxplot of mean reading achievement and teachers' use of a variety of approaches to organize their classroom instruction

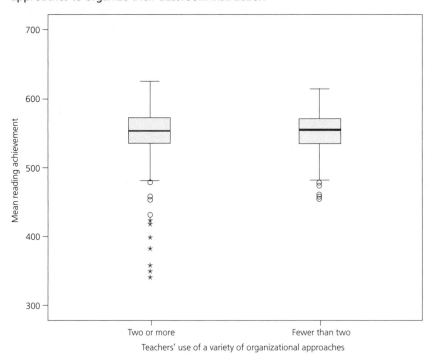

The Multivariate Analysis

Table 3 presents the findings of the multilevel analysis. Here, the baseline model represents the unconditional model. The following models include individual, composition, and process variables. In a multilevel model, the variance component of the two levels can be calculated by using the intra-class correlation, which gives an estimate of the proportion of variance that exists between the classes and can actually be explained by class-specific characteristics (Bryk & Raudenbush, 1992, p. 70). The inter-class correlation (ICC) for our data set was 21%, so the class that a student was attending apparently did make a difference. To put this another way, 21% of the variance was between the classes and could therefore be explained by class-level variables. This result is within the range of findings from other studies of student achievement (e.g., Ditton & Krüsken, 2006; Opdenakker, Van Damme, De Fraine, Van Landeghem, & Onghena, 2002; Westerbeek, 1999).

In the unconditional model, the mean reading achievement was 557.93 points. The second model, which accounted for the individual characteristics at Level 1, showed that boys did not score significantly lower than girls. With respect to the migration background, students whose parents were born in a country other than Germany achieved, on average, 28.28 score points fewer than students with parents who were both born in Germany. Students who had at least one parent born in Germany attained, on average, 15.86 score points fewer than students whose two parents were born in Germany. These findings represent a considerable achievement gap.

When we controlled for language spoken at home, we found an additional disadvantage for immigrant students. Students who never or sometimes spoke the test language at home had significantly lower scores on the reading test than students who always spoke the test language at home. Given that immigrants are twice as likely as nonimmigrants to be in a state of poverty (Beauftragte der Bundesregierung für Migration, Flüchtlinge und Integration, 2007), we can assume that these disadvantages in reading achievement for immigrant students in Germany can mainly be ascribed to the socioeconomic status of the family and, therefore, to the available resources that might be relevant to school learning. Students with medium and few home educational resources also scored significantly lower than students with high home educational resources. Students with low home educational resources especially showed (by more than 77 points) the highest disadvantage. Thus, socioeconomic status, migration background, and language spoken at home all had a significant influence on reading achievement.

After controlling for the individual variables, we introduced class-level variables to our (third) model in an attempt to explain the variance between the classes. In this third model, therefore, we considered the two composition variables. The proportion of students in a class who did not speak the test language showed a significant negative effect on reading achievement. The social composition of the class also exerted an effect on reading achievement. This variable was centered on its mean, which implies that in a class where 60% of the students have low educational resources, the reading

Table 3: Results of the HLM-Analysis

	Baseline model	Model with individual variables	Model with composition variables	Model with process variables
Reading achievement	557.93*** (2.55)	593.27*** (3.82)	591.52*** (3.79)	591.04*** (4.16)
Gender		-4.18 (2.47)	-4.20 (2.46)	-4.21 (2.46)
Language of test used at home (sometimes/never)		-9.50* (3.61)	-9.39* (3.95)	-9.39* (3.95)
One parent born in Germany		-15.86*** (3.95)	-15.40*** (3.99)	-15.42*** (4.00)
Neither parent born in Germany		-28.28*** (4.45)	-26.40*** (4.52)	-26.43*** (4.51)
Home educational resources (medium)		-26.74*** (3.70)	-27.06*** (3.59)	-27.06** (3.59)
Home educational resources (low)		-77.23*** (8.95)	-70.08*** (9.30)	-70.06*** (9.30)
Percentage of students who did not speak test language at home			-.56* (0.28)	-.56* (0.28)
Percentage of students with low educational resources at home			-1.41** (0.50)	-1.42** (0.51)
Teachers use a variety of organizational approaches (more than two)				1.55 (4.12)
Variance components				
Intercept	788.03***	541.94***	429.87***	432.48***
Level 1	2933.87	2674.13	2676.22	2675.76
R^2			.45	

achievement would be about 79 points lower than the average reading achievement in this calculated model. Both variables explained 45% of the variance of the intercept.

In our fourth and last model, we included the process characteristic denoting teachers' use of a variety of methods to organize their classroom teaching. As we observed earlier, a teacher who tends to use more than two methods (e.g., group work) offers students learning that is highly attuned to their individual learning needs and gives them access to different learning contents. This process characteristic showed a positive effect of about two points, but was non-significant. The linguistic composition of the class also had a non-significant effect.

SUMMARY AND DISCUSSION

The results show that most of the variance in this model was at the level of the individual. However, the proportion of variance that could be explained by class membership was 21%, indicating that the class a child ends up in does influence his or her learning achievement. We endeavored to explain this difference by using composition and process characteristics at the class level. Composition variables are many and varied. They can relate to the social composition of the class or school (e.g., socioeconomic status, percentage of immigrant students, percentage of girls) and to the cognitive or achievement composition of the class or school (e.g., mean reading achievement). In our analysis, we used the percentage of students who did not speak the instruction language and the percentage of students with low home educational resources to account for the social composition of the class.

At the level of the individual student, our analysis found that several variables had significant effects on student reading achievement. These included gender, language spoken at home, migration background, and home educational resources. The reading achievement of students was on the low side if they sometimes or never spoke the test language at home, had parents who were not born in Germany, and had only medium or low educational resources. Language spoken at home emerged as a significant predictor of reading difficulty for immigrant students.

These results indicate the existence of educational inequality for a large part of the German student population in elementary schools. They also support the findings of other research on educational inequality (e.g., Becker & Lauterbach, 2004; Diefenbach, 2003; Ditton & Krüsken, 2006; Kao & Thompson, 2003). The achievement differences that we found between students from immigrant backgrounds and students from nonimmigrant backgrounds correspond with results reported for German elementary school students by Kristen (2008, p. 241) that we cited earlier in this article. She found that students whose two parents were not born in Germany were the group of students most disadvantaged with respect to educational achievement. Kristen also showed that this disadvantage was especially pronounced for students of Turkish descent.

These educational inequalities were also evident, in our study, at the class level. In classes with a high percentage of students with low educational resources, students' reading achievement was significantly lower than the reading achievement of students in classes with a medium to high level of resourcing. The proportion of students in the class who did not speak the test language at home also had an effect on the reading achievement of the students in that class.

These results correspond in part with other analyses conducted relative to the German education system. We again refer to Kristen's work. Kristen (2008, p. 241) showed that, in German elementary schools, the percentage of students who spoke the instruction language at home did *not* exert an effect if the cognitive composition of the class was also taken into account. However, Kristen did not consider the social composition of the class with regard to socioeconomic resources. In his analysis of data on the reading achievement of students enrolled in Germany's secondary school system, Walter (2008, p. 177) found that cognitive composition had no effect if social composition and linguistic composition were also considered. The only significant composition effect that Walter found was social composition.

We can conclude from these findings that reading achievement depends on the social composition of the class, in particular the proportion of students in the class who have low educational resources. However, as is evident from our findings, the effect of composition variables such as this are often confounded, and we remain uncertain if other such variables are better (or not) predictors at the class level, such as mean reading achievement or student perception of school climate (e.g., how safe students feel at school).

Nonetheless, our findings suggest that educational inequality is a structural problem that affects the achievement of each student. Although we aimed, in this study, to gain a better understanding of the processes by which these composition effects may be transmitted, we were unable to offer new or additional explanation. And although we included in our analysis the process characteristic of teacher differentiation (i.e., teacher uses/does not use a variety of methods to meet the individual learning needs of students), we found no significant effect of a more learner-oriented teaching approach on reading achievement. Nor did this variable reduce composition effects: the effect of linguistic composition was no longer significant ($p = .050$), but it was not effectively reduced.

We cannot, as yet, easily determine the importance of our findings within the context of current research on composition effects because only a very few studies concentrate on the transmission mechanisms. In Germany, analysis of data from PISA conducted by Baumert and colleagues (2003) shows that composition effects apparently are not transferred by peer-culture (e.g., school satisfaction, acceptance of achievement norms). As is evident from our descriptive analysis, classes with a composition likely to disadvantage student achievement show a higher variance in their achievement scores. In addition, teachers in these classes use a variety of instructional methods to differentiate between achievement levels. Controlling for the variety of teacher instructional methods might therefore be insufficient; teacher and student interactions at the micro level may also be important factors, and we did not account for these.

One consequence of our present understanding of composition effects is that the higher- level variables, such as teachers' competencies and school policies, tend to be the target of policymaking decisions and efforts centered on ameliorating educational inequalities. Other possible steps could be taken to reduce the effects of the social class composition. One such step might be to change school district boundaries or regulations so that students from different social backgrounds can learn together. Another approach might be to require schools to have specified proportions of their school enrolments made up of students from various backgrounds. Such measures, though, require a huge amount of administrative effort and financial cost. The results of "busing" in the United States suggest that this approach is unlikely to be a promising one (see, for example, Thrupp, 1995). And the deregulation of school districts, which is already the case in some German Länder (states), could be counter-productive because parents might become even more prone to exercise choice over their child's school, thereby intensifying the homogeneous composition of the student body.

We consider, given the results of various studies in the elementary sector, that measures have to be taken to reduce achievement differences, especially those influenced by use of the instructional language, before children begin school. Also, at the class and school level, teachers and schools need more resources to cope with the learning needs of different student populations. Perhaps the "all-day school", a relatively new endeavor in Germany that aims to ensure student learning aligns with each student's individual learning needs, can be used to help enhance quality learning time and especially provide more time on task for students with few school-relevant resources and learning support at home. Another option might be to introduce mixed-age classes, where students with different ability levels learn together. Finally, more research is needed to determine the transmission mechanism of composition effects. Such research needs to take into account the normative and comparative culture of the class and teachers' expectations of student achievement.

References

Alba, R., Handl, J., & Müller, W. (1994). Ethnische Ungleichheit im deutschen Bildungssystem [Ethnic inequalities in the German education system]. *Kölner Zeitschrift für Soziologie und Sozialpsychologie, 46*, 209–237.

Ammermüller, A., & Pischke, J. (2006). *Peer-effects in European primary schools: Evidence from PIRLS*. Cambridge, UK: National Bureau of Economic Research.

Baumert, J., Stanat, P., & Watermann, R. (2006). Schulstruktur und die Entstehung differenzieller Lern-und Entwicklungsmilieus [School structure and the creation of differential learning and development milieus]. In J. Baumert, P. Stanat, & R. Watermann (Eds.), *Herkunftsbedingte Disparitäten im Bildungswesen: Differenzielle Bildungsprozesse und Probleme der Verteilungsgerechtigkeit* [Social inequalities in the educational system: Differential education processes and problems of distributional justice] (pp. 95–188). Wiesbaden: VS Verlag für Sozialwissenschaften.

Baumert, J., Trautwein, U., & Artelt, C. (2003). Schulumwelten: Institutionelle Bedingungen des Lehrens und Lernens [School environments: Institutional conditions of teaching and learning]. In Deutsches PISA-Konsortium (Ed.), *PISA 2000: Ein differenzierter Blick auf die Länder der Bundesrepublik Deutschland* [PISA 2000: A comparative view of the länder of the Federal Republic of Germany] (pp. 261–331). Opladen, Germany: Leske + Budrich.

Beauftragte der Bundesregierung für Migration, Flüchtlinge und Integration. (2007). 7. *Bericht der Beauftragten der Bundesregierung für Migration, Flüchtlinge und Integration über die Lage der Ausländerinnen und Ausländer in Deutschland* [7th report of the German Federal Commission for Migration, Refugees and Integration about the State of Resident Aliens in Germany]. Berlin, Germany: Author.

Becker, R., & Lauterbach, W. (2004). Dauerhafte Bildungsungleichheiten: Ursachen, Mechanismen, Prozesse und Wirkungen [Long-term education inequalities: Causes, mechanisms, processes and effects]. In R. Becker & W. Lauterbach (Eds.), *Bildung als Privileg? Erklärungen und Befunde zu den Ursachen der Bildungsungleichheit* [Education as a privilege? Explanations and results of the causes of education inequalities] (pp. 9–30). Wiesbaden, Germany: VS Verlag für Sozialwissenschaften.

Bos, W., Hornberg, S., Arnold, K.-H., Faust, G., Fried, L., Lankes, E.-M., ... & Valtin, R. (Eds.). (2008). IGLU-E 2006. *Die Länder der Bundesrepublik Deutschland im nationalen und internationalen Vergleich* [IGLU-E 2006: Selected länder of the Federal Republic of Germany—national and international comparisons]. Münster, Germany: Waxmann.

Bos, W., Lankes, E.-M., & Prenzel, M. (2004). *IGLU. Einige Länder der Bundesrepublik Deutschland im nationalen und internationalen Vergleich* [IGLU: Selected länder of the Federal Republic of Germany—national and international comparisons]. Münster, Germany: Waxmann.

Bos, W., Schwippert, K., & Stubbe, T. C. (2007). Die Kopplung von sozialer Herkunft und Schülerleistung im internationalen Vergleich [The link between students' social background and achievement: An international comparison]. In W. Bos et al. (Eds.), *IGLU 2006: Lesekompetenzen von Grundschulkindern in Deutschland im internationalen Vergleich* [IGLU 2006: Reading competence of primary school children in Germany and in international comparison] (pp. 225–247). Münster, Germany: Waxmann.

Bos, W., Valtin, R., Voss, A., Hornberg, S., & Lankes, E.-M. (2007). Konzepte der Lesekompetenz in IGLU 2006 [Concepts of reading competence in IGLU 2006]. In W. Bos et al. (Eds.), IGLU 2006: *Lesekompetenz von Grundschulkindern in Deutschland im internationalen Vergleich* [IGLU 2006: Reading competence of primary school children in Germany and in international comparison] (pp. 81–104). Münster, Germany: Waxmann.

Boudon, R. (1974). *Education, opportunity, and social inequality: Changing perspectives in western society*. New York: John Wiley.

Bryk, A., & Raudenbush, S. (1992). *Hierarchical linear models: Applications and data analysis methods*. Thousand Oaks, CA: Sage.

Burns, R., & Mason, D. A. (2002). Class composition and student achievement in elementary schools. *American Educational Research Journal, 39*, 207–233.

Caldas, S. J., & Bankston, C. (1998). The inequality of separation: Racial composition of schools and academic achievement. *Educational Administration Quarterly, 34*, 533–557.

Carroll, J. B. (1963). A model of school learning. *Teachers College Record, 64*, 723–733.

Coleman, J. S. (1966). *Equality of educational opportunity*. Washington, DC: Government Printing Office.

Corno, L., & Snow, R. E. (1986). Adapting teaching to individual differences among learners. In M. C. Wittrock (Ed.), *Handbook of research on teaching* (pp. 605–629). New York: Macmillan Publishing Company.

Cortina, K., Carlisle, J., & Zeng, J. (2008). Context effects on students' gains in reading comprehension in Reading First Schools in Michigan. Zeitschrift für Erziehungswissenschaft, 1, 47–66.

Creemers, B. (1994). *The effective classroom*. New York: Redwood Books.

Creemers, B., Scheerens, J., & Reynolds, T. (2000). Theory development in school effectiveness research. In C. Teddlie & D. Reynolds (Eds.), *The international handbook of school effectiveness research* (pp. 283–298). London, New York: Falmer Press.

Dar, Y., & Resh, N. (1994). Separating and mixing students for learning: Concepts and research. *Pedagogisch tijdschrift*, *19*, 109–126.

Diefenbach, H. (2003). Ethnische Segmentation im deutschen Schulsystem: Eine Zustandsbeschreibung und einige Erklärungen für den Zustand [Ethnic segmentation in the German school system: A description of conditions and some explanations for these]. In B. P. Forschungsinstitut Arbeit (Ed.), *Jahrbuch Arbeit, Bildung, Kultur* [Yearbook of work, education, culture] (Volume 21/22, pp. 225–255). Recklinghausen, Germany: FIAB.

Diefenbach, H. (2007). *Kinder und Jugendliche aus Migrantenfamilien im deutschen Bildungssystem. Erklärungen und empirische Befunde* [Children and adolescents from immigrant families in the German education system: Explanations and empirical findings]. Wiesbaden, Germany: VS Verlag.

Ditton, H., & Krüsken, J. (2006). Sozialer Kontext und schulische Leistungen: Zur Bildungsrelevanz segregierter Armut [Social context and school achievements: The educational relevance of segregated poverty]. *Zeitschrift für Soziologie der Erziehung und Sozialisation*, *26*, 135–157.

Dreeben, R., & Barr, R. (1988). Classroom composition and the design of instruction. *Sociology of Education*, *61*, 129–142.

Erikson, R., & Jonsson, J. (1996). *Can education be equalized? The Swedish case in comparative perspective*. Oxford: Westview Press.

Esser, H. (2006). *Migration, Sprache und Integration: AKI-Forschungsbilanz 4* [Migration, language, and integration: AKI research synopsis 4]. Berlin: Wissenschaftszentrum Berlin für Sozialforschung.

Foy, P., & Kennedy, A. (2008a). *PIRLS 2006 user guide, supplement 1*. Boston, MA: Boston College.

Foy, P., & Kennedy, A. (2008b). *PIRLS 2006 user guide, supplement 3*. Boston, MA: Boston College.

Hallinan, M. T. (1988). School composition and learning: A critique of the Dreeben-Barr model. *Sociology of Education*, *61*, 143–146.

Hanushek, E., Kain, J., Markman, J., & Rivkin, S. (2003). Does peer ability affect student achievement? *Journal of Applied Econometrics*, *18*, 527–544.

Harker, R., & Tymms, P. (2004). The effects of student composition on school outcomes. *School Effectiveness and School Improvement*, *15*, 177–199.

Hattie, J. (2002). Classroom composition and peer effects. *International Journal of Educational Research*, *37*, 449–481.

Hattie, J. (2003). *Teachers make a difference: What is the research evidence?* Retrieved March 3, 2009, from http://www.educationalleaders.govt.nz/Pedagogy-and-assessment/Building-effective-learning-environments/Teachers-Make-a-Difference-What-is-the-Research-Evidence.

Heath, A., & Brinbaum, Y. (2007). Explaining ethnic inequalities in educational attainment: Guest editorial. *Ethnicities, 7,* 291–305.

Helmke, A., Helmke, T., Heyne, N., Hosenfeld, A., Kleinbub, I., Schrader, F., & Wagner, W. (2007). Erfassung, Bewertung und Verbesserung des Grundschulunterrichts: Forschungsstand, Probleme und Perspektiven [Assessment, evaluation, and improvement of teaching in primary schools: Research evidence, problems, and perspectives]. In K. Möller, P. Hanke, Ch. Beinbrech, Th. Kleichmann, & R. Schlages (Eds.), *Qualität von Grundschulunterricht entwickeln, erfassen und bewerten* [Developing, assessing, and evaluating the quality of teaching in primary schools] (pp. 17–34). Wiesbaden, Germany: VS Verlag.

Hornberg, S., Bos, W., Buddeberg, I., Potthoff, B., & Stubbe, T. (2007a). Anlage und Durchführung von IGLU 2006 [Design and implementation of IGLU 2006]. In W. Bos et al. (Eds.), *IGLU 2006: Lesekompetenz von Grundschulkindern in Deutschland im internationalen Vergleich* [*IGLU 2006: Reading competence of primary school children in Germany and in international comparison*] (pp. 21–46). Münster, Germany: Waxmann.

Hornberg, S., Valtin, R., Potthoff, B., Schwippert, K., & Schulz-Zander, R. (2007b). Lesekompetenzen von Mädchen und Jungen im internationalen Vergleich [Reading competence of girls and boys: An international comparison]. In W. Bos et al. (Eds.), *IGLU 2006: Lesekompetenz von Grundschulkindern in Deutschland im internationalen Vergleich* [IGLU 2006: Reading competence of primary school children in Germany and in international comparison] (pp. 195–219). Münster, Germany: Waxmann.

Hox, J. (2002). *Multilevel analysis: Techniques and applications.* London: Lawrence Erlbaum Associates.

Joncas, M. (2007). PIRLS 2006 sample design. In M. Martin, I. Mullis, & A. Kennedy (Eds.), *PIRLS 2006 technical report* (pp. 35–49). Boston, MA: Boston College.

Kalter, F. (2008). Stand, Herausforderungen und Perspektiven der empirischen Migrationsforschung (State, challenges, and perspectives of empirical migration research). *Kölner Zeitschrift für Soziologie und Sozialpsychologie,* 11–36.

Kao, G., & Thompson, J. (2003). Racial and ethnic stratification in educational achievement and attainment. *Annual Review of Sociology, 29,* 417–442.

Kristen, C. (2008). Schulische Leistungen von Kindern aus türkischen Familien am Ende der Grundschulzeit. Befunde aus der IGLU-Studie. [School achievement of children from Turkish families at the end of primary school: Findings from the IGLU Study]. *Kölner Zeitschrift für Soziologie und Sozialpsychologie, 48,* 230–251.

Marsh, H. W., & Hattie, J. (1996). Theoretical perspectives on the structure of self-concept. In B. A. Bracken (Ed.), *Handbook of self-concept* (pp. 38–90). New York: Wiley.

Martin, M., Mullis, I., & Kennedy, A. (Eds.). (2007). *PIRLS 2006 technical report.* Boston, MA: Boston College.

Oakes, J. (2005). *Keeping track: How schools structure inequality*. New Haven, CT: Yale University Press.

Opdenakker, M. C., & Van Damme, J. (2001). Relationship between school composition and characteristics of school process and their effect on mathematics achievement. *British Educational Research Journal*, *27*, 407–432.

Opdenakker, M. C., Van Damme, J., De Fraine, B., Van Landeghem, G., & Onghena, P. (2002). The effect of schools and classes on mathematics achievement. *School Effectiveness and School Improvement*, *13*, 399–427.

Pallas, A., Entwisle, D., Alexander, K., & Slutka, M. (1994). Ability-group effects: Instructional, social or institutional? *Sociology of Education*, *67*, 27–46.

Portes, A., & Hao, L. (2004). The schooling of children of immigrants: Contextual effects on the educational attainment of the second generation. *Proceedings of the National Academy of Science*, *101*, 11920–11927.

Portes, A., & MacLeod, D. (1996). Educational progress of children of immigrants: The roles of class, ethnicity, and school context. *Sociology of Education*, *69*, 255–275.

Raudenbush, S., Bryk, A., Cheong, Y., & Congdon, R. (2004). *HLM 6: Hierarchical linear and nonlinear modeling (computer software)*. Lincolnwood IL: Scientific Software International.

Rüesch, P. (1998). *Spielt die Schule eine Rolle?* [Does school play a role?] Bern, Switzerland: Peter Lang.

Rumberger, R. W., & Palardy, G. (2005). Does segregation still matter? The impact of student composition on academic achievement in high school. *Teachers College Record*, *107*, 1999–2045.

Sharp, S., & Croxford, L. (2003). Literacy in the first year of schooling: A multilevel analysis. *School Effectiveness and School Improvement*, *14*, 213–231.

Stanat, P. (2006). Disparitäten im schulischen Erfolg: Forschungsstand zur Rolle des Migrationshintergrunds [Inequalities and school success: Research evidence on the importance of migration background]. *Unterrichtswissenschaft*, *36*, 98–124.

Stanat, P., & Christensen, P. (2006). *Where immigrant students succeed: A comparative review of performance and engagement in PISA 2003*. Paris: Organisation for Economic Co-operation and Development.

Stanat, P., & Lüdtke, O. (2008). Multilevel issues in international large-scale assessment studies. In F. van Vijver, D. van Hemmert, & Y. Poortinga (Eds.), *Multilevel analysis of individuals and cultures* (pp. 315–344). New York: Lawrence Earlbaum.

Statistisches Bundesamt. (2008). *Fachserie 11: Bildung und Kultur. Reihe 1.1, Private Schulen: Schuljahr 2007/08* [Series 1.1, Education and culture. Volume 1.1, private schools: School year 2007/08]. Wiesbaden, Germany: Federal Statistics Office.

Statistisches Bundesamt. (2009). *Fachserie 1: Bevölkerung und Erwerbstätigkeit. Reihe 2.2 Bevölkerung mit Migrationshintergrund: Ergebnisse des Mikrozensus 2007* [Series 1: Population and employment. Volume 2.2, immigrant population: Results of the micro census]. Wiesbaden, Germany: Federal Statistics Office.

Teddlie, C., Stringfield, S., & Reynolds, D. (2000). Context issues within school effectiveness research. In C. Teddlie & D. Reynolds (Eds.), *The international handbook of school effectiveness research* (pp. 160–185). London and New York: Falmer Press.

Thrupp, M. (1995). The school mix effect: The history of an enduring problem in educational research, policy, and practice. *British Journal of Sociology of Education, 16*, 183–203.

Walter, O. (2008). Ethno-linguale Kompositionseffekte in neunten Klassen: Befunde aus der Klassenstichprobe von PISA 2006 [Ethno-linguistic composition effects in ninth grade: Evidence of the PISA 2006 class sample]. *Zeitschrift für Erziehungswissenschaft Sonderheft 10-08*, 169–184.

Walter, O., & Stanat, P. (2008). Der Zusammenhang des Migrantenanteils in Schulen mit der Lesekompetenz: Differenzierte Analysen der erweiterten Migrantenstichprobe von PISA 2003 [The relationship between the proportion of immigrant students and reading competence: In-depth analyses of the extended immigrant sample in PISA 2003]. *Zeitschrift für Erziehungswissenschaft, 1*, 84–105.

Westerbeek, K. (1999). *The colours of my classroom: A study into the effects of the ethnic composition of classrooms on the achievement of pupils from different ethnic backgrounds.* Florence, Italy: European University Institute.

Wilkinson, I. (2002). Introduction: Peer-influences on learning. Where are they? *International Journal of Educational Research, 37*, 395–401.

Assessing fit of latent regression models

Sandip Sinharay, Zhumei Guo, and Matthias von Davier
Educational Testing Service, Princeton, NJ, USA[1]

Bernard P. Veldkamp
University of Twente, Enschede, The Netherlands

The reporting methods used in large-scale educational survey assessments such as the National Assessment of Educational Progress (NAEP) rely on a latent regression model. Research assessing the fit of latent regression models is lacking. This article suggests a simulation-based model fit procedure to assess the fit of such models. The procedure involves investigating whether the latent regression model adequately predicts basic statistical summaries. Application of the suggested procedure to an operational NAEP data set revealed important information regarding the fit of the latent regression model to the data.

---

1 The opinions expressed herein are those of the author and do not necessarily represent those of Educational Testing Service.

INTRODUCTION

The National Assessment of Educational Progress (NAEP), the only regularly administered and mandated national assessment program in the United States (see, for example, Beaton & Zwick, 1992), is an ongoing survey of the academic achievement of school students in the United States in a number of subject areas, such as reading, writing, and mathematics. In 1984, researchers reporting NAEP results began using a statistical model consisting of two components: (i) an item response theory (IRT) component, and (ii) a linear regression component (see, for example, Beaton, 1987; Mislevy, Johnson, & Muraki, 1992). Researchers conducting other large-scale educational assessments, such as the International Adult Literacy Study (IALS; Kirsch, 2001), the Trends in Mathematics and Science Study (TIMSS; Martin & Kelly, 1996), and the Progress in International Reading Literacy Study (PIRLS; Mullis, Martin, Gonzalez, & Kennedy, 2003) adopted a very similar model. This model is often referred to as a *latent regression model* (LRM). The DGROUP set of programs (Rogers, Tang, Lin, & Kandathil, 2006), which is a product of Educational Testing Service (ETS), can be used to estimate the parameters of this model.

Standard 3.9 of the *Standards for Educational and Psychological Testing* (American Psychological Association, National Council on Measurement in Education, & American Educational Research Association, 1999) demands evidence of model fit when an IRT model is used to make inferences from a data set. It is therefore important to assess the fit of the LRM used in NAEP to ensure quality control and an overall improvement in the long term. Although some model-checking procedures have been applied to the NAEP model (e.g., Beaton, 2003; Dresher & Thind, 2007; Li, 2005), there is scope for further work in this area.

In this article, we recommend use of a simulation-based procedure to assess fit of the LRM used in NAEP and other large-scale assessments. The procedure involves investigating whether the model adequately predicts several summary statistics of the observed data. The suggested procedure, which generates predicted data sets under the assumption that the model is true, involves use of the NAEP operational software, and it compares several summary statistics computed from the observed data set to those computed from the predicted data sets. Our procedure is therefore similar to the parametric bootstrap (e.g., Efron & Tibshirani, 1993) and the posterior predictive model checking method (e.g., Gelman, Carlin, Stern, & Rubin, 2003).

We provide, in Section 1 of this article, background information on the current NAEP statistical model and estimation procedure, and on the existing NAEP model-checking procedures. We then, in Sections 2 and 3, describe our suggested model checks and the NAEP data set that we used for our study. In the fourth section, we explore the Type I error rates of the suggested procedure. We provide a real data example in the fifth section. In the final section of the article (Section 6), we present conclusions and suggestions for future work.

1. THE NAEP LATENT REGRESSION MODEL AND ESTIMATION

1.1 The Model

In NAEP, the latent proficiency variable for student i is assumed to be p-dimensional, where p could be between 1 and 5. Let us denote it as $\theta_i = (\theta_{i1}, \theta_{i2},...\theta_{ip})'$.

Let us denote the response vector to the test items for student i as $y_i = (y_{i1}, y_{i2},...y_{ip})$, where y_{ik}, a vector of responses, contributes information about θ_{ik}. For example, y_{ik} could be responses of student i to algebra questions in a mathematics test and θ_{ik} the algebra skill variable of the student. Let us denote the item parameters of the items that are designed to elicit information on θ_{ik}'s (i.e., items that measure the k-th subscale) as β_k. Suppose $\beta = (\beta_1, \beta_2,...\beta_p)$. The likelihood for a student is given by

$$f(y_i|\theta_i,\beta) = \prod_{k=1}^{p} f_1(y_{ik}|\theta_{ik},\beta_k) \equiv L(\theta_i,\beta;y_i). \tag{1}$$

The expressions $f_1(y_{ik}|\theta_{ik},\beta_k)$, above, consist of factors contributed by a univariate IRT model, usually the two- or three-parameter logistic (2PL, 3PL) model for dichotomous items and the generalized partial-credit model (GPCM) for polytomous items.

Suppose $x_i = (x_{i1}, x_{i2},...x_{im})$ are m covariates for the i-th student. Typically, NAEP collects information on demographic and educational characteristics, converts them to numerical variables, and then uses a principal component analysis for extraction of principal components that explains 90% of the variance of these variables (see, for example, Allen, Donoghue, & Schoeps, 2000); the values of the principal components play the role of the x_{ij}'s in further analyses. Conditional on x_i, the student proficiency vector θ_i is assumed to follow a multivariate normal distribution, that is,

$$\theta_i|x_i,y_i,y,\beta,\Gamma,\Sigma \sim N(\Gamma'x_i,\Sigma). \tag{2}$$

Together, Equations 1 and 2 form the LRM or *conditioning model* employed in NAEP. Equations 1 and 2 imply that

$$p(\theta_i|y_i,x_i,\beta,\Gamma,\Sigma) \propto L(\theta_i,\beta;y_i) N(\Gamma'x_i,\Sigma). \tag{3}$$

where $p(\theta_i|y_i,x_i,\beta,\Gamma,\Sigma)$ is the conditional posterior distribution of θ_i. (For further details, see, for example, von Davier, Sinharay, Oranje, & Beaton, 2006).

1.2 Estimation

NAEP uses a three-stage estimation process for fitting the above-mentioned LRM to the data.

1. The first stage, *scaling*, uses the PARSCALE software (Allen et al., 2000) to fit the model given by Equation 1 to the student response data and to estimate the item parameters. During this stage, the prior distributions of the components of the student proficiency are assumed to be independent, discrete univariate distributions.

2. The second stage, *conditioning*, assumes that the item parameters are fixed at the estimates found in the scaling stage and that they fit the model given by (1) and (2) to the data, and estimates Γ and Σ. The following versions of the DGROUP program perform this conditioning step differently.

- BGROUP (Beaton, 1987) is employed when $p \leq 2$ and uses numerical quadrature.
- CGROUP (Thomas, 1993) is employed when $p > 2$ and uses Laplace approximations.
- NGROUP (Mislevy, 1985) is employed to find the starting values for BGROUP or CGROUP and uses a normal approximation of $L(\theta_i; y_i)$.[1]

3. The third stage of the NAEP estimation process generates *plausible values* (imputed values of the proficiency variables) for all the students using the parameter estimates obtained from the scaling and conditioning stages. The plausible values are generated according to the following three-step process:

- Draw $\Gamma \sim N(\hat{\Gamma}, \hat{S}(\hat{\Gamma}))$, where $\hat{\Gamma}$ and $\hat{S}(\hat{\Gamma})$ are estimates of Γ and the corresponding standard deviation, respectively, and are obtained using DGROUP.
- Compute from Equation 3 the posterior mean and the covariance of θ_i, conditional on the generated value of Γ and the fixed variance matrix $\Sigma = \hat{\Sigma}$.
- Draw θ_i from a multivariate normal distribution, with the mean and variance computed in the above step.

The plausible values are used to estimate student subgroup averages. The third stage also estimates the variances corresponding to the student subgroup averages as the sum of two terms—the variance due to the latency of θ_is and the variance due to sampling of students. The computation of the second term involves the use of a jackknife approach, while the computations of both terms involve the plausible values generated in the conditioning step.

1.3 Existing Work on Assessing Fit of the NAEP Model

NAEP researchers rigorously monitor data quality and employ a number of qualitative checks of the results of their statistical analyses. When conducting first-level checks, NAEP researchers employ several plausibility analyses. (These involve examining the computer outputs to make sure that they make sense.) The researchers also conduct computer-based checks at different stages of the statistical analysis; these ensure that the data analysis process is working as intended. The first-level checks involve working through several carefully designed checklists, such as an item analysis checklist and a DGROUP conditioning checklist. However, these first-level checks provide quality control measures that are necessary but not sufficient. Thus, even if the checks reveal no problems and show that the programs are running as expected on the appropriate data sets, the inferences may be problematic if the model does not adequately explain the data. Therefore, as second-level checks, additional steps are taken to ensure the appropriateness and quality of the IRT model (Allen et al., 2000, p. 233).

---

1 Because the item parameters are assumed to be known in this step, the symbol of the item parameters does not appear in this expression for the likelihood.

This check involves examination of item parameter estimates—extreme estimates often indicate problems—and use of differential-item-functioning (DIF) analyses to examine issues of multidimensionality (see, for example, Roussos & Stout, 1996, for the connection between DIF and multidimensionality). Those conducting NAEP operational analyses also employ graphical item fit analyses. These require use of residual plots and a related χ^2-type item fit statistic (Allen et al., 2000, p. 233) that provides guidelines on how to treat the items, such as collapsing categories of polytomous items, treating adjacent-year data separately in concurrent calibration, or dropping items from the analysis. However, the null distribution of these residuals and of the χ^2-type statistic are unknown, as Allen et al. (2000) acknowledge (p. 233).

Another second-level check used in NAEP operational analyses is comparison of observed and model-predicted proportions of students obtaining a particular score on an item (Rogers, Gregory, Davis, & Kulick, 2006). These analyses, however, do not use the variability of the quantities involved. We considered it would be useful to make the comparison of the observed and predicted proportions more meaningful by providing a methodology that incorporates the variability. As will be clear later, our work partially addressed this issue.

Beaton (2003) suggests item fit measures involving sums and sum of squares of residuals obtained from the responses of each student to each question. Assuming that Y_{ij} denotes the response of the i-th student to the j-th item, Beaton's fit indices are of the form

$$\sum W_i \frac{(Y_{ij} - E(Y_{ij}|\Theta))^k}{(\sqrt{Var(Y_{ij}|\Theta)})^k}$$

where k could be 1 or 2, Θ is the collection of all model parameters, and W_i is the NAEP sampling weight (Allen et al., 2000, pp. 161–225). A bootstrap method is then used to determine the null distribution of these statistics. Li (2005) used Beaton's statistics when analyzing operational test data sets in order to determine the effect of accommodations on students with disabilities. Dresher and Thind (2007) used Beaton's statistics when analyzing 2003 NAEP and 1999 TIMSS data. Dresher and Thind also employed the χ^2-type item fit statistic provided by the NAEP-PARSCALE program, but computed the null distribution of the statistic from its values for one simulated data set. These methods have their limitations, however. For example, Sinharay (2005, p. 379) argues that fit statistics based on examinee-level residuals are unreliable because of their excessive variability, a limitation that applies to Beaton's fit statistics. (See also Li, Bolt, & Fu, 2006, who found such statistics questionable.)

With any practical application of model fit analysis, it is important that analysts use suitable test statistics to examine the appropriate aspects of the model. The standard recommendation (see, for example, Gelman et al., 2003, p. 172) is that those checking a model in an application should focus on aspects of the model that are relevant to the purposes for which the inference will be applied. For example, if we were interested in using a statistical model to estimate the mean income of a population, we would need to focus the model fit analysis on the mean.

This issue has received little attention with respect to the IRT model fit in general (e.g., Sinharay, 2005) and with respect to NAEP in particular. Thus, there is substantial scope for further work directed at assessing the fit of LRMs that use NAEP data. Note that such work has to take full account of the idiosyncrasies of the NAEP model and of data such as the matrix sampling (so that each student sees only some of the questions), sampling weights, and missing values.

2. THE SUGGESTED PROCEDURE

During our study, we applied a simulation-based model fit procedure to NAEP statistical analysis to investigate whether the LRM used for NAEP adequately predicts several data summaries (or *test statistics*).

2.1 Description of the Procedure

The determination of the null distribution (or the computation of the *p*-values) of a test statistic is not straightforward, given the complicated nature of the LRM applied in NAEP. Because of this, we employed a simulation-based procedure that used existing NAEP software programs to determine the null distribution of the test statistics and to perform the model fit assessment. The steps in the procedure follow:

1. Computation, from the original NAEP data set, of several test statistics (such as biserial correlation). We describe these statistics in Section 2.2.

2. Estimation, using PARSCALE, of item parameters (as in the scaling stage of the NAEP three-stage estimation process).

3. Generation, using the DGROUP program of plausible values (as in the third stage of the NAEP estimation process). The operational NAEP estimation process generated five plausible values for each candidate, but we generated 200 plausible values for each candidate. These are like draws of θ_i from its posterior distribution.

4. Simulation, from the model given by Equation 1, of 200 data sets, using the generated plausible values and the item parameters estimated in Step 2, above. The simulated data sets can be considered to be those predicted by the model, that is, those we would observe if the model were valid.

5. Computation of the values of several test statistics for each of the 200 simulated data sets (resulting in 200 *simulated/predicted values* for each statistic). We then compared the predicted values of each statistic to the corresponding observed values in order to judge the goodness of fit of the model. An observed value that is extreme with respect to the distribution of the predicted values indicates model misfit. We performed the comparison of the observed and predicted values of the statistics graphically, by plotting the observed and predicted values of the statistics. An observed value located at the tail of the distribution of the predicted values indicates that the model does not adequately predict the corresponding statistic. We also computed *p*-values for the statistics. A *p*-value is the proportion of the predicted values of a statistic that is greater than the corresponding observed value. A very low or a very high *p*-value indicates that the model does not adequately predict the corresponding statistic.

The flowchart in Figure 1 provides a graphical description of the procedure for the average group score statistic (described below).

Figure 1: Steps of the simulation procedure to determine the null distribution of the average group score statistic

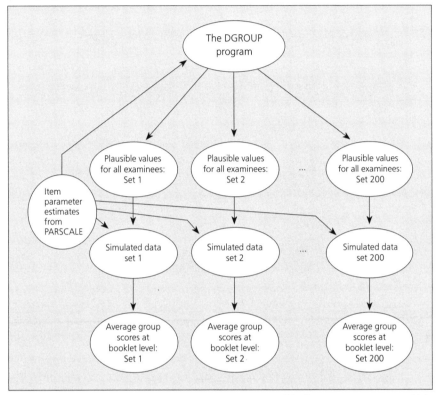

Note: The item parameter estimates from PARSCALE were used in the DGROUP program, which generates 200 sets of plausible values. The plausible values and the item parameter estimates were used to generate 200 simulated data sets, which resulted in 200 simulated/predicted average group scores for each booklet for each student group. Each booklet-level-observed average group score was then compared to the corresponding 200 simulated values for model fit assessment.

The procedure just described is an approximation of the posterior predictive model-checking (PPMC) method (e.g., Gelman et al., 2003; Sinharay, 2005), a popular Bayesian model-checking procedure. The PPMC method involves the following four steps:

1. Generating a sample of size n, mostly using a Markov chain Monte Carlo method (Gelman et al., 2003) from the joint posterior distribution of the model parameters;

2. Simulation of n data sets using the generated parameter values;

3. Computation of the values of a test statistic of interest for each of these n simulated data sets; and

4. Comparison of the observed value of the corresponding test statistic with the *n* values computed in the above step.

Because our suggested procedure required us to perform the last three of these steps, the procedure is similar to the PPMC method. However, it is only an approximation of the PPMC method. This is because we performed only part of the first step involved in a PPMC: we drew plausible values (which are approximate draws from the student posterior distribution), but we did not draw item parameter values and assumed that these were fixed at their estimates (obtained from the scaling state of the NAEP estimation process). Sinharay (2005) and Sinharay, Johnson, and Stern (2006) successfully used the PPMC method to detect misfit of simple IRT models. Our suggested procedure involved application of several fit statistics similar to those recorded in these two articles.

Our procedure is also similar to the parametric bootstrap method (e.g., Efron & Tibshirani, 1993) that has been successfully applied to assess the fit of IRT models and other similar models (see, for example, Stone, 2000; von Davier, 1997). We consider our procedure fairly easy to understand because it is similar to two popular model-checking methods. In addition, because it uses existing NAEP software, operational implementation of the procedure is straightforward.

2.2 Description of the Test Statistics

With NAEP, unlike several other large-scale assessments, not all students are asked all items; instead, each student has to answer the items in one of several booklets. (A booklet is a collection of test items.) We computed all the test statistics separately for each booklet.

Researchers van der Linden and Hambleton (1997, p. 16) recommend collecting a wide variety of evidence about model fit and then making an informed judgment about model fit and usefulness of a model with a particular set of data for assessing the fit of two- and three-parameter IRT models. Sinharay (2005) and Sinharay et al. (2006) took heed of this recommendation when assessing the fit of simple IRT models. They used a variety of simple summaries of the data—similar to the ones listed below—to do this. The recommendation put forward by van der Linden and Hambleton (1997) is equally appropriate for any IRT model, including the one employed in NAEP.

Our suggested procedure, together with the statistics described below, provides a tool kit that researchers can use to collect a variety of evidence to determine the fit of the LRM to NAEP data.

- *Average group score:* Let Y_{ij} denote the response of the *i*-th student to the *j*-th item in a booklet. For a dichotomous item, Y_{ij} is 0 or 1. For a *k*-category polytomous item, Y_{ij} takes one from among the values 0, 1, ... *k*–1. NAEP encounters a substantial percentage of omitted and not-reached responses. In NAEP, not-reached items are treated as not-presented items. An omitted response is assigned a fractional score equal to the reciprocal of the number of options if the item is multiple-choice and is assigned the score for the lowest scoring category if the item is a constructed-response item (Allen et al., 2000, pp. 231–232). To obtain a statistic that appropriately takes into account the omitted and not-reached responses, we defined

$$s_i = \sum_j Y_{ij} / R_i$$

as the proportion-correct score of student i, where R_i is the sum of the maximum raw score points for the items that the i-th student reached. We then computed the weighted average of the s_is for a student group as

$$A_g = \frac{\sum_{i \in g} W_i s_i}{\sum_{i \in g} W_i}$$

where g denotes a student group (such as all students or male students, or White students). The statistic A_g denotes the average proportion score in a booklet for the g-th group. Note that if student i omitted item j, Y_{ij} is $1/m$ for a m-option multiple-choice item and is equal to the lowest scoring category for a constructed-response item. Because student subgroup means are reported in NAEP, the decision to examine how the NAEP model predicts the statistic A_g is a natural one.

- *Average item score:* We used the weighted average item score for item j,

$$p_j = \frac{\sum_i W_i Y_{ij}}{\sum_i W_i}$$

as a test statistic. This statistic is closely related to the proportion score statistic used by Rogers et al. (2006). The main difference between the two is that p_j is defined for a booklet.

- *Biserial correlation coefficients:* Because of the way the NAEP operational analysis treats the omitted and the not-reached items, the standard definition of the biserial correlation is not appropriate here. Accordingly, for each item in a booklet, we computed the correlation between the vector of responses to an item and the vector of proportion-correct scores s_i (using the notation introduced earlier). We used the sampling weights W_i in the computations.

- *Item pair correlation:* This is the correlation between the response vectors for two items. We again used the sampling weights W_i in the computations.

We chose the above statistics not only because they are simple data summaries but also because Sinharay (2005) and Sinharay et al. (2006) found results similar to these in their research. The average group score statistic deserves special mention. Ideally, model checking in an application should focus on those aspects of the model that are relevant to the purposes for which the inference will be applied (Gelman et al., 2003, p. 172). Because the quantities of primary interest in NAEP are the mean scale scores for the different subgroups, it is necessary to determine if the model adequately predicts these quantities. The ideal would be to compare the observed value[2] of a test statistic based on the mean scale scores to the model-predicted values of the test statistic. However, because mean scale scores are functions of model-estimated student proficiency variables, it is impossible to obtain a test statistic based on mean

---

2 When we refer to an "observed value," we mean a value that can be computed from the data set before an appropriate model is fitted to it.

scale scores that will have an observed value. The average group scores of student subgroups of interest are thus best-possible observed proxies of the mean scale scores of these subgroups. We can expect that these average group scores, although simple to compute, will have strong correlations with their corresponding mean scale values. Accurate prediction of the average scores of important student subgroups by the NAEP model should thus provide strong evidence that the subgroup estimates provided by the NAEP model are accurate.

3. DATA

We obtained a data set from the NAEP 2002 reading assessment for Grade 12. This set contained data for about 15,000 students. Our primary reasons for choosing the reading assessment were that reading is a No Child Left Behind[3] subject and that reading items have typically been more likely than mathematics items to display problematic item fit (mathematics is another No Child Left Behind subject). The reading assessment considered here measured three skills—reading for literary experience, reading for information, and reading to perform a task.

The reading assessment had 38 booklets. Each of the first 36 booklets was given to a few hundred students, while each of the last two booklets was given to a few thousand students. In addition, each of the last two booklets consisted of one long block (out of a total of two long blocks) of items,[4] whereas each of the first 36 booklets consisted of two shorter blocks (out of a total of nine short blocks) of items. The number of items in a booklet was approximately 20 (about one-third multiple-choice items and about two-thirds constructed-response items) for the first 37 booklets and about 10 (all constructed-response items) for the last booklet. About 50% of all students taking the reading assessment were male, approximately 65% were White, and about 15% were Black. The proportion of omitted and not-reached responses ranged from 4% to 10% for the various booklets.

4. STUDYING THE TYPE I ERROR RATE OF THE SUGGESTED PROCEDURE

Studying the Type I error rate of any statistic used for model checking is important. As we noted earlier, our suggested procedure is similar to the bootstrap method (Efron & Tibshirani, 1993) and the posterior predictive model checking method (Gelman et al., 2003). Researchers have found that both of these methods have Type I error rates close to the nominal level for a wide variety of models, including IRT models. However, we performed a limited study to make sure that the Type I error rate of our suggested procedure was not too high.

---

3   The No Child Left Behind Act of 2001 requires states to develop assessments in basic skills to be given to all students in certain grades, if those states are to receive federal funding for schools.

4   In NAEP, the item pool is divided into several blocks of items; each booklet typically consists of three blocks of items.

When carrying out our study, we began by simulating a data set from the NAEP model, using the techniques described in Section 2 of this article. Let us denote this simulated data set as *D*. The structure of *D* is the same as that described in Section 3 of this article. For example, *D* has responses from about 15,000 students to questions in 38 booklets (remember that each student worked on just one booklet).[5] We performed the model fit analysis (this involved running PARSCALE and DGROUP, simulating 200 data sets, computing the test statistics, and computing the *p*-values) described in Section 2 on *D*. Because *D* was simulated from the NAEP model, the model fitted *D* perfectly. So, ideally, we would have expected not to see any sign of misfit of the NAEP model to this data set.

The proportion of significant *p*-values was close to the nominal level of 5% for all the statistics—average group score, average item score, biserial correlation, and item-pair correlation. Figure 2 provides an example—a histogram of all 744 *p*-values for the biserial correlation statistic. The y-axis in this figure shows the relative frequency (frequency of an interval divided by the total frequency). Note the two vertical lines drawn at values .025 and .975. The figure shows that the *p*-values are more or less uniformly distributed between 0 and 1. Six percent of the *p*-values were greater than .975 or less than .025, very close to the nominal level. This outcome points to the acceptable Type I error rate of our suggested procedure.

Figure 2: The *p*-values for the biserial correlations in the Type I error study

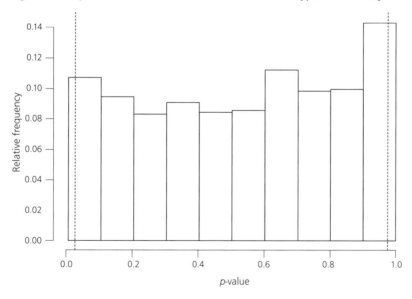

---

5   This simulated data set is one of those simulated for the next section, where we study the fit of the NAEP model
    to the NAEP data set described in Section 3.

45

However, for the average group score statistic and the average item score statistic, the *p*-values did not seem to follow a uniform distribution and had a mean less than .5, as is evident in Figure 3. This figure shows all the *p*-values for the average group score statistic for four groups—male students, White students, Black students, and all students.[5] Each panel displays 38 points, and each point denotes the *p*-value for a booklet. The horizontal dashed line in each panel denotes the value of .025; a *p*-value below this indicates that the predicted values of the statistic were significantly lower than the corresponding observed value. The range of the y-axis is the same in all four panels of Figure 3. Figure 4 presents a histogram of all the 744 *p*-values for the average item score statistic.

Figure 3: The p-values for the average group score statistic in the Type I error study

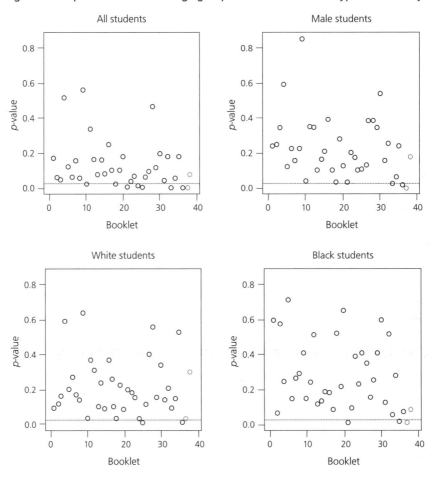

_____

5   The first three of these groups are actually important subgroups in NAEP reporting.

Figure 4: The p-values for the average item score statistic in the Type I error study

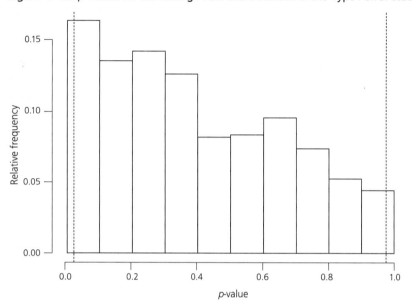

Figures 3 and 4 show that the distribution of these p-values is not uniform; for example, more than half of the p-values are less than .5 for each of these statistics. However, because we were studying the misfit of the model to a data set that was simulated from the model, we would have expected the distribution of these p-values to be uniform, and the proportion of the p-values that are less than .5 to be very close to .5. Further research is needed on this issue. Fortunately, the percentage of p-values for these two statistics that was greater than .975 or less than .025 was close to 5, the nominal level.

We repeated all the analyses reported in this section using another simulated data set. The results, however, were similar to the preceding analysis; that is, the distribution of these p-values was not uniform.

5. RESULTS FROM THE ANALYSIS OF DATA FROM THE 2002 NAEP READING ASSESSMENT

In this section, we describe the results of our application of the procedure suggested in Section 2 to the 2002 NAEP reading data set described in Section 3. We first provide results for the four statistics and then provide a discussion of the results.

5.1 Average Group Score

Figure 5, which is similar to Figure 3, presents the p-values for the average group score statistic for all the booklets as well as for male students, White students, Black students, and all students. The figure shows the following:

1. *Some evidence of misfit for all students (top left panel):* about half of the *p*-values lie below .025.

2. *Most of the p-values in all panels lie below .5, which indicates that the predicted values were generally lower than the observed value of the statistic:* the *p*-values in Figure 5 are substantially smaller overall than those observed in Figure 3. Hence, even if we consider the distribution observed in Figure 3 as the true null distribution of *p*-values, the model seems to under-predict the average group score statistic in Figure 5.

3. *Little evidence of misfit in the plots for the male, White, and Black students:* however, note that most of the *p*-values corresponding to the last two booklets are 0.0 in these plots.

Figure 5: The *p*-values for the average group score statistic for the 2002 NAEP reading data set

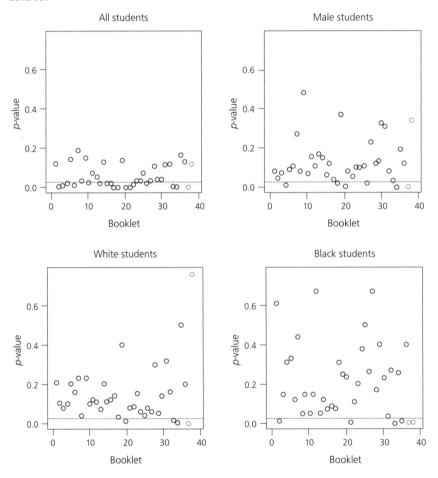

Figure 6 shows the observed value and the predicted value of the average score statistic for four booklets (1, 2, 37, and 38) for all the students, male students, White students, and Black students. Each row corresponds to a booklet and has four panels. In each panel, the histogram denotes the predicted value, and the vertical dashed line denotes the observed value. There are some differences in the figure in the observed and predicted values of the test statistic, especially for Booklets 2 and 37. However, the magnitude of these differences is not too large, even for Booklet 37, where we found the largest differences. For example, for Booklet 37, for all students (the first panel in the third row in Figure 6), the observed value of the average score statistic is about .58, while the mean of the predicted values is approximately .57. As such, the differences between the observed and predicted values, while statistically significant, are likely to have little practical significance. Further research to study the practical significance of these differences would be beneficial.

Figure 6: The observed and the predicted values of the average group score statistic for Booklets 1, 2, 37, and 38 for the 2002 NAEP reading data set

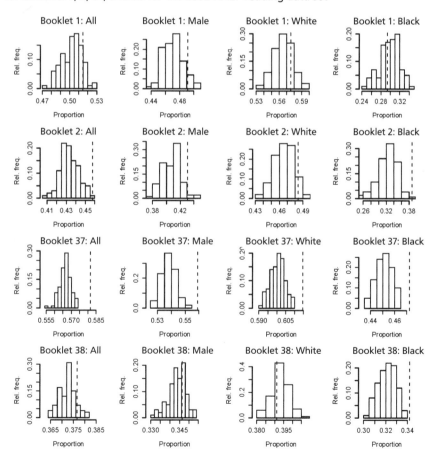

5.2 Average Item Score

Figure 7 presents all 744 p-values for the average item score statistic. Note the two vertical lines drawn at values .025 and .975. Note also that an item which appeared in two different booklets is treated as two different items and so has two p-values associated with it. The figure shows that just over half of the p-values were less than .5. The percentage of p-values greater than .975 or is less than .025 is 9, not much more than the nominal level.

Figure 7: The p-values for the average item score statistic for the 2002 NAEP reading data set

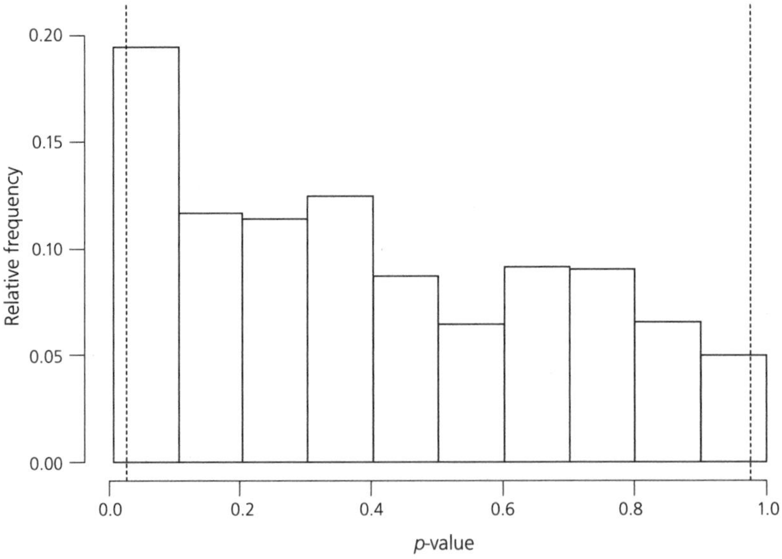

5.3 Biserial Correlation

Figure 8 presents all 744 p-values for the biserial correlation. Note the two vertical lines drawn at values .025 and .975. Note also that an item which appeared in two different booklets was treated as two different items and so has two p-values associated with it. The figure shows only a few extreme p-values for the biserial correlation, which means that the NAEP model adequately predicted the statistic. The percentage of p-values greater than .975 or less than .025 is 10, not much more than the nominal level.

Figure 8: The *p*-values for the biserial correlations for the 2002 NAEP reading data set

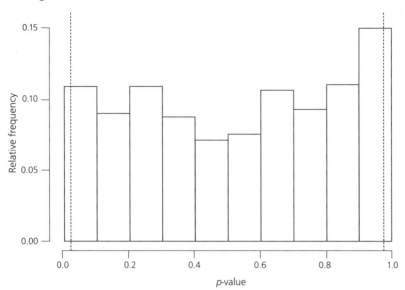

5.4 Item-pair Correlation

Figure 9 shows all 13,784 *p*-values for the item-pair correlation statistic. Note the two vertical lines drawn at values .025 and .975. Note also that an item which appeared in two different booklets was treated as two different items. The figure shows only a few extreme *p*-values for the item-pair correlations. The percentage of *p*-values greater than .975 or less than .025 is 9, not much more than the nominal level.

5.5 Discussion of the Results from the 2002 NAEP Reading Data Set

The results show that the LRM employed in NAEP adequately predicted the average item score, the biserial correlation, and the item-pair correlation. The model did not appear to adequately predict the average group scores of the students; it often under-predicted these scores. However, because the differences between the observed scores and the predicted scores seemed negligible, they were probably not practically significant. Overall, the model adequately predicted several summaries of the NAEP data. We can therefore conclude that the NAEP operational model was adequate for the NAEP data analyzed in this study.

Figure 9: The *p*-values for the item-pair correlations for the 2002 NAEP reading data set

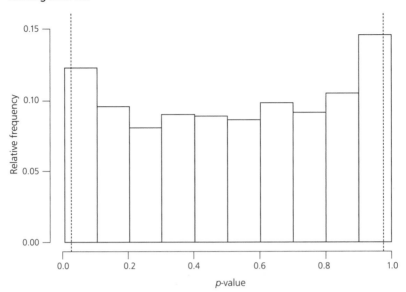

6. CONCLUSIONS

To ensure quality control and overall improvement of the NAEP statistical analysis, it is important to frequently assess the fit of the NAEP statistical model. The task is far from straightforward, given the complex nature of the NAEP statistical model and estimation procedure.

As documented in this article, we applied a simulation-based model fit procedure to NAEP data to investigate whether the LRM employed in this assessment adequately predicts basic statistical summaries, such as the average group scores. Our suggested procedure is easily understood. Also, because it permits use of existing NAEP software, operational implementation of the procedure is simple. Analysis of a real data set provided us with some evidence of a misfit of the NAEP model. However, the magnitude of the misfit was small, which means that the misfit probably had no practical significance.

We found that the distribution of the *p*-values for the average group score and the average item score statistics under the null model were non-uniform and not centered around .5; the model seems to under-predict these quantities. We do not have an explanation for this phenomenon as yet and intend to conduct further research on this potential issue. It is possible that the phenomenon may be associated with how NAEP generates plausible values, or with the discrepancy between the scaling stage (where the ability parameters are assumed to follow independent univariate distributions) and the conditioning stage (where the ability parameters are assumed to follow a multivariate regression model) of NAEP estimation.

Another possible reason could be associated with the inclusion of several hundred principal components as covariates in the latent regression model. The smaller eigenvalues associated with the principal components were usually very small, which may have contributed to some level of instability of these components. This issue is likely to be a particular concern whenever large numbers of eigenvalues and associated principal components are involved. Anderson's (1963) asymptotic theory for principal component analysis and Krzanowski's (1987) jackknife-based standard errors for eigenvalues in principal component analysis may prove useful when assumptions necessary for deriving asymptotic results are not met.

It is not uncommon for simulation-based p-values to have non-uniform null distributions. Von Davier (1997) found that the bootstrap-based null distribution is non-uniform for each of two goodness-of-fit statistics. Researchers such as Sinharay and Stern (2003) and Sinharay et al. (2006) found PPMC-based p-values have non-uniform null distributions. Conceptually, it is possible to apply a double-simulation procedure to calibrate non-uniform p-values in order to obtain calibrated p-values that follow a uniform distribution.[6] However, this approach is too time-consuming if applied to a typical NAEP data set.

We would like to see several related issues studied in the future. In our limited examination, we found some evidence of misfit (which means that the procedure has some power), and we found the Type I error rate to be satisfactory. However, we consider it necessary to conduct a more detailed study of Type I error rate and the power of the suggested procedure. We also found greater misfit for the average group score statistic for the last two booklets, which were given to several thousand students, in contrast to the first 36 booklets, which were given to a few hundred. A possible reason for the misfit is the greater power of model fit measures for larger samples. Another reason could be that the last two booklets have one long block each, whereas the first 36 booklets have two short blocks each.

It is possible to examine raw-score-based graphical item-fit analyses, such as that conducted by Sinharay (2006). Because we examined booklet-level statistics only, it may be informative to study test statistics that combine information from several booklets. We could, for example, obtain an overall average item score by combining information across booklets and a weighted average of booklet averages for a group. Also, because NAEP reports the percentage of students at or above different performance levels (e.g., *basic*, *proficient*, etc.), it would be helpful to focus on a statistic related to percentages. Running an MCMC algorithm and then employing the PPMC method (Gelman et al., 2003) to assess the fit of the NAEP model could be another avenue of future research, especially given relatively recent work on an MCMC algorithm for fitting the NAEP model (see, for example, Johnson & Jenkins, 2004).

---

9   Hjort, Dahl, and Steinbakk (2006), for example, obtained uniformly distributed calibrated PPMC-based p-values.

References

Allen, N. L., Donoghue, J. R., & Schoeps, T. L. (2000). *The 1998 NAEP technical report.* Washington, DC: U. S. Department of Education.

American Psychological Association, National Council on Measurement in Education & American Educational Research Association. (1999). *Standards for educational and psychological testing.* Washington DC: American Educational Research Association.

Anderson, T. W. (1963). Asymptotic theory for principal components analysis. *Annals of Mathematical Statistics, 34*, 122–148.

Beaton, A. (1987). *The NAEP 1983–84 technical report.* Princeton, NJ: Educational Testing Service.

Beaton, A. (2003). *A procedure for testing the fit of IRT models for special populations: Draft.* Unpublished manuscript.

Beaton, A., & Zwick, R. (1992). Overview of the National Assessment of Educational Progress. *Journal of Educational and Behavioral Statistics, 17*, 95–109.

Dresher, A. R., & Thind, S. K. (2007, April). *Examination of item fit for individual jurisdictions in NAEP.* Paper presented at the annual meeting of the American Educational Research Association, Chicago, IL, USA.

Efron, B., & Tibshirani, R. J. (1993). *An introduction to the bootstrap.* London: Chapman & Hall.

Gelman, A., Carlin, J. B., Stern, H. S., & Rubin, D. B. (2003). *Bayesian data analysis.* New York: Chapman & Hall.

Hjort, N. L., Dahl, F. A., & Steinbakk, G. (2006). Post-processing posterior predictive p values. *Journal of the American Statistical Association, 101*, 1157–1174.

Johnson, M. S., & Jenkins, F. (2004). *A Bayesian hierarchical model for large-scale educational surveys: An application to the National Assessment of Educational Progress* (ETS Research Report No. RR-04-38). Princeton, NJ: Educational Testing Service.

Kirsch, I. (2001). *The International Adult Literacy Survey (IALS): Understanding what was measured* (ETS Research Report No. RR-01-25). Princeton, NJ: Educational Testing Service.

Krzanowski, W. J. (1987). Cross-validation in principal component analysis. *Biometrics, 43*, 575–584.

Li, J. (2005). *The effect of accommodations for students with disabilities: An item fit analysis.* Paper presented at the annual meeting of the National Council on Measurement in Education, Montreal, Canada.

Li, Y., Bolt, D. M., & Fu, J. (2006). A comparison of alternative models for testlets. *Applied Psychological Measurement, 30*, 3–21.

Martin, M. O., & Kelly, D. L. (1996). *TIMSS technical report: Vol. I. Design and development.* Chestnut Hill, MA: Boston College.

Mislevy, R. (1985). Estimation of latent group effects. *Journal of the American Statistical Association, 80*, 993–997.

Mislevy, R., Johnson, E., & Muraki, E. (1992). Scaling procedures in NAEP. *Journal of Educational and Behavioral Statistics*, *17*, 131–154.

Mullis, I. V. S., Martin, M. O., Gonzalez, E. J., & Kennedy, A. M. (2003). *PIRLS 2001 international report: IEA's study of reading literacy achievement in primary schools.* Chestnut Hill, MA: Boston College.

Rogers, A., Gregory, K., Davis, S., & Kulick, E. (2006). *User's guide to NAEP model-based p-value programs.* Unpublished manuscript. Princeton, NJ: ETS.

Rogers, A., Tang, C., Lin, M.-J. & Kandathil, M. (2006). *DGROUP* (computer software). Princeton, NJ: Educational Testing Service.

Roussos, L., & Stout, W. (1996). A multidimensionality-based DIF analysis paradigm. *Applied Psychological Measurement*, *20*, 355–371.

Sinharay, S. (2005). Assessing fit of unidimensional item response theory models using a Bayesian approach. *Journal of Educational Measurement*, *42*, 375–394.

Sinharay, S. (2006). Bayesian item fit analysis for dichotomous item response theory models. *British Journal of Mathematical and Statistical Psychology*, *59*(2), 429–449.

Sinharay, S., Johnson, M. S., & Stern, H. S. (2006). Posterior predictive assessment of item response theory models. *Applied Psychological Measurement*, *30*(4), 298–321.

Sinharay, S., & Stern, H. S. (2003). Posterior predictive model checking in hierarchical models. *Journal of Statistical Planning and Inference*, *111*, 209–221.

Stone, C. A. (2000). Monte Carlo based null distribution for an alternative goodness-of-fit test statistic in IRT models. *Journal of Educational Measurement*, *37*(1), 58–75.

Thomas, N. (1993). Asymptotic corrections for multivariate posterior moments with factored likelihood functions. *Journal of Computational and Graphical Statistics*, *2*(3), 309–322.

van der Linden, W. J., & Hambleton, R. K. (1997). *Handbook of modern item response theory.* New York: Springer.

von Davier, M. (1997). Bootstrapping goodness-of-fit statistics for sparse categorical data: Results of a Monte Carlo study. *Methods of Psychological Research, 2*(2), 29–48.

von Davier, M., Sinharay, S., Oranje, A., & Beaton, A. (2006). Marginal estimation of population characteristics: Recent developments and future directions. In C. R. Rao & S. Sinharay (Eds.), *Handbook of statistics. Vol. 1. Psychometrics* (pp. 1039–1055). Amsterdam, The Netherlands: Elsevier.

School quality and student achievement in 21 European countries

The Heyneman-Loxley effect revisited

Sonia Ilie
University of Cambridge, Cambridge, UK

Petra Lietz
Australian Council for Educational Research, Adelaide, Australia[1]

The Heyneman-Loxley effect (1982, 1983) refers to an effect moderating the degree to which school quality affects student achievement. This moderating effect was found to relate to a country's economic productivity. More specifically, the effect is one in which school quality has a greater impact on student achievement in countries that are less developed economically than in countries that are more highly developed. This article presents a reexamination of this effect using hierarchical linear modeling (HLM) analyses of data for 21 European countries that participated in the Trends in International Mathematics and Science Study (TIMSS) in 2003. Two models are analyzed. The first is a three-level model that includes each country's economic status at the highest level, school resources at the middle level, and students' respective family backgrounds at the lowest level. The second is a two-level model that includes school and student context variables only and examines these separately for each country. Results indicate little evidence to support the Heyneman-Loxley effect in the selected group of countries in 2003.

---

1 The authors undertook the work reported in this article while at Jacobs University Bremen, Germany.

INTRODUCTION

Because education plays an important role in shaping an individual's life opportunities, it is generally agreed that the higher a person's achieved educational status, the higher the returns for that person in terms of economic and social status (see, for example, Levin 2001a, 2001b). However, what is less clear are which factors shape educational attainment, and how they operate. Teasing out these factors and their effects is extremely complex.

In order to explain differences in educational attainment, one needs to consider a number of factors frequently considered important at various levels of education systems. The economic status of a country, region, or city serves as a proxy for a system's available resources and tends to be located at the macro level of an education system. Among the factors considered to operate at the intermediate levels are those associated with the school and teachers and those associated with students' families and caregivers. The first group includes factors such as school leadership and resources, quality of instruction, and the commitment of teachers and other staff toward making the most of the available resources. The second group, pertaining as it does to students' locus of initial upbringing, includes core values and attitudes, including emphasis on educational attainment. It also covers resources relevant to education within the family and the assistance that family members are able to provide students with respect to their learning. At the micro level, factors such as student gender, ability, and attitudes toward school and future education, as well as behaviors such as self-confidence, persistence, and effort, are regarded as being essential to any attempt to explain differences in educational attainment. In the next section of this article, we list and discuss some of the relevant research pertaining to hypothesized reasons for variations in school achievement.

Reseachers conducting international comparative studies are faced with the question of whether these factors should be analyzed with a view to determining how they affect educational attainment across countries or within countries. In other words, should an international comparative study be directed at developing a universal model in which factors are examined that have significant effects on attainment across countries, or should it be directed at developing separate models that allow examination of how the different factors in the different countries influence attainment in each of those countries?

Heyneman and Loxley (1982) took the latter view. Employed by the World Bank at the time of their research, the authors focused on separate analyses of countries. Their aim was to obtain information about which factors affect attainment in specific nations, particularly low-income countries. This information would then inform policies related to the World Bank's allocation of funds to low-income countries. The two authors used multiple regression analysis to reanalyze data from the First International Science Study (FISS), undertaken by the International Association for the Evaluation of Educational Achievement (IEA) (Comber & Keeves, 1973). They entered variables into the analyses in four blocks: preschool, school track, school program, and school. The preschool variables included measures of parental education and occupation, number of books and use of dictionary at home, and student gender and age. School track (usually academic or vocational) was included only for those countries (e.g., Germany) offering students this option. School program captured the distinction between types of school (e.g., private or public). School variables included, for example, total student enrolment, percentage of science teachers, opportunity to learn, availability of science text-books, and hours of homework per week.

In line with the aims of the initial analysis of the IEA data, Comber and Keeves (1973) retained a variable only if its average standardized regression coefficients on science achievement was greater than |.05| across the 18 countries they considered for this particular analysis. Heyneman and Loxley (1982), in contrast, and in line with their aims, analyzed the data for each country separately. Their approach led to different variables being retained for each country. However, in the Comber and Keeves' analysis, each block contained the same variables. In the Heyneman and Loxley reanalysis, each block contained different variables because the categorization included only those variables found, in each country, to have a significant effect on achievement.

Results revealed considerable differences across countries in the number and overall explanatory power of variables, particularly those in the school variables block. The most dramatic differences were recorded for Chile and India. While 10 variables were included across all countries in the initial analysis, 19 were included for Chile and India in the reanalysis. The variance in science achievement explained by this block of school variables also increased from 6% (initial analysis) to 20% (reanalysis) in Chile and 8 to 28% in India.

These findings gave rise to the so-called Heyneman-Loxley effect, which states that the quality of schools has a greater impact on achievement in low-income countries than it does in high-income countries. At the same time, the effects on achievement of the family context tend to be weaker in low-income countries than in higher-income countries. While the study presented in this article is not an exact replication of the Heyneman-Loxley analysis, our aim was to examine the relative effects of the family and the school on achievement in different countries. We did this by undertaking hierarchical linear modeling (HLM) analyses of data from the successor of FISS, namely IEA's Trends in International Science and Mathematics Study (TIMSS) 2003.

This article is structured as follows. First, we give a brief overview of conceptual frameworks for analyzing factors influencing educational attainment. We also offer some insights into what is known about the different aspects of these frameworks. Second, we describe the data and our method of analysis. Third, we present and discuss the results of our analyses. We finish with a summary of our study and some conclusions.

REASONS FOR VARIATIONS IN STUDENT ACHIEVEMENT: AN OVERVIEW

Carroll (1963) developed an influential general model of school learning. The model posited three factors (aptitude, ability, and perseverance) as internal to the learner, and two factors (opportunity to learn and quality of instruction) as external to the learner. Carroll's work served as the basis for other models that emphasized various factors, such as student aptitude (Reynolds & Walberg, 1991), student environment (Bloom, 1976), instruction (Harnishfeger & Wiley, 1976), and teacher characteristics and instructional delivery (Anderson, 2004). Keeves (1972) presented a model that recognized the nested nature of educational settings and identified three levels in the educational environment of a student. These were the home, the peer group, and the school.

Lietz (1996), combining the elements of several of these models, developed a conceptual framework of variables on school learning made up of a two-way matrix. The rows of the matrix described the levels in which education is embedded. The columns of the matrix indicated the different dimensions. The levels, starting from the highest, were country, followed by community, school, classroom/teacher, home, and student. The dimensions, starting from the left, covered structure/demographics, resources, values, practices/behaviors, and outcomes. This framework allowed any variable to be placed in the matrix according to its location in terms of level and dimension. It also assisted with placing variables in models of factors influencing educational attainment. In general, variables at a higher level and further to the left were considered to influence variables at lower levels and further to the right. Thus, for example, GDP (gross domestic product), positioned as a resource variable at the country level, was considered to influence the number of public libraries. The libraries, in turn, formed a resource variable at the community level—a variable that could be considered to influence community values relating to literacy and literary enjoyment. Finally, outcomes considered at the student level included student learning, achievement, attitudes, and interests. Although these variables could be aggregated to other levels, Lietz argued that, in a conceptual framework of school learning, any educational effort has to be judged by its effects on students.

While the aforementioned frameworks endeavored to conceptualize the many factors that play a role in school learning, Buchmann and Hannum (2001) reviewed the results of relevant research into different aspects of these frameworks in order to delineate the areas encompassed by the research. Figure 1 illustrates the findings of this review. Buchmann and Hannum's comprehensive research review provided insights into the areas that still needed to be addressed to advance understanding of how the many factors within education systems influence student performance. One area that seemed to require further attention was community factors, which, either separately or in connection with family or school background, was assumed to affect educational outcomes, especially in economically less developed countries. Another area was the joint influence of school factors and family factors on educational outcomes, given that most research seemed to focus on one or the other.

Figure 1: Summary of findings of review of research into factors influencing student achievement

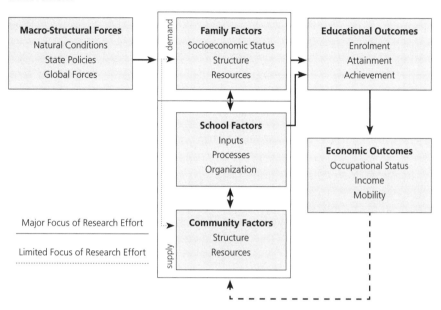

Source: Buchmann and Hannum (2001, p. 79).

Buchmann and Hannum (2001) considered that country-level reasons for differences in academic achievement related to educational policy that defined the length of the educational process, accessibility to it, and the financial resources the system needed to enable individuals to attend primary, secondary, and tertiary education. What could also be influenced at the country level (see also Fuller & Robinson, 1992) was how the people within the country perceived and understood the benefits of education. In other words, countries could differ with regard to the extent to which they fostered attitudes and behaviors conducive to providing high levels of educational provision and high levels of educational achievement. The authors furthermore argued that providing incentives for people to attain higher levels of education also contributes positively to a country's economy. This is because people with higher levels of educational attainment generally secure higher-paid employment (Ganzeboom, De Graaf, & Treiman, 1992), and they, in turn, benefit their country's economy by providing a highly educated and competent labor force.

Economic explanations of differential attainment also seemed extremely plausible on the basis of the research available at the time. One theory arising out of research examining the effects of economic development on students' learning posits that richer countries create an environment more conducive to learning. Findings reported by Entwisle and Alexander (1995), for example, suggested that because students from wealthier countries and families tend to have and to use more books and more learning materials than their less well-resourced peers, they have higher levels of educational achievement. Entwisle and Alexander (1995) also suggested that families in poorer countries frequently need to augment their income through child labor, which reduces even further the opportunity for these children to learn and to achieve at levels commensurate with those of children who do not have these restraints on their learning.

Baker, Goesling, and LeTendre (2002) provide evidence in support of this claim. They concluded from their study that students with more resources—regardless of whether these are books, family income, or teacher attention—have more opportunities to learn and to translate their knowledge into higher scores on tests and examinations. What these findings suggest, in terms of country-wide educational policy, is that ensuring a fair distribution of resources to students is a crucial starting point for achieving more positive outcomes (see also Chiu & Khoo, 2005, in this regard). Another study, by Schiller, Khmelkov, and Wang (2002), explored the effect of family characteristics on mathematics achievement and the relationship of this effect to a country's economic development level. Using data from TIMSS 1995, Schiller et al. found that "the positive effect of higher parents' education on middle-school students' mathematics test scores is remarkably consistent among the 34 nations examined" (p. 25).

The cultural approach to explaining differences in student achievement differentiates between societies that are structured in either an egalitarian or a hierarchical manner. The argument put forward under this approach is that people in hierarchical societies tend to "obey superiors" while those in egalitarian ones "interact as equals" (Chiu & Khoo, 2005). According to scholars such as Bond et al. (2004) and Hofstede (2001), the level of educational achievement that students attain is largely rooted in the context within which they are raised, generally the family, which not only conveys but also reflects the structures and values of a society.

Family has always been regarded as one of the most prominent factors influencing educational achievement (Elder, 1965; Rosen, 1961). Studies conducted at the high point of this theory in the 1960s and 1970s reinforced the idea that variations in family socialization practices account for differences in student achievement. Anderson and Evans (1976) compared Grade 9 students—students generally one year older than the eighth graders who participate in TIMSS—from Mexican-American and Anglo-American backgrounds. One of Anderson and Evans' main findings was that "parental independence training," operationalized as "the granting of enough autonomy to make decisions and to accept responsibility for success or failure" (p. 6), is associated with a significant increase in academic performance. Students who were guided toward an egalitarian work ethos, which prompted them to accept responsibility for their actions, autonomy, and independence, as opposed to relying on a clear command structure, seemed to fare better in achievement tests and overall performance than those working within a work ethos characterized by a clear command structure. The authors argued that the former group of students had a greater sense of confidence in their abilities, which stemmed from and contributed to their capacity to cope with economic, social, and educational challenges.

The individual student and the characteristics that influence his or her academic results are thus located within the family. Intelligence, readiness to work and learn, and analytical and synthetic cognitive abilities are obvious factors influencing a student's results in a formal educational setting. These characteristics tend, however, to be ones that are difficult to measure. IQ tests, for example, have come under scrutiny with respect to what they really measure and whether they can be validly related to other student characteristics (Francis et al., 2005; Weinberg 1989).

What has been examined in some detail, though, is the impact of attitudes on achievement—on whether students with more positive attitudes toward learning actually perform at a higher level than their less positive peers (e.g., Gardner, 1991; Singh, Granville, & Dika, 2002). The converse effect, which assumes that attitudes influence achievement, has also been studied (e.g., Kotte, 1992; Mickelson, 1990; Papanastasiou & Zembylas, 2002; Schibeci & Riley, 2006). The study by Papanastasiou and Zembylas (2002), conducted in Cyprus, identified a relationship between attitudes and achievement. The final model of factors influencing the science achievement of students in that country showed a complex set of interrelationships, including the degree of importance that students' parents accorded science-based subjects (e.g., biology, chemistry, earth science) and the extent to which the students themselves liked these subjects. Papanastasiou and Zembylas found a directional relationship between students' attitudes toward science and students' scores on the TIMSS test. The standardized path coefficient of .56 was one of the largest coefficients in the entire model. In percentage terms, the coefficient explained 16% of the overall science achievement score.

Another family influence concerns aspects that are more structural and financial in nature. A large family, for example, appears to hinder educational attainment because students with many siblings have to share and compete for resources (Blake, 1989; Downey, 2001; Steelman & Powell, 1989). The "resource dilution hypothesis" supported by these studies emphasizes that physical resources (such as number of books, time spent working with a computer) and parental control and attention are divided among the children of a household, which means that each successive child leads to decreases in academic achievement for the children of that household. Analyses have both confirmed (e.g., Pong, 1997, in Malaysia) and refuted this theory (e.g., Buchmann, 2000, in Kenya). This theory appears, though, to overlook one important factor that aids academic achievement, and that is cultural background. Sibling socialization and respect for elders, for example, can have a beneficial influence on the behavior and responsibility-related actions of children, attributes that have been shown to be associated with educational success (e.g., Galindo & Escamilla, 1995; Wang & Taylor, 2000).

Another culturally based theory is the "formative years" theory posited by Inglehart, Basanez, Diez-Medrano, Halman, and Luijkx (2004). If we connect this theory, as the authors did, to their claim of a growing trend of individualization worldwide, we face a large array of challenges in the field of educational determinants. If people are indeed focusing on themselves, their desires, and needs rather on than the collective or the group, this focus will be apparent in students' behavior, but how it plays out in terms of learning and achievement is, as yet, unclear. Modern teaching methods emphasize group work, team work, and cooperation. The question of whether such teaching methods mediate the individualistic tendencies of students to the detriment or advancement of their educational achievement has yet to be answered.

Chiu and McBride-Chang (2006) offer a family-focused explanation that has economic underpinnings. They suggest that one possible cause of variations in educational achievement is the likelihood that, especially in richer countries, physical public resources (such as libraries) have a positive influence on family resources because the former raises the value of the latter. Chiu and McBride-Chang's subsequent analysis of data from 43 countries provides evidence that interaction within the family has an impact on student achievement, particularly with respect to the parents' contribution to their children's knowledge about and understanding of the world.

Chiu and McBride-Chang's (2006) work brings in considerations relating to family structure. The increase in "non-traditional" households (e.g., single-parent, same-sex parents) (Akresh, 2007) has led to an increase in research on students from such backgrounds. Much of this research has focused on single-mother families, and has found a negative association between this type of family structure and achievement, as well as school attendance. Seltzer (1994), having reviewed research in this area, concluded that one causal element is the economic situation of such families, which are generally poorer than two-parent households. He also suggested a cultural component to the problem, namely the low levels of social capital within these families, which can sometimes be traced back to microeconomic aspects, such as increased working hours for the single mother and extensive use of external child-care services.

In summary, educational achievement is mediated by a large number of factors that operate at the country, school, family, and individual levels. Our aims during our study were twofold. Our first was to organize factors from each of these levels within a model of students' academic achievement in mathematics. Our second was to relate our findings from that process to the research undertaken by Heyneman and Loxley (1982, 1983) and to their eponymous effect, which suggests that a country's economic situation interacts with the relationship between school quality and student achievement. We also, during our analysis, took into consideration the results of the analyses of TIMSS data undertaken by Baker et al. (2002), who modeled the effects of country, school, and family background characteristics on achievement, and the results of the analyses conducted by Chiang (2006), who examined correlations between GDP and achievement across countries.

METHOD

TIMSS Sample

TIMSS 2003 defined two target populations. The first targeted students who had completed four years of formal schooling. The second targeted students who had completed eight years of formal schooling. For most countries, the two populations included students in Grade 4 and Grade 8. An international sampling referee oversaw the complex sampling procedures in order to ensure that the samples were of high quality and representative of the two target populations in each participating country. Countries could choose to have one or both populations take part in the study (Martin, Mullis, & Chrostowski, 2004).

Although the TIMSS 2003 sampling strategy differed across countries in some respects, it involved two stages. The first stage involved selection of schools. The second involved random selection of one intact class within each school. In order to increase sampling precision, the TIMSS analysts employed, for stratification purposes, any available information in a country that related to achievement and had been sanctioned for such use by that country. In many countries, this included information relating to geographical or administrative regions, school type (e.g., private or government), and school size. (For further details regarding sampling procedures employed in TIMSS 2003, see Foy & Joncas, 2004.)

European Sample

The present analysis was conducted with data from all 21 European countries that participated in the 2003 TIMSS assessment. The total number of participating students and the total number of participating schools across these countries were 82,403 and 3,922, respectively. For the purpose of the analyses, Europe was defined to include Cyprus and, as an extension, the Russian Federation. England and Scotland were considered as separate education systems, as was the Basque Country in Spain. At the time of the survey, Serbia and Montenegro still formed one country; this situation has since changed.

The original analysis by Heyneman and Loxley (1982) included 18 nations, their 1983 study focused on 29 countries, and the Baker et al. (2002) model expanded the initial sample to include 36 countries. (Table 1 lists the countries included in each analysis.) Our analysis, as noted, involved 21 countries—all European but not all members of the European Union. Our rationale for this choice was that previous research investigating the Heyneman-Loxley effect focused on either politically, geographically, or economically diverse samples, such as the ones detailed in Table 1, or on independent analyses of low GDP-per-capita countries. At the time of the 2003 TIMSS data collection, Europe—and particularly the countries of the European Union— was in the beginning stages of wide-reaching educational reform (e.g., the Bologna Declaration of 1999). Because of these reforms and the 2004 and 2007 accession to the European Union of several of the countries included in our analysis, the region is likely to experience pronounced change in terms of cross-country variation in student outcomes, educational expectations, educational policy, and economic situation. Given this context, our analysis could act as the initial stage of a larger comparative study of the interactions of state, family, and school variables on student achievement after a period of educational policy integration.

Our sample reflected the wide spread of GDP per capita observed in the Heyneman-Loxley (1982, 1983) and the Baker et al. (2002) studies. The GDP per capita, reported on the basis of purchasing power parity (PPP) in 2003, of the countries in our analysis ranged from $1,800 in Moldova to $37,700 in Norway. In the original analysis by Heyneman and Loxley (1982), the GDP per capita ranged from $117 in India to $5,362 in the United States of America.

Table 1: Countries considered in TIMSS data analyses focused on factors influencing student achievement

Heyneman and Loxley (1982)	Heyneman and Loxley (1983)	Baker et al. (2002)	Present study
Australia	Argentina	Australia	Basque Ct.
Belgium (Flemish)	Australia	Austria	Belgium (Flemish/French)
Belgium (French)	Belgium (Flemish)	Belgium (Flemish)	Bulgaria
Chile	Belgium (French)	Belgium (French)	Cyprus
England	Bolivia	Canada	England
Finland	Botswana	Colombia	Estonia
Germany	Brazil	Cyprus	Hungary
Hungary	Chile	Czech Republic	Italy
India	Colombia	Denmark	Latvia
Iran	Egypt	England	Lithuania
Italy	El Salvador	France	Macedonia
Japan	England	Germany	Moldova
Netherlands	Finland	Greece	Netherlands
New Zealand	Germany	Hong Kong	Norway
Scotland	Hungary	Hungary	Romania
Sweden	India	Iceland	Russia
Thailand	Iran	Ireland	Scotland
USA	Italy	Israel	Serbia-Montenegro
	Japan	Korea	Slovakia
	Mexico	Kuwait	Slovenia
	Netherlands	Latvia	Sweden
	New Zealand	Lithuania	
	Paraguay	Netherlands	
	Peru	New Zealand	
	Scotland	Norway	
	Sweden	Portugal	
	Thailand	Romania	
	Uganda	Russian Federation	
	USA	Singapore	
		Slovakia	
		Slovenia	
		Spain	
		Sweden	
		Switzerland	
		Thailand	
		USA	

Analyses

Although similar in pattern to the analysis reported by Baker et al. (2002), our analyses departed from their approach in several ways. First, we applied several models to the existing data. These included a two-level model for each individual country in order to account for interactions between the two levels (school and student) of the data, and a three-level model that included all 21 nations and also specified all cross-level interactions. Second, we did not include two of the background variables (at the school level) used in the Baker et al. study because these two were not included in the TIMSS 2003 background questionnaire (Martin, 2005a). As such, the current analyses do not represent a strict replication of the two major previous works, but they are similar enough to warrant comparisons, albeit in light of the different sampling strategy explained above.

Independent Variables

In this section, we briefly describe the independent variables employed in the analyses, first at the country, then at the school, and finally at the student level. Table 2 provides a summative account of these variables.

At the country level, we used GDP per capita as an indicator of a country's wealth. Because the data in the analyses were gathered in 2003, we took the 2003 value of the GDP for each country from the *CIA World Factbook* (Central Intelligence Agency, 2004) and measured it in terms of purchasing power parity (PPP) in 2003 US dollars.

At the school level, we employed the series of variables considered in the TIMSS 2003 survey. We began by using the 11-item index measuring shortages of school resources that was created from the TIMSS data (Martin, 2005b). Principals participating in TIMSS 2003 were asked to indicate the extent to which instruction in their schools was affected by a shortage of supply budget, school building space, instructional space, lighting and heating, computer hardware and software, library resources, calculators, laboratories, and audiovisual equipment. We then considered school-level information about the students. This included the percentage of students absent on a typical day from school and the percentage of students who completed the school year. This second variable indicated drop-out rates; principals were asked to indicate the "percentage of students who are still enrolled at the end of the school year, compared to the beginning of the year."

We also took into account a variable that focused on the principal's perception of the school climate. The assumption underlying this variable was that a safe learning environment, that is, one less affected by absenteeism, bullying, and/or disruptive behavior, would allow students to concentrate on their academic work. This TIMSS 2003 variable replaced the variable of "time spent by the principal discussing curriculum and school-wide issues with teachers" that Baker et al. (2002) used.

Although we would have been interested in doing so, we were unable to include a variable that was used in both the Heyneman-Loxley and the Baker et al. analyses but was not included in the TIMSS 2003 school questionnaire. This variable was the number of teachers who had been at the school for more than five years.

Table 2: Independent variables used in the current analyses

TIMSS variable	Variable name	Variable label	Coding
COUNTRY LEVEL			
GDPPERCA	GDP	GDP per capita in 2003	2003 U.S.$ (PPP)
SCHOOL LEVEL			
BCBGASTD	ABSENT from school	Percentage of students absent on a typical day	1 = < 5%; 2 = 5–10%; 3 = 11–20%; 4 = > 20%
BCBGENRS	RETENTION academic year	Percentage of students still enrolled at the end of the	1 = 96–100%; 2 = 90–95%; 3 = 80–89%; 4 = < 80%
BCDMST	RESOURCES	Availability of school resources for mathematics instruction	Is your school capacity to provide instruction affected by a shortage or an inadequacy of any of the following? a = Instructional materials (e.g., textbook) b = Budget for supplies (e.g., paper, pencils) c = School buildings and grounds d = Heating/cooling and lightening systems e = Instructional space (e.g., classrooms) g = Computers for maths instruction h = Computer software for maths instruction i = Calculators for maths instruction j = Library materials for maths instruction k = Audio-visual resources for maths instruction 1 = none, 2 = a little, 3 = some, 4 = a lot Three levels assigned to this variable: 1 = High: Average value of a–e is < 2 AND the average value of g–k is < 2 3 = Low: Average value of a–e ≥ 3 AND the average value of g–k ≥ 3 2 = Medium: All other combinations

Table 2: Independent variables used in the current analyses (contd.)

TIMSS variable	Variable name	Variable label	Coding
COUNTRY LEVEL			
BCDGCH	CLIMATE	School climate	Computed from principals' responses to eight items regarding school climate using a 4-point Likert scale (1 = v. high, 2 = high, 3 = med., 4 = low, 5 = v. low)
			How would you characterize each of the following within your school? (SCQ2_7)
			The question consisted of 8 items:
			a = Teachers' job satisfaction
			b = Teachers' understanding of the school's curricular goals
			c = Teachers' degree of success in implementing the school's curriculum
			d = Teachers' expectations for student achievement
			e = Parental support for student achievement
			f = Parental involvement in school activities
			g = Students' regard for school property
			h = Students' desire to do well in school.
			An index was calculated by averaging the responses for the above eight categories and assigning three levels to the variable:
			1 = High: Average value is ≤ 2
			2 = Medium: Average value is > 2 AND ≤ 3
			3 = Low: Average value is > 3.
STUDENT LEVEL			
ITSEX	GENDER	Student gender	1 = Girl, 2 = Boy
BSBGOLAN	LANGUAGE	Language at home different from language of instruction	1 = Always, 2 = Almost always, 3 = Sometimes, 4 = Never
BSBGBOOK	BOOKS	Number of books in the home	1 = 0–10, 2 = 11–25, 3 = 26–100, 4 = 101–200, 5 = more than 200
BSDAGE	AGE	Student's age in months	Age in months
BSDGEDUP	PARENTS	Highest educational level of either parent	1 = Finished university or equivalent or higher (ISCED 7,8)
			2 = Finished post-secondary vocational/technical education but not university (ISCED 5,6)
			3 = Finished upper secondary schooling (ISCED 4)
			4 = Finished lower secondary schooling (ISCED 3)
			5 = No more than primary schooling (ISCED 1,2)

Variables at the student level included the educational status of parents and the number of books in a student's home. We also took into account background information, by including, as independent variables in the analyses, age, gender, and whether or not the language of instruction was the same as the one spoken at home.

Dependent Variable

The dependent variable that we used in the analyses consisted of the five plausible values calculated for each student as an estimate of his or her mathematics proficiency. Plausible values were first proposed by Mislevy, Beaton, Kaplan, & Sheehan (1992), who based their work on work conducted by Rubin (1987).[2] According to the American Institutes for Research (2008), plausible values are:

> ... imputed values that resemble individual test scores and have approximately the same distribution as the latent trait being measured. Plausible values were developed as a computational approximation to obtain consistent estimates of population characteristics in assessment situations where individuals are administered too few items to allow precise estimates of their ability. Plausible values represent random draws from an empirically derived distribution of proficiency values that are conditional on the observed values of the assessment items and the background variables.

In order to apply the five plausible values (BSMMAT01-05) as the outcome variable, we used the "plausible value outcome variable" option in the "estimation settings" of the HLM6 software (Raudenbush, Bryk, Cheong, Congdon, & du Toit, 2004) that was used for the multilevel modeling undertaken in this study. From here on, we refer to this dependent variable as MATH. However, it is important to note that we estimated each parameter for each of the five plausible values and subsequently averaged the five estimates in the HLM. Finally, we calculated standard errors for the average, using the approach put forward by Little and Rubin (1987; see also Little & Schenker, 1995).

The Models

As we mentioned earlier, we ran two types of model. In the first model, we simultaneously analyzed data from all 21 countries in a three-level HLM, with student data included at Level 1, school data at Level 2, and country data at Level 3. The equations for the three-level model[3] (without interactions) follow:

- *Level 1 model:* MATH = π_0 + π_1(GENDER) + π_2(LANGUAGE) + π_3(BOOKS) + π_4(AGE) + π_5(PARENTS) + e
- *Level 2 model:* π_0 = β_{00} + β_{01}(ABSENT) + β_{02}(RETENTION) + β_{03}(RESOURCES) + β_{04}(CLIMATE) + r_0
- *Level 3 model:* β_{00} = γ_{000} + γ_{001}(GDP) + u_{00}

---

2 For a primer on the rationale for using plausible values in survey assessments such as TIMSS, see von Davier, Gonzalez, and Mislevy (2009).

3 Unless otherwise stated, all variables were grand-mean centered. House weight (HOUWGT) was used at Level 1 and school weight (SCHWGT) was used at Level 2.

Because hierarchical linear modeling with HLM6 did not allow for missing data at the second and third levels, we had a small reduction in cases when analyzing the model. This reduction meant that we analyzed data from 71,829 students and 2,634 schools. In regard to the Level 3 model, the absence of a significant direct link between countries' economic levels of development and mathematics performance would not in itself negate the existence or persistence of the Heyneman-Loxley effect. Rather, as illustrated by the conceptual frameworks discussed above, GDP might operate through constructs at lower levels to influence performance. We therefore specified an additional three-level model that included interactions between GDP per capita and all variables at the second and third levels. The equations were as follows:

$$MATH = \pi_0 + \pi_1(GENDER) + \pi_2(LANGUAGE) + \pi_3(BOOKS) + \pi_4(AGE) + \pi_5(PARENTS) + e$$

$$\pi_0 = \beta_{00} + \beta_{01}(ABSENT) + \beta_{02}(RETENTION) + \beta_{03}(RESOURCES) + \beta_{04}(CLIMATE) + r_0$$

$$\pi_1 = \beta_{10} + r_1$$

$$\pi_2 = \beta_{20} + r_2$$

$$\pi_3 = \beta_{30} + r_3$$

$$\pi_4 = \beta_{40} + r_4$$

$$\pi_5 = \beta_{50} + r_5$$

$$\beta_{00} = \gamma_{000} + \gamma_{001}(GDP) + u_{00}$$

$$\beta_{01} = \gamma_{010} + \gamma_{011}(GDP) + u_{01}$$

$$\beta_{02} = \gamma_{020} + \gamma_{021}(GDP) + u_{02}$$

$$\beta_{03} = \gamma_{030} + \gamma_{031}(GDP) + u_{03}$$

$$\beta_{04} = \gamma_{040} + \gamma_{041}(GDP) + u_{04}$$

$$\beta_{10} = \gamma_{100} + \gamma_{101}(GDP) + u_{10}$$

$$\beta_{20} = \gamma_{200} + \gamma_{201}(GDP) + u_{20}$$

$$\beta_{30} = \gamma_{300} + \gamma_{301}(GDP) + u_{30}$$

$$\beta_{40} = \gamma_{400} + \gamma_{401}(GDP) + u_{40}$$

$$\beta_{50} = \gamma_{500} + \gamma_{501}(GDP) + u_{50}$$

We estimated the next model—the two-level model with data from students analyzed at the first level and information from schools included at the second level—separately for each country. The equations for this model follow:

- *Level 1 model:* $MATH = \beta_0 + \beta_1(GENDER) + \beta_2(LANGUAGE) + \beta_3(BOOKS) + \beta_4(AGE) + \beta_5(PARENTS) + r$

- *Level 2 model:* $\beta_0 = \gamma_{00} + \gamma_{01}(ABSENT) + \gamma_{02}(RETENTION) + \gamma_{03}(RESOURCES) + \gamma_{04}(CLIMATE) + u_0$

As with the three-level analyses, missing data were not permitted at the higher level of the two-level analyses. This situation resulted in fewer cases in the latter. However, in most countries, a sufficient number of cases remained to warrant analysis. In three countries, missing data led to information for just under 80% of the schools being retained in the analyses. These countries were Moldova (73% valid cases), England (63% valid cases), and Scotland (68% valid cases). This information needs to be kept in mind when interpreting the results. In addition, in Cyprus and Slovenia, the variable "percentage of students still enrolled at the end of the academic year" (RETENTION) had a constant value of 1 (the code attributed to the approximately 96% or students still enrolled). We excluded this variable from the analyses for these two countries.

So that we could take into account the initial TIMSS sample design, we weighted cases by house weight (HOUWGT) at the student level, and by school weight (SCHWGT) at the school level. Using the HLM6 software (Raudenbush et al., 2004) to normalize these weights allowed us to address the concerns regarding their use expressed by Rutkowski, Gonzalez, Joncas, and von Davier (2010). We did not conduct weighting at the country level because we knew that each country would contribute equally to the final results.

RESULTS AND DISCUSSION

We present and discuss the results in two parts. In the first part, we focus on cross-country variations in student achievement in mathematics. In the second part, we present the results by country. We compare these results in both sections to the results of the studies reported by Heyneman and Loxley (1982) and Baker et al. (2002).

Cross-Country Variation in Student Achievement in Mathematics: The Three-Level Model

No significant direct effect of GDP per capita on mathematics achievement ($p = .52$) emerged from the analysis (see Tables 3 and 4). Once the other factors in the model were taken into account, there was no evidence that students in countries with a higher GDP per capita performed at a higher level in mathematics than students in countries with a lower GDP per capita. The only other variable whose direct effect was also not significant ($p = .49$) was GENDER, indicating that male and female students performed at similar levels in mathematics, a finding that aligns with other reported TIMSS results (e.g., Neuschmidt, Barth, & Hastedt, 2008).

As is evident from Tables 3 and 4, the direct effects of the other predictors of achievement emerged as significant. Thus, at the student level, significant effects were observed for the frequency with which students spoke the language of instruction at home (LANGUAGE; π_{02} = -3.31), the number of books in the home (BOOKS; π_{03} = 11.07), the student's age (AGE; π_{04} = -18.94), and parental education (PARENTS; π_{05} = -9.80). When we took into consideration the direction of the effects and the coding of the variables (see Table 2 above), these results indicated that students who spoke the language of instruction more frequently at home, who had more books at home, who were younger, and who had more highly educated parents achieved at a higher level than their peers. These effects held after all other significant effects in the model had been considered. Thus, books at home appears to have a separate, identifiable positive effect on performance even after the educational level of parents is taken into account.

Table 3: Final estimation of fixed effects, model without interactions

Fixed effect	Standard coefficient	Error	Approx. t-ratio	D.F.	p-value
For INTRCPT$_1$, π_0					
For INTRCPT$_2$, β_{00}					
INTRCPT$_3$, γ_{000}	500.565	3.466	144.434	19	0.000
GDP, γ_{001}	-0.000	0.000	-0.648	19	0.525
For ABSENT, β_{01}					
INTRCPT$_3$, γ_{010}	-9.862	1.563	-6.308	2629	0.000
For RETENTION, β_{02}					
INTRCPT$_3$, γ_{020}	2.813	0.591	4.763	2629	0.000
For RESOURCES, β_{803}					
INTRCPT$_3$, γ_{030}	-7.227	1.632	-4.429	2629	0.000
For CLIMATE, β_{04}					
INTRCPT$_3$, γ_{040}	-11.297	0.850	-13.289	2629	0.000
For GENDER slope, π_1					
For INTRCPT$_2$, β_{10}					
INTRCPT$_3$, γ_{100}	-1.533	2.240	-0.685	55777	0.493
For LANGUAGE slope, π_2					
For INTRCPT$_2$, β_{20}					
INTRCPT$_3$, γ_{200}	-3.313	1.182	-2.803	55777	0.006
For BOOKS slope, π_3					
For INTRCPT$_2$, β_{30}					
INTRCPT$_3$, γ_{300}	11.066	1.140	9.706	55777	0.000
For AGE slope, π_4					
For INTRCPT$_2$, β_{40}					
INTRCPT$_3$, γ_{400}	-18.939	0.529	-35.795	55777	0.000
For PARENTS slope, π_5					
For INTRCPT$_2$, β_{50}					
INTRCPT$_3$, γ_{500}	-9.802	0.627	-15.625	55777	0.000

Table 4: Final estimation of variance components, model without interactions

Random effect	Standard deviation	Variance component	Chi-square	D.F.	p-value
INTRCPT$_1$, r_0	34.501	1190.305	25868.272	2599	0.000
LEVEL 1, e	60.453	3654.523			
INTRCPT$_1$/INTRCPT$_2$, u_{00}	12.266	150.467	223.684	19	0.000

73

Significant effects for the school-level variables on achievement were also detected for the percentages of students absent on a typical day from school (ABSENT; β_{01} = -9.86) and still enrolled at the end of the school year (RETENTION; β_{02} = 2.81), the availability of school resources for mathematics instruction (RESOURCES; β_{03} = -7.23), and the nature of the school climate (CLIMATE; β_{04} = -11.30). Thus, once we had taken student characteristics into account, it was apparent that students who were achieving at the higher levels were those attending schools with lower absenteeism, where instruction was less affected by shortages of school resources, and where principals reported a positive school climate in terms of teachers' job satisfaction, involvement, and expectations as well as parental support and students' desire to do well.

The positive effect for RETENTION appears somewhat counterintuitive because, given its coding, this result suggests that students in schools with a lower percentage of students enrolled at the end of the academic year perform at a higher level. A more probable explanation, however, could be that it is the lower-achieving students who have dropped out, resulting in a higher performance within these schools compared to those schools that manage to retain the lower-performing students.

The above results are meaningful, but they do not directly address the core feature of the Heyneman-Loxley effect, namely the cross-level interactions. The absence of a significant direct relationship between a country's economic situation and mathematics performance would not by itself negate the existence or persistence of the Heyneman-Loxley effect. Indeed, it would appear to be the main underlying tenet that the effects of school quality and family context on achievement differ depending on countries' levels of economic development. While Heyneman and Loxley were unable to use multilevel modeling to test this hypothesis in 1982 and 1983, advances in statistical analysis programs have since made such a test possible. We therefore introduced cross-level interactions of GDP per capita on school-level and student-level variables in the initial model, in an effort to determine if the effects of these variables on mathematics achievement would vary depending on the level of countries' economic development. Tables 5 and 6 present the results of this analysis.

In their 2002 article, Baker et al. reported no significant interaction effects between GDP per capita and any of the school-level variables, which led the authors to conclude that "the effects of school resources do not vary significantly across countries with different levels of economic development" (p. 303). Our analysis confirmed this absence of significant interaction effects between GDP and the school-level variables, with the exception of RETENTION (i.e., the percentage of students still enrolled at the end of the academic year). The positive interaction effect observed for this variable suggests that the differences in mathematics performance of students in schools with varying drop-out rates are greater in low-income countries.

However, care must be exercised when comparing the two slightly different conclusions, for two reasons. First, the Baker et al. (2002) study used two other school-level variables in the analysis (as discussed above) and did not include the school climate variable (CLIMATE) used in the present study. Second, while the interaction effect was statistically significant ($p = .00$), a substantive interpretation would appear inappropriate given the size of this effect ($\gamma_{021} = -0.001$).

Table 5: Final estimation of fixed effects, model with interactions

Fixed effect	Standard coefficient	Error	Approx. t-ratio	D.F.	p-value
For INTRCPT$_1$, π_0					
For INTRCPT$_2$, β_{00}					
INTRCPT$_3$, γ_{000}	501.274	3.516	142.56	19	0.000
GDP, γ_{001}	-9.999	0.000	-0.635	19	0.533
For ABSENT, β_{01}					
INTRCPT3, γ_{010}	-10.707	1.960	-5.462	40	0.000
GDP, γ_{011}	0.000	0.000	0.355	99	0.723
For RETENTION, β_{02}					
INTRCPT$_3$, γ_{020}	-4.746	2.236	-2.212	408	0.034
GDP, γ_{021}	-0.001	0.000	-3.910	1178	0.000
For RESOURCES, β_{803}					
INTRCPT$_3$, γ_{030}	-6.615	1.614	-4.097	67	0.000
GDP, γ_{031}	-0.000	0.000	-0.543	1028	0.587
For CLIMATE, β_{04}					
INTRCPT$_3$, γ_{040}	-9.998	2.041	-4.898	31	0.000
GDP, γ_{041}	-0.000	0.000	-0.821	78	0.414
For GENDER slope, π_1					
For INTRCPT$_2$, β_{10}					
INTRCPT$_3$, γ_{100}	0.841	1.555	0.541	39	0.591
GDP, γ_{101}	0.000	0.000	2.409	17	0.028
For LANGUAGE slope, π_2					
For INTRCPT$_2$, β_{20}					
INTRCPT$_3$, γ_{200}	-4.334	1.030	-4.207	13	0.001
GDP, γ_{201}	-0.000	0.000	-3.569	186	0.001
For BOOKS slope, π_3					
For INTRCPT$_2$, β_{30}					
INTRCPT$_3$, γ_{300}	11.334	1.002	11.313	124	0.000
GDP, γ_{301}	-0.000	0.000	-0.536	128	0.593
For AGE slope, π_4					
For INTRCPT$_2$, β_{40}					
INTRCPT$_3$, γ_{400}	-16.921	1.563	-10.898	16	0.000
GDP, γ_{401}	0.000	0.000	1.980	26	0.058
For PARENTS slope, π_5					
For INTRCPT$_2$, β_{50}					
INTRCPT$_3$, γ_{500}	-9.352	0.496	-18.868	110	0.000
GDP, γ_{501}	0.000	0.000	2.501	134	0.014

Table 6: Final estimation of variance components, model with interactions

Random effect	Standard deviation	Variance component	Chi-square	D.F.	p-value
INTRCPT$_1$, r_0	35.188	1238.206	26404.763	2599	0.000
LEVEL 1, e	61.162	3740.803			
INTRCPT$_1$/INTRCPT$_2$, u_{00}	11.884	141.233	206.149	19	0.000

The same comment applies to the picture that emerged at the student level. While a number of statistically significant interaction effects between GDP and student-level constructs were apparent in the current analyses, the sizes of the effects were so small (i.e., would result in changes to the mathematics score in the fourth decimal place) that they do not warrant substantive interpretation. Therefore, the results of the current analyses can be seen to support Baker and colleagues' (2002) report of no significant interaction effects of GDP on the relationship between student-level constructs and achievement.

The percentages of variance explained by the model at each level and overall are given in Table 7. Here, the calculations were based on the formulae developed by Bryk and Raudenbush (1996, p. 13), which state that the variance available to be explained at each of the two levels can be calculated by dividing the variance component associated with the intercept by the sum of that variance component plus the variance component associated with the slope. The same authors also offered a formula for calculating the percentages of explained variance at each level by dividing the difference between the variance component associated with the fully unconditional (null) model and the variance component from the full model to the former. In order to arrive at the final variance explained by the model, the two results are multiplied. Thus, in the current analysis, the model explained 44% of the variance associated with the school level (i.e., 24%). This outcome translated into school-level variables explaining 11% of the total variance (i.e., 0.44*0.24). In addition, the student-level variables explained 8% of the nearly three-quarters of the between-student variance (i.e., 6% of the overall variance) while GDP accounted for about one-third (39%) of the variance between countries (3%), which translated into 1% of the overall variance. As a consequence, the total variance accounted for in mathematics achievement by all variables in the three-level model was 18%.

Table 7: Variance components, three-level model

	Variance available to be explained (1) (%)	Variance explained by model (2) (%)	Final variance explained by model (1)*(2) (%)
Between students	0.73	0.08	0.06
Between schools	0.24	0.44	0.11
Between countries	0.03	0.39	0.01
Total variance explained by final model			0.18

Country-by-Country Student Achievement in Mathematics: The Two-Level Models

Table 8 shows which variables had a significant relationship with achievement in each country, listed in ascending order of GDP per capita. As is evident from the table, the degree of variance that the model explained between students within schools ranged from 2% in Latvia, Lithuania, and the Netherlands to 10% in Norway. The variance explained between schools revolved around 13% in most countries, with Moldova (1%), Norway (4%), and Romania (5%) being exceptionally low. Again, no pattern in support of the Heyneman-Loxley effect emerged. If such an effect had been apparent, we would have seen an increase in the amount of variance explained by the student-context variables and a decrease, as GDP increased, in the amount of variance in achievement explained by school-level variables.

Table 8: Significant direct effects in two-level model, by country ($p < .05$)

Country	Student-level context variables			School-level context variables			
	LANGUAGE	BOOKS	PARENTS	RETENTION	CLIMATE	RESOURCES	ABSENT
Moldova		X	X				
Serbia-Montenegro		X	X				
Cyprus	X	X	X		X		X
Bulgaria		X	X			X	
Macedonia	X	X	X				X
Romania		X	X				
Russia		X	X	X			X
Latvia		X	X				
Lithuania		X	X				
Estonia	X	X	X				
Slovakia		X	X	X	X		X
Hungary	X	X	X	X			
Slovenia	X	X	X				
Basque Ct.		X	X				X
Italy	X	X	X	X	X		
Sweden	X	X	X				X
England		X		X			
Scotland		X	X				X
Netherlands	X	X			X		
Belgium	X	X	X	X	X		X
Norway		X	X	X			

77

Because the countries in Table 8 are listed in ascending order, we would expect a larger number of crosses—indicating a significant effect of a school-level variable—to emerge in the upper right-hand side of the table. At the same time, and assuming the Heyneman-Loxley effect applied to the countries under review, we would expect fewer crosses, indicating significant effects of school variables on achievement for countries lower down the table, given that these are the higher-income countries.

No such pattern emerged. Indeed, for the two countries with the lowest GDP—Moldova and Serbia-Montenegro—none of the school-level variables had a significant relationship with achievement. However, for Belgium, the country with the second-highest GDP, three of the four school-level variables had a significant effect on achievement, and three significant effects emerged for Slovakia, one of the countries with a medium-size GDP. At the same time, no significant school-level effects emerged for Latvia, Lithuania, and Estonia, which also are located in the middle in terms of economic development. Thus, no pattern of effects in support of the Heyneman-Loxley effect emerged from our analysis.

When we considered two of the three student-level context variables, a consistent pattern became apparent. The number of books in the home had a significant effect on achievement in all 21 countries, while a high level of educational attainment by one or both parents had a significant effect in all countries except England and the Netherlands. The frequency with which students spoke the language of instruction at home had a significant effect in only nine of the 21 countries. Taken together, these results do not support the greater importance of family context variables for achievement in countries with higher GDP that is suggested by the Heyneman-Loxley effect.

Overall, it appears that, across all 21 countries, student-level predictors were more consistently related to mathematics achievement than were school-level predictors (see Table 9).

Table 9: Country-specific explained variance and GDP per capita

Country	PPP for GDP per capita (2003)	Variance explained between students, within schools (1)	Variance explained between schools (2)	Total variance explained (1)+(2)
Moldova	1,800	0.04	0.01	0.05
Serbia-Montenegro	2,300	0.05	0.17	0.22
Cyprus	5,600	0.06	0.17	0.23
Bulgaria	6,600	0.04	0.10	0.14
Macedonia	6,700	0.03	0.15	0.19
Romania	6,900	0.04	0.05	0.09
Russia	8,900	0.04	0.12	0.16
Latvia	10,100	0.02	0.13	0.15
Lithuania	11,200	0.02	0.17	0.19
Estonia	12,300	0.07	0.12	0.19
Slovakia	13,300	0.04	0.17	0.21
Hungary	13,900	0.06	0.17	0.23
Slovenia	18,300	0.05	0.12	0.17
Basque Ct.	22,000	0.05	0.17	0.22
Italy	26,800	0.05	0.12	0.18
Sweden	26,800	0.08	0.16	0.24
England	27,700	0.04	0.13	0.18
Scotland	27,700	0.04	0.14	0.19
Netherlands	28,600	0.02	0.10	0.12
Belgium	29,000	0.03	0.12	0.15
Norway	37,700	0.10	0.04	0.14

CONCLUSION

In summary, the results of the analysis of the three-level model provided little support for the Heyneman-Loxley effect for three main reasons.

First, no direct effect of GDP on achievement emerged from the data used in the models tested in this study. In other words, mathematics performance did not systematically differ in relation to GDP once other factors in the model were taken into account.

Second, and more importantly, the effects of three of the four school-level variables on achievement did not differ systematically in relation to country GDP—the main assumption of the Heyneman-Loxley effect. Thus, no interaction effects emerged for GDP and the relationships between student absenteeism, school mathematics resources, school climate, and students' achievement. The exception was the percentage of students still enrolled at the end of the academic year. Here, the interaction effect of GDP indicated that the performance differences across schools with different drop-out rates were greatest in countries with lower levels of economic development.

The third reason relates to the Heyneman-Loxley assertion that the importance of school quality decreases for higher-income countries as the importance of family context increases. The results of our three-level analyses supported this assertion in only one instance—number of books in the home. This outcome suggests that the likelihood of students from homes with more books performing at a higher level in mathematics becomes more pronounced as a country's GDP rises. In contrast, the negative interaction effect of GDP with language of instruction not being spoken at home suggests that the likelihood that students who speak the language of instruction at home will perform at a higher level than their peers is less pronounced in higher-income countries.

The analyses of the two-level model for each of the 21 countries provided no evidence in support of the Heyneman-Loxley effect. The school-level variables were no more likely to have significant effects on achievement in low-income countries than they were in high-income countries, and they did not account for the variance in achievement in these countries. At the same time, two of the three student context variables—books in the home and parental education—consistently related to achievement across 19 of the 21 countries, regardless of those countries' levels of economic development. This finding points to the continuing universal importance relative to student achievement of the context in which students are raised.

In conclusion, the results of the analysis of TIMSS 2003 data for 21 European countries at quite different stages of economic development presented in this article provide little, if any, support for the existence of the Heyneman-Loxley effect, which maintains that school quality is of greater importance and family context is of lower importance in low-income countries than in high-income countries. In this respect, the current results support findings reported by Baker et al. (2002), who also found no evidence in support of the Heyneman-Loxley effect in their analysis of TIMSS 1995 data.

What the current analyses do emphasize, however, is the consistent and continuing importance of the home environment for student achievement across countries. An example of a possible response to the finding that a large proportion of the differences in student achievement relate to individual student rather than school characteristics can be found in South Australia. The Innovative Community Action Networks (ICAN) (Government of South Australia, 2008) is a program targeted at 12- to 19-year-old students who are at risk of dropping out of school or who have left school without a formal qualification and who have not enrolled in further education or started employment. The program takes a case-management approach in that it assesses each student's individual circumstances and then requires the school and home in partnership to develop and manage learning opportunities suited to that student's needs.

In order to provide and deliver these opportunities, the South Australian Department of Education and Children's Services has entered partnerships with a variety of community groups, including youth groups, employer groups, health services, local councils, theatre and arts groups, local businesses, justice teams, parents, schools, vocational training colleges, universities, and volunteer organizations. In this way, students in the program are provided with the kinds of opportunities and experiences that other students enjoy as a result of their more advantaged home backgrounds. The Australian initiative, and the likely many other such examples, suggest that in line with the ongoing quest to assist all students to reach their full potential, future policy decisions regarding the allocation of resources might be more fruitfully aimed at developing creative ways to support the educational efforts and resources to which students are exposed not only within schools but also outside them.

References

Akresh, R. (2007). *School enrolment impacts of non-traditional household structure*. Unpublished manuscript, University of Illinois at Urbana–Champagne. Retrieved from https://netfiles.uiuc.edu/akresh/www/Research/Akresh_SchoolEnrollment.pdf

American Institutes for Research. (2008). *Plausible values imputation: Draft version*. Retrieved from http://am.air.org/help/NAEPTextbook/htm/oplausiblevalue simputations.htm

Anderson, J. G., & Evans, F. B. (1976). Family socialization and educational achievement in two cultures: Mexican-American and Anglo-American. *Sociometry*, *39*(3), 209–222.

Anderson, L. W. (2004). *Increasing teacher effectiveness* (2nd ed.). Paris: UNESCO International Institute for Educational Planning.

Baker, D. P., Goesling, B., & LeTendre, K. G. (2002). Socioeconomic status, school quality, and national economic development: A cross-national analysis of the "Heyneman-Loxley effect" on mathematics and science achievement. *Comparative Education Review*, *46*(3), 291–312.

Blake, J. (1989). *Family size and achievement*. Berkeley, CA: University of California Press.

Bloom, B. (1976). Human characteristics and school learning. New York: McGraw Hill.

Bologna Declaration (1999). *Joint declaration of the European ministers of education*. Retrieved from http://www.bologna-bergen2005.no/Docs/00-Main_doc/990719BOLOGNA_DECLARATION.PDF

Bond, M. H., Leung, K., Au, A., Tong, K.-K., de Carrasquel, S. R., Murakami, F. M., Yamaguchi, S. ... Lewis, J. R. (2004). Cultural dimensions of social axioms. *Journal of Cross-Cultural Psychology*, *35*(5), 548–570.

Bryk, A. S., & Raudenbush, S. W. (1996). *HLM: Hierarchical linear modeling with HLM/2L and HLM/3L programs*. Chicago, IL: Scientific Software International Press.

Buchmann, C. (2000). Family structure, parental perceptions and child labor in Kenya: What factors determine who is enrolled in school? *Social Forces*, *78*, 1349–1379.

Buchmann, C., & Hannum, E. (2001). Education and stratification in developing countries: A review of theories and research. *Annual Review of Sociology*, *27*, 77–102.

Carroll, J. P. (1963). A model of school learning. *Teachers College Record*, *64*(8), 723–733.

Central Intelligence Agency (CIA). (2004). *The 2003 world factbook*. Retrieved April 1, 2008, from https://www.cia.gov/library/publications/download/download-2003/index. html

Chiang, F. S. (2006). *Student learning and national economic development: A re-examination of the Heyneman-Loxley effect using TIMSS 1999 and 2003 data*. Paper presented at the 2005 annual meeting of the Comparative and International Educational Society (West) at the University of British Columbia, Vancouver, Canada.

Chiu, M. M., & Khoo, L. (2005). Effects of resources, distribution inequality, and privileged bias on achievement: Country, school, and student level analyses. *American Educational Research Journal*, *42*, 575–603.

Chiu, M. M., & McBride-Chang, C. (2006). Gender, context and reading: A study of students in 43 countries. *Scientific Studies of Reading*, *10*(4), 331–362.

Comber, L. C., & Keeves, J. P. (1973). *Science education in nineteen countries*. Stockholm, Sweden: Almqvist & Wiksell.

Downey, D. B. (2001). Number of siblings and intellectual development: The resource dilution explanation. *American Psychologist*, *56*(6–7), 497–504.

Elder, G. H. Jr. (1965). Family structure and educational attainment: A cross-national analysis. *American Sociological Review*, *30*, 81–96.

Entwisle, D. R., & Alexander, K. L. (1995). A parent's economic shadow: Family structure versus family resources as influences on early school achievement. *Journal of Marriage and the Family*, *57*(2), 399–409.

Foy, P., & Joncas, M. (2004). TIMSS 2003 sampling design. In M. O. Martin, I. V. S. Mullis, & S. J. Chrostowski (Eds.), *TIMSS 2003 technical report* (pp. 108–123). Chestnut Hill, MA: Boston College.

Francis, D. J., Fletcher, J. M., Stuebing, K. K., Lyon, G. R., Shaywitz, B. A., & Shaywitz, S. E. (2005). Psychometric approaches to the identification of LD: IQ and achievement scores are not sufficient. *Journal of Learning Disabilities*, *38*(2), 98.

Fuller, B., & Robinson, R. (1992). *The political construction of education*. New York: Praeger.

Galindo, R., & Escamilla, K. (1995). A biographical perspective on Chicano educational success. *The Urban Review*, *27*(1), 1–29.

Ganzeboom, H. B. G., De Graaf, P. M., & Treiman, D. J. (1992). A standard international socio-economic index of occupational status. *Social Science Research*, *21*, 1–56.

Gardner, R. C. (1991). Attitudes and motivation in second language learning. In A. G. Reynolds (Ed.), *Bilingualism, multiculturalism, and second language learning* (pp. 43–64). Hillsdale, NJ: Lawrence Erlbaum Associates.

Government of South Australia. (2008). *Innovative Community Action Networks (ICAN)*. Retrieved from http://www.decs.sa.gov.au/portal/students.asp?group=stayingschool&id =ican

Harnishfeger A., & Wiley, D. E. (1976). Conceptual issues in models of school learning. *Curriculum Studies*, *10*(3), 215–231.

Heyneman S. P., & Loxley, W. A. (1982). Influences on academic performance across high- and low-income countries: A re-analysis of IEA data. *Sociology of Education*, *55*, 13–21.

Heyneman S. P., & Loxley, W. A. (1983). The effect of primary school quality on academic achievement across twenty-nine high- and low-income countries. *American Journal of Sociology*, *88*, 1162–1194.

Hofstede, G. (2001). *Culture's consequences: Comparing values, behaviors, institutions and organizations across nations* (2nd ed.). Thousand Oaks, CA: Sage Publications.

Inglehart, R., Basanez, M., Diez-Medrano, J., Halman, L., & Luijkx, R. (2004). *Human beliefs and values*. Ann Arbor, MI: University of Michigan Press.

Keeves, J. P. (1972). *Educational environment and student achievement*. Stockholm, Sweden: Almqvist and Wiksell.

Kotte, D. (1992). *Gender differences in science achievement in 10 countries: 1970/71 to 1983/84*. Frankfurt, Germany: Peter Lang.

Levin, H. M. (2001a). High-stakes testing and economic productivity. In M. L. Kornhaber & G. Orfield (Eds.), *Raising standards or raising barriers?* New York: Century Foundation.

Levin, H. M. (2001b). Waiting for Godot: Cost-effectiveness evaluation in education. In R. J. Light (Ed.), *Evaluation findings that surprise: New directions for evaluation* (pp. 55–65). San Francisco, CA: Jossey-Bass.

Lietz, P. (1996). *Changes in reading comprehension across countries and over time*. New York: Waxmann.

Little, R., & Rubin, D. B. (1987). *Statistical analysis with missing data*. New York: John Wiley & Sons.

Little, R., & Schenker, N. (1995). Missing data. In G. Arminger, C. C. Clogg, & M. E. Sobel (Eds.), *Handbook of statistical modeling for the social and behavioral sciences* (pp. 39–76). New York: Plenum Press.

Martin, M. O. (Ed.). (2005a). *TIMSS 2003 user guide for the international data base*. Chestnut Hill, MA: Boston College. Retrieved from http://timss.bc.edu/timss2003i/userguide.html

Martin, M. O. (Ed.). (2005b). *Variables derived from the student, teacher and school questionnaires*. Chestnut Hill, MA: Boston College. Retrieved from http://timss.bc.edu/timss2003i/PDF/t03_ug_s3.pdf

Martin, M. O., Mullis, I. V. S., & Chrostowski, S. J. (Eds.). (2004). *TIMSS 2003 technical report*. Chestnut Hill, MA: Boston College.

Mickelson, R. A. (1990). The attitude–achievement paradox among black adolescents. *Sociology of Education*, *63*, 44–61.

Mislevy, R. J., Beaton, A. E., Kaplan, B., & Sheehan, K. M. (1992). Estimating population characteristics from sparse matrix samples of item responses. *Journal of Educational Measurement*, *29*(2), 133–161.

Neuschmidt, O., Barth, J., & Hastedt, D. (2008). Trends in gender differences in mathematics and science (TIMSS 1995–2003). *Studies in Educational Evaluation, 34*(2), 56–72.

Papanastasiou, E. C., & Zembylas, M. (2002). The effect of attitudes on science achievement: A study conducted among high school pupils in Cyprus. *International Review of Education, 48*(6), 469–484.

Pong, S. L. (1997). Sibship size and educational attainment in peninsular Malaysia: Do policies matter? *Sociological Perspectives, 40*, 227–242.

Raudenbush, S., Bryk, A., Cheong, Y. F., Congdon, R., & du Toit, M. (2004). *HLM6: Linear and non-linear modeling*. Lincolnwood, IL: Scientific Software International.

Reynolds, A. J., & Walberg, H. J. (1991). A structural model of science achievement. *Journal of Educational Psychology, 83*(1), 97–107.

Rosen, B. C. (1961). Family structure and achievement motivation. *American Sociological Review, 26*, 574–585.

Rubin, D. B. (1987), *Multiple imputation for nonresponse in surveys.* New York: John Wiley & Son.

Rutkowski, R., Gonzalez, E., Joncas, M., & von Davier, M. (2010). International large-scale assessment data: Issues in secondary analysis and reporting. *Educational Researcher, 39*(2), 142–151.

Schibeci, R. A., & Riley, J. P. (2006). Influence of students' background and perceptions on science attitudes and achievement. *Journal of Research in Science Teaching, 23*(3), 177–187.

Schiller, K. S., Khmelkov, V. T., & Wang, X. Q. (2002). Economic development and the effects of family characteristics on mathematics achievement. *Journal of Marriage and the Family, 64*(3), 730–742.

Seltzer, J. A. (1994). Consequences of marital dissolution for children. *Annual Review of Sociology, 20*, 235–266.

Singh, K., Granville, M., & Dika, S. (2002). Mathematics and science achievement: Effects of motivation, interest and academic engagement. *The Journal of Educational Research, 95*(6), 323–332.

Steelman, L. C., & Powell, B. (1989). Acquiring capital for college: The constraints of family configuration. *American Sociological Review, 54*, 844–855.

von Davier, M., Gonzalez, E., & Mislevy, R. (2009). What are plausible values and why are they useful? *IERI Monograph Series: Issues and Methodologies in Large-Scale Assessments, 2*, 9–36. Hamburg, Germany: IERInstitute.

Wang, M. C., & Taylor, R. D. (2000). *Resilience across contexts: Family, work, culture, and community*. Mahwah, NJ: Lawrence Erlbaum Associates.

Weinberg, R. A. (1989). Intelligence and IQ: Landmark issues and great debates. *American Psychologist, 44*(2), 98–104.

One approach to detecting the invariance of proficiency standards over time

Jiahe Qian[1]
Educational Testing Service, Princeton, NJ, USA[2]

This study explores the use of a mapping technique to test the invariance of proficiency standards over time for state performance tests. The first step involved mapping the state proficiency standards onto the National Assessment of Educational Progress (NAEP) scale. During the second step, no attempt was made to determine a direct deviation in proficiency standards. Instead, this step involved testing the invariance of the NAEP equivalents of the state standards over time. The basis of the mapping technique is an enhanced method that was originally designed for comparing performance standards for public school students set by different states when the state tests are comparable. This approach can also be used to detect score inflation over time for state tests.

1 The author thanks Shelby Haberman, Henry Braun, Sandip Sinharay, and William Monaghan for their suggestions and comments. The author is particularly grateful to Daniel Eignor for his help in clarifying the psychometric meaning of the statistical techniques. The author would also like to thank Bruce Kaplan, Sailesh Vezzu, and Xiaoke Bi for their computational assistance and Kim Fryer for editorial assistance. The opinions expressed herein are solely those of the author and do not necessarily represent those of the Educational Testing Service. This work was supported by the National Center for Education Statistics, Contract # ED-02-CO-0023.

2 The opinions expressed herein are those of the author and do not necessarily represent those of Educational Testing Service.

INTRODUCTION

In the United States, the stability of state education performance test standards has recently become a concern. The reason is that, under the No Child Left Behind Act (NCLB), each state can select its own tests and set its own proficiency standards for reading and mathematics, thereby determining its standing with respect to the national requirements of adequate yearly progress (American Federation of Teachers, 2006). The study presented here was designed to develop an approach to test the level of invariance in proficiency standards over time for state tests or analogous assessments.

Proficiency standards—specific levels of mastery of knowledge and skills in education— are usually anchored by cutoff points on a test scale. These cutoff points classify student performance into several achievement categories, such as *basic, proficient*, and *advanced*. State tests usually use an equating process to ensure numerical cutoff points reflect proficiency standards, provided that no substantial changes occur in the assessment. However, over time, proficiency standards can deviate from the achievement levels on the original scale on which they were established, such that each cutoff point no longer anchors to the same ability level. This phenomenon is called *deviation in proficiency standards* (DPS) or *proficiency standard deviation*. Many researchers have found DPS in performance assessments when they compare these assessments with other stable assessments such as the National Assessment of Educational Progress (NAEP) (Cannell, 1987; Grissmer, Flanagan, Kawata, & Williamson, 2000; Klein, Hamilton, McCaffrey, & Stecher, 2000; Neill & the Staff of FairTest, 1997; Smith, 1991). Another concept, *scale drift*, also relates to the stability of a test scale. However, as Angoff (1984) notes, scale drift usually relates to inadequate equating of a new form of a test to "one or more of the existing forms for which conversions to the reference scale (i.e., the reporting scale) are already available" (p. *viii*).

DPS can be caused by many factors, such as score inflation, scale drift, alteration of the test instrument, changes in assessment format, reform of the subject framework, content modification, or differential performance gains (Koretz, 2007; Madaus, 1988b). However, if other factors are not present, DPS can serve as an indicator of score inflation, meaning that students gain higher test scores than before at each given level of academic achievement (Arenson, 2004; Koretz, 1988; Linn, 2000; Potter, 1979). The section of this paper headed "Application to Empirical Data" discusses a procedure for detecting score inflation by proxy: detect the presence of DPS, a necesssary condition for score inflation.

The approach developed in this study to test the invariance of proficiency standards is based on an enhanced mapping technique that was originally designed for comparing performance standards that different states set for public school students when the tests are comparable (Braun & Qian, 2007a). Testing whether the proficiency standard deviates from its original scale by simply observing the changes of scores on a test itself is difficult. However, it becomes feasible when a test with potential DPS is compared with another test that has no DPS. For example, many educators have compared state tests with the NAEP assessments. They found that test score improvements shown on state tests used for high-stakes decisions tend not to be corroborated by score improvements on the NAEP (Haney, 2002; Linn, Graue, & Sanders, 1990). This study employs an analogous strategy to measure the invariance of proficiency standards. This strategy transforms the scale of state tests to the well-established NAEP scale and then uses the NAEP scale as a benchmark to detect whether the proficiency standards of state tests are invariant over time.

To implement the approach developed by this study, the state proficiency standards were first mapped onto the NAEP scale. (These mapped proficiency standards of state tests are called the *NAEP equivalents to the state standards* or *NAEP equivalents*.) Next, a related solution—the invariance of the NAEP equivalents over time—was examined. This was done in preference to effort focused on directly detecting invariance of proficiency standards. The mapping makes the comparison effective because, as a benchmark, NAEP is generally regarded as meeting high standards with respect to test design, test content, and psychometric quality. In addition, NAEP is the only nationally standardized test that is administered in a uniform and stable manner across states. Also, NAEP scores are not influenced by factors such as grade inflation. (For a general introduction to NAEP, see Jones & Olkin, 2004.)

Although the literature demonstrates, for a number of reasons, that linking state tests to NAEP assessments at the student level does not result in an appropriate or a valid linking (Feuer, Holland, Green, Bertenthal, & Hemphill, 1998; Koretz, Bertenthal, & Green, 1999), studies show that mapping the proficiency standards on state tests to NAEP equivalents is valid (Braun & Qian, 2007b; McLaughlin & Bandeira de Mello, 2003). Because the schools in the sample used in this study take both NAEP and state tests, there is an overlapping of student populations between the two assessments. Moreover, the test instruments used for NAEP and the state tests are similar but not the same. These features ensure that the mapping procedure provides a valid assessment of state standards in terms of stability. Therefore, most of the heterogeneity across states in the NAEP equivalents to the state standards can be attributed to differences in the stringency of proficiency standards set by the states.

If a significant change in the NAEP equivalents is found over time, then it is likely that the proficiency standards of the state test have deviated from its original scale. In this paper, it is suggested that parties interested in confirming the causes of significant DPS, especially serious claims such as score inflation, form a committee, with members consisting of test experts and subject-matter specialists able to judge the reasons for an observed change.

The next section of this paper describes the estimation method that is used to map the proficiency standards of state tests. This section also introduces some properties of the mapped proficiency standards over time. The following section introduces the data used in the study, namely the 2003 and 2005 fourth- and eighth-grade state tests of reading and mathematics. It also presents the empirical results from testing the invariance of state standards. The penultimate section documents the application of the approach used to detect score inflation for state tests. The final section offers a summary and some conclusions.

METHODOLOGY

A. Outline of the Methodology for Mapping State Standards to the NAEP Scale

As described in Braun and Qian (2007a), the mapping procedure is carried out separately for each state that participates in NAEP and is represented in the National Longitudinal School-Level State Assessment Score Database[2] (for the corresponding academic year). To make the comparisons of the NAEP equivalents over time effective, both the state tests and the NAEP assessments need to comply with standard conditions (see below).

The statistical analysis presented in this study involves the sample design of NAEP assessments, school weights, and target estimation, among other features. In NAEP, state samples are obtained through a two-stage probability sampling design. To account for the unequal probabilities of selection and to allow for adjustments for non-response, each school and each student is assigned separate sampling weights. This study applied appropriate weights when estimating the proportion of students in the state who scored above the standard. The statewide target proportion of students meeting the standard is estimated by a ratio estimator. Appendix A provides a description of the weights, the target estimation, and the variance estimation.

Let P denote the state-wide proportion of students meeting a particular standard. Let F denote the score distribution on the NAEP assessment for the state and the $(1-P)$th quantile on F be $\xi = F^{-1}(1-P)$. The estimate of the $(1-P)$th quantile, $\hat{\xi}$, can also be denoted as $\hat{\xi}_{WAM}$, where the abbreviation WAM stands for "weighted aggregate mapping." Braun and Qian (2007a) followed the steps below when mapping state standards to the NAEP scale:

1. Based on the proportions of students who meet a given state's performance standard on that state's own assessment in NAEP-sampled schools, estimate the proportion of students in the state as a whole who meet the state's standard. First, identify the schools in the state's NAEP sample and match the schools with their records in the NLSLSASD. For each school, obtain the proportion of students meeting the state standard.

   Using the school weights from the NAEP design allows one to obtain an estimate of P via a ratio estimator, $\bar{p}_w$, which is a weighted average estimate of the number of students meeting the standard over a weighted average estimate of the number of eligible students. (For a more detailed description of the weights and the ratio estimator, see Appendix A.)

2. Based on the NAEP sample of schools and students within schools, estimate the distribution of scores on the NAEP assessment for the state as a whole. This

---

2 The National Longitudinal School-Level State Assessment Score Database (NLSLSASD; www.schooldata.org) is constructed and maintained by the American Institutes for Research (AIR) for the National Center for Education Statistics (NCES). Its purpose is to collect and validate data from state testing programs across the United States. It contains assessment data for approximately 80,000 public schools in the United States and is updated annually.

procedure is carried out in order to generate the results contained in the report that is issued after each NAEP assessment. Let $\hat{F}$ denote the empirical distribution of F, which can be obtained from the NAEP sample.

3. Find the point on the NAEP score scale at which the estimated proportion of students in the state scoring above that point equals the proportion of students in the state meeting the state's own performance standard. After estimating by $\bar{p}_w$ the proportion P of students meeting the state's own performance standard (defined with respect to the state test score scale) and calculating the NAEP score distribution as in Steps 1 and 2, map the performance standard to the NAEP scale by finding the point $\hat{\xi}$ on the NAEP scale that is the $(1-\bar{p}_w)$th quantile:

$$\hat{\xi}_{WAM} = \hat{F}^{-1}(1-\bar{p}_w). \tag{1}$$

The estimated NAEP equivalent to the state standard is taken to be $\hat{\xi}_{WAM}$, which is an estimate of ξ. If the state employs more than one standard, this procedure can be repeated for each one.

4. Compute an estimate of the variance of the estimated NAEP equivalent. Given NAEP's complex sample design and latent ability measurement, this computation is developed according to the NAEP jackknife methods used to obtain variance estimates (Allen, Donoghue, & Schoeps, 2001).

Figure 1 illustrates the mapping procedure. The dashed curve on the left-hand side represents an estimate of the state distribution of scores on the state test, based on the scores of all students in the schools selected for the state's NAEP sample. The area in the upper tail of this distribution above the state standard is an estimate of the proportion of students in the state meeting or exceeding that standard, and is denoted by $\hat{p}_w$. In practice, it is necessary to obtain only $\hat{p}_w$ from the data. The curve on the right-hand side represents the estimated distribution of NAEP scores for the state. This is the usual reported NAEP distribution that is estimated based on the performance of students in the state's NAEP sample who took the NAEP assessment.

Figure 1: The schematic of the mapping procedure

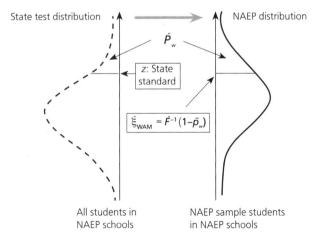

The estimated NAEP equivalent to the state standard, $\hat{\xi}$, is the point on the NAEP scale where the corresponding upper tail area of the NAEP distribution also equals $\hat{p}_w$. For a given distribution of state test scores and a specific distribution of NAEP assessment scores, by the monotone property of equipercentile linking, a larger $\hat{p}_w$ corresponds to a lower $\hat{\xi}$ and vice versa.

B. Testing the Invariance of State Standards Over Time

Mapping State Standards to the NAEP Scale Over Time

As I pointed out in the introductory section, the validity of the mapping methodology requires that the state test and the NAEP assessment be reasonably equivalent with respect to their test instruments, including subject frameworks, assessment format, psychometric characteristics of the tests, norms, and so on. The standard conditions involved with the procedure are then described, and the following is assumed: (a) there are no considerable changes in the state test instrument over time; (b) the state tests maintain their numerical cut points related to the standards over time (via score equating); and (c) the distributions of state test scores over time maintain the same shape and spread, but there is allowance for horizontal shifting of the distribution curve. The same assumptions are applied to the NAEP assessments. These standard conditions are reasonable even though they may appear to be stringent.

Let z_A and z_B be the state test standards of Time Point A and Time Point B, respectively. Because state tests are assumed to maintain their standards over time, $z_A = z_B$. Let ξ^A and ξ^B be the images of z_A and z_B for Time Point A and Time Point B, respectively. Their estimates are $\hat{\xi}^A$ and $\hat{\xi}^B$. The variance estimation of $\hat{\xi}^A$ or $\hat{\xi}^B$ is the same as that for $\hat{\xi}$ in Section A of the Methodology.

Let P^A be the proportion of students meeting the standard z_A for Time Point A, and let P^B be the proportion for Time Point B. The two empirical curves on the left side of Figure 2 illustrate a change between two time points, whereas $\hat{\xi}^A$ and $\hat{\xi}^B$ on the right-hand side of the figure are the results of mapping procedure.

Figure 2: The mapping procedure for a state test over two time periods

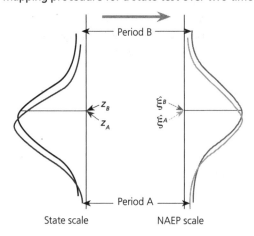

Let $P^B = P^A + \Delta P^S$, where ΔP^S is the change in the proportion of students meeting the standard in the state test. When $\Delta P^S > 0$, it means that a higher proportion of students met the standard at Time Point B. A higher proportion meeting the standard at Time Point B could occur for one of two possible reasons: there has been real progress in education or there is DPS in the testing results. If there has been progress in education, we can assume that the students will show a similar degree of progress in both the state test and the corresponding NAEP assessment.

Some Properties of the NAEP Equivalents Over Time

Let F^A and F^B denote the estimated distributions on the NAEP scale for Time Point A and Time Point B. As given in (1), the NAEP equivalent for Time Point A, the image of P^A, is the $(1 - P^A)$th quantile on F^A:

$$\xi^A = F^{-1,A}(1-P^A), \tag{2}$$

and the image of P^B on F^B is

$$\xi^B = F^{-1,B}(1-P^B) = F^{-1,B}(1-(P^A + \Delta P^S)). \tag{3}$$

Let P^α be the true proportion of students whose scores are greater than the point of ξ^A in the NAEP assessment at Time Point B, that is,

$$\xi^A = F^{-1,B}(1-P^\alpha). \tag{4}$$

Because of the changes in performance over time, P^α is usually not equal to P^A. Thus, $P^\alpha = P^A + \Delta P^N$, where ΔP^N is the changed proportion in NAEP above ξ^A at Time Point B.

First, assume $\Delta P^S = \Delta P^N$. Thus, for the time period, students show the same change in achievement in both the state test and the corresponding NAEP assessment. This assumption implies that $P^\alpha = P^A + \Delta P^S$. Because of (4) and

$$\xi^B = F^{-1,B}(1-(P^A + \Delta P^S)) = F^{-1,B}(1 - P^\alpha), \tag{5}$$

thus $\xi^B = \xi^A$. This outcome indicates that when $\Delta P^S = \Delta P^N$, the NAEP equivalent is invariant over time. Accordingly, ξ^A can be viewed as being an *invariant equivalent*. Figure 2 illustrates how the mapping procedure for both the state test and the NAEP assessment performs for the time period in question. When the NAEP scale is used as the benchmark for comparison, invariance of NAEP equivalents over time under the standard conditions is equivalent to the invariance of state proficiency standards over time.

Second, assume $\Delta P^S > \Delta P^N$, that is, $P^A + \Delta P^S > P^A + \Delta P^N$, so the proportion of students meeting the standard on the state test is higher than that on the NAEP assessment. Because

$$\xi^A = F^{-1,B}(1 - P^\alpha) = F^{-1,B}(1-(P^A + \Delta P^N)) \tag{6}$$

and the monotone property of $F^{-1,B}(\cdot)$, it follows that

$$\xi^B = F^{-1,B}(1-(P^A + \Delta P^S)) < F^{-1,B}(1-(P^A + \Delta P^N)) = \xi^A. \tag{7}$$

This indicates that the NAEP equivalent at Time Point B is lower than ξ^A. It shows an occurrence of DPS, a deviation in proficiency standard. Figure 3 illustrates the empirical mapping procedure indicating that the state test performs differentially from the NAEP assessment over time.

Third, assume $\Delta P^S < \Delta P^N$, that is, $P^A + \Delta P^S < P^A + \Delta P^N$, so the proportion of students meeting the standard in the state test is lower than that in the NAEP assessment. Because of (6) and the monotone property of $F^{-1,B}(\cdot)$, it follows that

$$\xi^B = F^{-1,B}\left(1-\left(P^A + \Delta P^S\right)\right) > F^{-1,B}\left(1-\left(P^A + \Delta P^N\right)\right), \tag{8}$$

hence $\xi^B > \xi^A$. This is a trivial case, although it shows an occurrence of DPS.

Figure 3: The mapping procedure with score inflation in the state test for Period B

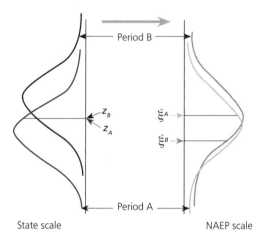

State scale   NAEP scale

Test of the Invariance of NAEP Equivalents Over Time
In this study, the evaluation procedure employs both statistical significance tests and effect size criteria. For the statistical approach, the hypothesis serves as a check of the invariance of the NAEP equivalents over time under the standard conditions. The null hypothesis can be expressed as $H_o : \xi^B = \xi^A$. An equivalent hypothesis is whether the proportion of students passing ξ^B at Time Point B equals the proportion passing the invariant equivalent at Time Point B: $P^B = P^\alpha$. This study employed two significance tests in the analysis. The first test required use of a t-type statistic to check the difference of two proportions. The second statistic is the log-odds ratio (Haberman, 1978).

Let n_B be the sample size in consideration for Time Point B. Let $\hat{\xi}^B$ and $\hat{\xi}^A$ be the estimates of ξ^B and ξ^A, respectively. In Table 1, let n_{11} and n_{21} be the numbers of students whose scores are greater than $\hat{\xi}^B$ and $\hat{\xi}^A$, respectively, and n_{12} and n_{22} be the numbers of students who failed to meet the standards. Let $\hat{p}_w^B = n_{11}/n_B$ be the estimate of P^B, and $\hat{p}_w^\alpha = n_{21}/n_B$ be the estimate of P^α. Let $\hat{p}^B = n_{.1}/n$ and $\hat{q} = 1 - \hat{p}$.

Define the Z_c statistic as

$$Z_c = \frac{\left| \hat{p}_w^\alpha - \hat{p}_w^\beta \right| - 1/n_{B.}}{\sqrt{2\hat{p}\hat{q}/n_{B.}}} \; . \tag{9}$$

The term, $1/n_{B.}$, in (9) is the Yates' correction for continuity (Yates, 1934). The log-odds ratio is defined as

$$L = \log \left(\frac{n_{11} n_{22}}{n_{12} n_{21}} \right), \tag{10}$$

and an estimate of its standard error is

$$SE\,(L) = \sqrt{\frac{1}{n_{11}} + \frac{1}{n_{12}} + \frac{1}{n_{21}} + \frac{1}{n_{22}}} \; . \tag{11}$$

Because the NAEP state data are collected by a two-stage sampling approach, the formulas for simple random sampling underestimate the variances employed in the test statistics. The variance estimation for complex data usually uses replicate resampling approaches (Wolter, 1985). To simplify computations and count the effects of complex sampling, the variances are estimated by multiplying a variance estimate by a design effect, which Kish (1965) introduced as a ratio of the variance of a statistic from complex samples over the variance of the statistic from simple random samples. Based on previous NAEP analyses, 2.5 is used as the approximate design effect for computation purposes. A .05 alpha level is then used in the analyses of the statistical tests.

Table 1: Number of NAEP students whose scores were greater than ξ^B and who passed ξ^A at Time Point B

	Proficiency standard		
	Pass	Fail	Total
ξ^B	n_{11}	n_{12}	$n_{B.}$
ξ^A	n_{21}	n_{22}	$n_{B.}$
Total	$n_{.1}$	$n_{.2}$	N

When the hypothesis is rejected, it means that there is a significant difference in the NAEP equivalents over time, which implies a significant DPS. It also means that the students in the state test performed differently from how they would have on the NAEP assessment. However, DPS cannot be considered equivalent to score inflation because other possible factors could cause such differences, including differential performance gains and style of classroom instruction. Only when other potential factors can be dismissed can DPS be taken as an indication of score inflation.

For practical purposes, the effect size criterion is also used to evaluate the difference of two proportions drawn from independent samples, or the differences between a single proportion and any specified hypothetical value. The effect size for comparison of proportions is called the *H* index. To provide a better scale for looking at differences on which effect sizes for proportions are comparably detectable, Cohen (1988) applied the arcsine transformation to the proportions before calculating their difference.

Let the arcsine transformation be $\varphi = 2\arcsin\sqrt{p}$. The *H* index for proportions is then defined as $H = |\varphi_1 - \varphi_2|$. To count as an intermediate effect size, the absolute value of the *H* index has to be at least 0.20 in the measuring differences of two proportions.

C. Evaluating the Test Results

When a significant DPS is detected, it is important to find the causes of this deviation in respect of proficiency standards. To assess the test results, a committee of test experts and subject-matter specialists should be assembled. This process is analogous to the review process that happens with a NAEP differential item functioning (DIF) analysis (Allen et al., 2001).

The process of judging the causes of the deviation in the NAEP equivalents over time consists of two phases. The initial phase involves executing the relevant computations and statistical tests. The second phase involves assessing the results and determining the factors that could cause the deviation in proficiency standards over time. The expert committee will need to check the standard condition assumptions, review the results of the findings, discuss the possible causes for the differences, and draw conclusions. Only if all competing potential causes are eliminated can the results be attributed to score inflation.

APPLICATION TO EMPIRICAL DATA

Data

To detect the deviation in proficiency standards over time, this study analyzed two sets of data: (a) the 2003 and 2005 NAEP mathematics and reading assessment samples for Grade 4 (G4) and Grade 8 (G8) students; and (b) the 2003 and 2005 state test samples of mathematics and reading for G4 and G8 students. The information on the proportions of students meeting state test standards for 2003 and 2005 was retrieved from the NLSLSASD. This database contains the proportions of students, by school, meeting each of the state's standards for nearly all states, beginning as early as the academic year 1994. However, it does not contain scores for individual students. The NLSLSASD typically presents, for each school, the percentage of students meeting or exceeding each achievement standard established by the state.[3]

---

3 For almost all states, some schools in the NAEP school sample were either missing from the NLSLSASD or the required datum was not listed. In these cases, the number of schools available for estimation was smaller than the number of schools in the NAEP school sample. For each subject and grade combination, there were four to five jurisdictions in which the proportion of NAEP sample schools employed in the estimation was less than 0.9.

Empirical Results

The analysis involved first completing the mapping procedure described in the section of this paper headed "Outline of the Methodology for Mapping State Standards to the NAEP Scale." The report prepared by Braun and Qian (2007b) contains the tables of the estimates of the statewide proportion of proficient students, the estimated NAEP equivalents to the state standard, and the estimated standard error of the NAEP equivalent for the 2005 G4 and G8 reading and mathematics state tests, respectively. The same report also contains the results for the 2003 G4 and G8 reading and mathematics state tests, respectively. For each state, each table also displays the number of schools in the NAEP sample and the number of schools employed in the mapping. This last quantity is simply the number of schools in the NAEP sample that could be matched to the schools with usable state test performance data. The notes under each of the tables list issues concerning data in this present analysis.

Appendix B contains four figures pertaining to the ordered estimated NAEP score equivalents together with their estimated standard errors for the four subject and grade combinations (reading, Grades 4 and 8; mathematics, Grades 4 and 8). The estimated standard errors in these figures are relatively small compared to the range of the estimated NAEP score equivalents. The error bands in the figures extend plus or minus 1.96 standard errors on either side of the estimated NAEP equivalent for the state.

As shown in Figure B1, for reading at G4 in 2005, the largest estimated NAEP score equivalent of 234 (Massachusetts) is 73 points higher than the lowest one, 161 (Mississippi). The other figures, B2 to B4, also show similarly wide ranges of the estimated NAEP score equivalents. The large discrepancies in the mapped states' assessment standards make it difficult to gauge where states currently are in terms of reaching the goal delineated by the No Child Left Behind Act (Lewin, 2007) and how far they have to go to reach that goal.

For the G4 reading analysis, this study used, for comparative purposes, the data from 21 of the 25 states that had both 2005 and 2003 data. To align the state test and the NAEP reading assessments, this study dropped state data if the relevant state assessment was labeled "English/Language Arts" rather than "Reading." The study only considered and later discussed those states that showed an increase in the proportion of students meeting the state standards. The outcome of both the statistical tests and the effect size check showed significant results for two states. These two (States 1 and 2) are listed in Table 2.

Note that the names of all the states listed in Table 2 are unspecified because the possible causes for the deviation in proficiency standards have yet to be investigated. For example, the State 1 test shows a large increase in the proportions of students meeting the state's standards. In the 2005 NAEP sample for State 1, the proportion of the students who passed ξ^B is 0.71, and the proportion of those who passed ξ^A is about 0.60. The images of $\bar{p}_w^A$ on $\hat{F}^A(0.60)$ and $\bar{p}_w^B$ on $\hat{F}^B(0.71)$ show significant variation in the NAEP scale over time. This pattern indicates the presence of a significant DPS, or a deviation in state proficiency standards.

Table 2: Results of statistical testing and *H* index checking, including significance, for Grade 4 reading and mathematics

State	2005 Estimate of proportion passing $\hat{\xi}^B, \hat{p}_w^B$	2005 Estimated NAEP equivalent, $\hat{\xi}^B$	2005 Estimate of proportion passing $\hat{\xi}^A, \hat{p}_w^A$	2003 Estimated NAEP equivalent, $\hat{\xi}^A$	Z_c statistic	Log-odds ratio	*H* index
			Grade 4 reading				
1	0.71	202	0.60	212	6.61	0.21	0.23
2	0.80	197	0.67	210	6.89	0.29	0.30
			Grade 8 reading				
3	0.63	244	0.52	256	5.15	0.19	0.22
4	0.82	235	0.73	247	5.24	0.23	0.22
5	0.72	245	0.63	256	5.56	0.18	0.19
6	0.30	276	0.19	285	6.02	0.27	0.26
7	0.57	254	0.43	267	6.48	0.25	0.28
			Grade 4 mathematics				
8	0.85	218	0.76	226	5.72	0.25	0.23
9	0.80	224	0.65	234	6.79	0.33	0.34
10	0.91	207	0.78	217	8.50	0.45	0.37
			Grade 8 mathematics				
11	0.61	269	0.52	278	4.35	0.18	0.20
12	0.53	276	0.44	286	4.51	0.17	0.20
13	0.74	258	0.64	268	4.68	0.20	0.22
14	0.70	266	0.53	280	8.24	0.32	0.35
15	0.65	277	0.44	293	8.82	0.37	0.42

In the G8 reading analysis, this study used, in the comparison, data from 28 of the 30 states that had both 2005 and 2003 data. Significant results relative to both the statistical testing and the effect size check emerged for five states (States 3 to 7). Table 2 displays the results for these five states.

In the G4 mathematics analysis, this study used data from 24 of the 25 states with both 2005 and 2003 data. After the first phase of the analysis, three of the states (States 8 to 10) listed in Table 2 showed significant differences in the NAEP equivalents as an outcome of the statistical testing and the effect size checks. Of the three state tests, the State 8 test showed a substantial increase in the proportions of students meeting its standards. Seventy-four percent and 85% of the students passed its standards in 2003 and 2005, respectively.

In the 2005 NAEP sample for State 8, the proportion of the students who passed its ξ^A is 0.76. The tests produced a significant outcome for the variation of the images of $\bar{p}_w^A$ on $\hat{F}^A$ (0.76) and $\bar{p}_w^B$ on $\hat{F}^B$ (0.85). This variation implies that the G4 State 8 mathematics test has a significant DPS and thus a deviation in state proficiency standards.

To confirm the cause of these changes in achievement level percentages, further investigation is needed, and final approval must be acquired from an expert committee during a second-phase analysis.

In the G8 mathematics analysis, this study used data from 25 of the 32 states with both 2005 and 2003 data. Significant results emerged for five states (States 11 to 15) with respect to the statistical testing and the effect size check.

AN APPLICATION: DETECTING SCORE INFLATION IN THE STATE TESTS

An important application of this approach is detecting score inflation in state tests. If other factors causing DPS can be excluded, a significant DPS indicates score inflation. DPS is thus a necessary condition for the demonstration of score inflation.

Over recent years, score inflation has become an increasing concern for many educators because it compromises efforts to improve education and accountability in assessments (Bromley, Crow, & Gibson, 1973; Hambleton et al., 1995; Rosovsky & Hartley, 2002; Shepard, 1988). Score inflation can be tied to a variety of situations. For non-linked or poorly equated tests, lack of adequate equating can result in what might be considered to be grade inflation. But even if the scale of a test is well linked or equated, score inflation can still be present.

A typical situation occurs when classroom instruction is test-driven or when students are focused on learning content specific to the questions asked in a standardized test. Because students at different achievement levels know the content of questions because they have memorized the same answers, the resulting scores will not necessarily indicate the real academic level of individual students. In particular, students at a lower proficiency level often achieve test scores that are higher than their relative aptitude in such environments would predict (Haladyna, Nolan, & Haas,

1991; Madaus, 1988a; Phelps, 2005). Such situations result in assessments that fail to adequately measure student levels of achievement; even efforts to align tests closely with curricular standards are insufficient to guard against this sort of score inflation (Koretz, 2005).

The principle applied to test score inflation is to check whether score improvements on NAEP corroborate score improvements on the state tests. The stability of NAEP scales is thus the basis of such comparisons. If a DPS is detected, an expert panel should then be asked to determine if the cause of the deviation is likely due to score inflation.

Of the two cases of DPS discussed in the section above on testing the invariance of state standards over time, only one gave an indicator of score inflation. When $\Delta P^s > \Delta P^N$, it implied that the proportion of students meeting the standard on the state test was higher than that on the NAEP assessment. The NAEP equivalent at Time Point B was lower than ξ^A, that is, $\xi^B < \xi^A$. This case of significant DPS accordingly provided a scenario for possible score inflation. In the second case, where $\Delta P^s < \Delta P^N$, the implication was $\xi^B > \xi^A$. This case of significant DPS was not an indicator of score inflation. It may have occurred because of failure to satisfy standard conditions or because of a change in testing conditions.

To reemphasize, in order for analysts to formally claim score inflation, they must ensure that the causes of DPS are evaluated by an expert committee, and they must discuss potential factors other than score inflation. Although analysis of the 2005 and 2003 G4 and G8 reading and mathematics data presented in Table 2 demonstrated significant DPS, specific causes of DPS, including possible score inflation, were not determined because these results had not been reviewed by an expert committee.

Finally, it is possible that the changes in NAEP equivalents over time were caused by a combination of factors: they may have been partly due to modification of the item formats and test structures and partly due to score inflation. Resolving this situation and drawing conclusions will necessitate the collection of additional data in further studies.

CONCLUSIONS

The study presented in this paper developed an approach for testing the invariance of state proficiency standards over time for state tests or other analogous assessments. This approach is based on the methodology originally developed for making useful comparisons between state standards at one time point. In both the original and the current development, the NAEP scale was used as the benchmark.

The approach developed in this paper arose from the need to deal with practical testing issues. It is well known that, over time, factors such as score inflation, scale drift, differential performance gains, test instrument structure changes, content modification, and style of classroom instruction can all contribute to a deviation in test scores (Thissen, 2007). Apparently, the concept of deviation in test scores is broader than a deviation in proficiency standards.

The entire process of this method involves detecting DPS over time, verifying that standard test conditions have been met, and having the causes of changes evaluated by an expert committee. Under standard conditions, a substantial difference in NAEP equivalents over time indicates possible score inflation. However, the reality of this situation can only be determined after discounting other factors related to changes in test conditions, such as content modification and changes in test instruments.

As mentioned in the section of this paper titled "Evaluating the Test Results," it is possible that differentiation of NAEP equivalents over time may be caused in part by changes in testing conditions and in part by score inflation. The existence of a combination of such causes makes investigation of this matter more difficult. When only limited information is available, individuals wanting to make inferences concerning score inflation with respect to this scenario should do so with due caution.

APPENDIX A: NAEP SAMPLE DESIGN, SCHOOL WEIGHTS, AND TARGET ESTIMATION

NAEP Sample Design and School Weights

State NAEP samples are obtained through a two-stage probability sampling design. The first stage constitutes a probability sample of schools containing the relevant grade. The second stage involves the selection of a random sample of students within each school. To account for the unequal probabilities of selection and to allow for adjustments for non-response, each school and each student is assigned a separate sampling weight.[4] If these weights are not employed in the computation of the statistics of interest, the resulting estimates can be biased.

Because of this caution, appropriate weights are applied in the estimation of the proportion of students in the state above the standard. In general, the school weight equals the inverse of the approximate school selection probability, and the student weight is inversely proportional to the product of the school selection probability and the student selection probability. A more detailed description of school weights can be found in Braun and Qian (2007a).

Because school weights are not retained in the NAEP database, this study computed the school weights in two steps. First, the sum of the student design weights for each school was calculated. This sum was then divided by the number of grade-eligible students.[5]

Details of the creation of school design weights for NAEP can be found in the *NAEP 1998 Technical Report* (Qian, Kaplan, Johnson, Krenzke, & Rust, 2001, Chapter 11).

---

4 Students with disabilities and English language learners who cannot be assessed, even with the accommodations that NAEP provides, are not considered non-respondents but are excluded from the population of inference. Their performance is not included in estimates of the NAEP score distributions.

5 Note that this calculation was carried out only for the subset of NAEP sample schools with complete data. School and student weights were not adjusted for schools lost from the NAEP school sample due to non-response.

The Ratio Estimator for the Target Proportion

Let P_k be the proportion of students achieving the standard at school k, and let w_k be the corresponding school weight. The total number of students meeting the standard is $\sum_{l=1}^{N} P_l \cdot M_l$, where N is the total number of public schools in the state containing the relevant grade and M_l is the number of students who were grade-eligible at school l (including all students with disabilities and English language learners). The statewide target proportion of students meeting the standard is approximately

$$P = \frac{\sum_{l=1}^{N} P_l \cdot M_l}{\sum_{l=1}^{N} M_l} .$$

Horvitz–Thompson estimators (Cochran, 1977) are used to estimate the numerator and denominator of P separately from the state's NAEP school sample. For example, $\sum_{l=1}^{n} w_l M_l$ estimates the total number of eligible students in the state, and $\sum_{l=1}^{n} w_l (P_l \cdot M_l)$ estimates the total number of students meeting the standard. The target proportion, P, of students meeting the standard can be estimated by a ratio estimator:

$$\bar{p}_w = \frac{\sum_{l=1}^{n} w_l (P_l \cdot M_l)}{\sum_{l=1}^{n} w_l M_l} .$$

Variance Estimation

When survey variables are observed without error from every respondent in relation to a stratified and clustered sample such as NAEP, the usual complex-sample variance estimators quantify the uncertainty associated with sample statistics (Skinner, Holt, & Smith, 1989). The fact that a specific NAEP score is not assigned to individual students participating in the NAEP assessments (even those who responded to the cognitive items) requires additional statistical analyses to properly quantify the uncertainty associated with inferences about score distributions (Allen et al., 2001; Wolter, 1985).

The total variance of the estimate of the NAEP equivalent to a state standard consists of two components: (a) the error due to sampling schools and students, and (b) the error of measurement that reflects the uncertainty in an assessed student's performance. The sampling error is estimated by applying the jackknife replicate re-sampling (JRR) approach to the mapping procedure. The estimation involves the corresponding schools on the state data and on the NAEP data. The measurement error due to unobservability is estimated by utilizing the variability among the five sets of plausible values generated for each assessed student (Rubin, 1987).

APPENDIX B: RESULTS OF MAPPING STATE STANDARDS FOR THE 2005 NAEP READING AND MATHEMATICS ASSESSMENTS

Figure B1: NAEP score equivalents of states' proficiency standards for reading at Grade 4 (2005)

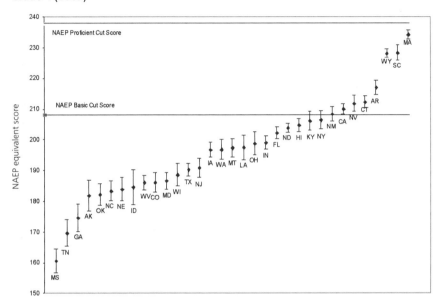

Source:

US Department of Education, Institute of Education Sciences, National Center for Education Statistics, National Assessment of Educational Progress (NAEP), 2005 Reading Assessment, and National Longitudinal School-Level State Assessment Score Database (NLSLSASD).

Figure B2: NAEP score equivalents of states' proficiency standards for reading at Grade 8 (2005)

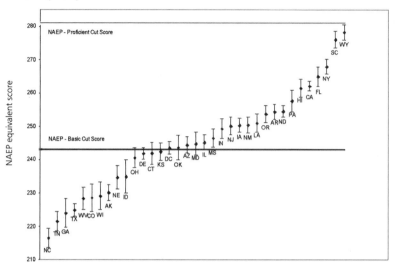

Source:

U.S. Department of Education, Institute of Education Sciences, National Center for Education Statistics, National Assessment of Educational Progress (NAEP), 2005 Reading Assessment, and National Longitudinal School-Level State Assessment Score Database (NLSLSASD).

Figure B3: NAEP score equivalents of states' proficiency standards for mathematics at Grade 4 (2005)

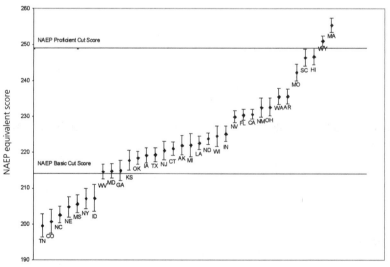

Source:

U.S. Department of Education, Institute of Education Sciences, National Center for Education Statistics, National Assessment of Educational Progress (NAEP), 2005 Reading Assessment, and National Longitudinal School-Level State Assessment Score Database (NLSLSASD).

Figure B4. NAEP score equivalents of states' proficiency standards for mathematics at Grade 8 (2005)

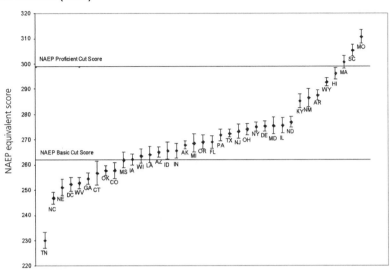

Source:

U.S. Department of Education, Institute of Education Sciences, National Center for Education Statistics, National Assessment of Educational Progress (NAEP), 2005 Reading Assessment, and National Longitudinal School-Level State Assessment Score Database (NLSLSASD).

References

Allen, N., Donoghue, J., & Schoeps, T. (2001). *The NAEP 1998 technical report* (NCES 2001-509). Washington DC: National Center for Education Statistics.

American Federation of Teachers. (2006). *Smart testing: Let's get it right.* Unpublished review retrieved from http://www.aft.org/pubs-reports/downloads/teachers/Testingbrief.pdf.

Angoff, W. H. (1984). *Scales, norms, and equivalent scores.* Princeton, NJ: Educational Testing Service.

Arenson, K. W. (2004, April 18). Is it grade inflation, or are students just smarter? *New York Times*, p. WK2.

Braun, H. I., & Qian, J. (2007a). An enhanced method for mapping state standards onto the NAEP scale. In N. J. Dorans, M. Pommerich, & P. W. Holland (Eds.), *Linking and aligning scores and scales* (pp. 313–338). New York: Springer.

Braun, H. I., & Qian J. (2007b). *Mapping 2005 state proficiency standards onto the NAEP scales* (NCES Research and Development Report No. NCES 2007–482). Washington DC: National Center for Education Statistics.

Bromley, D. G., Crow, H. L., & Gibson, M. S. (1973). Grade inflation: Trends, causes, and implications. *Phi Delta Kappan, 59*(10), 694–697.

Cannell, J. J. (1987). *Nationally normed elementary achievement testing in America's public schools: How all fifty states are above the national average*. Daniels, WV: Friends for Education.

Cochran, W. G. (1977). *Sampling techniques* (3rd ed.). New York: John Wiley & Sons.

Cohen, J. (1988). *Statistical power analysis for the behavioral sciences* (2nd ed.). Hillsdale, NJ: Erlbaum.

Feuer, M. J., Holland, P., Green, B. F., Bertenthal, M. W., & Hemphill, F. (Eds.). (1998). *Uncommon measures: Equivalence and linkage among educational tests*. Washington, DC: National Academy of Science.

Grissmer, D., Flanagan, A., Kawata, J., & Williamson, S. (2000). *Improving student achievement: What state NAEP test scores tell us* (Rand Corporation Rep. No. MR-924-EDU). Santa Monica, CA: Rand Corporation.

Haberman, S. J. (1978). *Analysis of qualitative data: Vol. 1, Introductory topics*. New York: Academic Press.

Haladyna, T., Nolen, S., & Haas, N. (1991). Raising standardized achievement test scores and the origins of test score pollution. *Educational Researcher, 20*(5), 2–7.

Hambleton, R. K., Jaeger, R. M., Koretz, D., Linn, R. L., Millman, J., & Phillips, S. E. (1995). *Review of the measurement quality of the Kentucky Instructional Results Information System, 1991–1994*. Frankfort, KY: Office of Education Accountability, Kentucky General Assembly.

Haney, W. (2002). Ensuring failure: How a state's achievement test may be designed to do just that. *Education Week, 56*, 58.

Jones, L., & Olkin, I. (2004). *The nation's report card: Evolution and perspectives*. Bloomington, IN: Phi Delta Kappa International.

Kish, L. (1965). *Survey sampling*. New York: John Wiley & Sons.

Klein, S. P., Hamilton, L. S., McCaffrey, D. F., & Stecher, B. M. (2000). What do test scores in Texas tell us? *Education Policy Analysis Archives, 8*, 49.

Koretz, D. M. (1988). Arriving in Lake Wobegon: Are standardized tests exaggerating achievement and distorting instruction? *American Educator, 12*(2), 8–15, 46–52.

Koretz, D. M. (2005). Alignment, high stakes, and the inflation of test scores. *Yearbook of the National Society for the Study of Education, 104*(2), 99–118.

Koretz, D. M. (2007). Using aggregate-level linkages for estimation and validation: Comments on Thissen and Braun & Qian. In N. J. Dorans, M. Pommerich, & P. W. Holland (Eds.), *Linking and aligning scores and scales* (pp. 339–353). New York: Springer.

Koretz, D. M., Bertenthal, M. W., & Green, B. F. (Eds.). (1999). *Embedding questions: The pursuit of a common measure in uncommon tests*. Washington, DC: National Academy of Sciences.

Lewin, T. (2007, June 8). States found to vary widely on education. *New York Times*, p. WK2.

Linn, R. L. (2000). Assessments and accountability. *Educational Researcher, 29*(2), 4–16.

Linn, R. L., Graue, M. E., & Sanders, N. M. (1990). Comparing state and district results to national norms: The validity of the claims that "Everyone is above average." *Educational Measurement: Issues and Practice, 9*(3), 5–14.

Madaus, G. F. (1988a). The distortion of teaching and testing: High-stakes testing and instruction. *Peabody Journal of Education, 65*(3), 29–46.

Madaus, G. F. (1988b). The influence of testing on the curriculum. In L. Tanner (Ed.), *Critical issues in curriculum* (pp. 83–121). Chicago, IL: University of Chicago Press.

McLaughlin, D., & Bandeira de Mello, V. (2003, June). *Comparing state reading and math performance standards using NAEP.* Paper presented at the National Conference on Large-Scale Assessment, San Antonio, TX.

Neill, M., & the Staff of FairTest. (1997). *Testing our children: A report card on state assessment systems.* Cambridge, MA: National Center for Fair & Open Testing.

Phelps, R. P. (2005). The source of Lake Wobegon. *Third Education Group Review, 1,* 2.

Potter, W. P. (1979). Grade inflation: Unmasking the scourge of the seventies. *College and University, 55*(1), 19–26.

Qian, J., Kaplan, E., Johnson, E., Krenzke, T., & Rust, K. (2001). State weighting procedures and variance estimation. In N. Allen, J. Donoghue, & T. Schoeps (Eds.), *The NAEP 1998 technical report* (pp. 193–225). Washington, DC: National Center for Education Statistics.

Rosovsky, H., & Hartley, M. (2002). *Evaluation and the academy: Are we doing the right thing? Grade inflation and letters of recommendation.* Cambridge, MA: American Academy of Arts and Sciences.

Rubin, D. B. (1987). *Multiple imputation for nonresponse in surveys.* New York: John Wiley & Sons.

Shepard, L. A. (1988, April). *The harm of measurement-driven instruction.* Paper presented at the annual meeting of the American Educational Research Association, Washington, DC.

Skinner, C., Holt, D., & Smith, T. (1989). *Analysis of complex surveys.* New York: John Wiley & Sons.

Smith, M. L. (1991). Meanings of test preparation. *American Educational Research Journal, 28*(3), 521–542.

Thissen, D. (2007). Linking assessments based on aggregate reporting: Background and issues. In N. J. Dorans, M. Pommerich, & P. W. Holland (Eds.), *Linking and aligning scores and scales* (pp. 287–312). New York: Springer.

Wolter, K. (1985). *Introduction to variance estimation.* New York: Springer.

Yates, F. (1934). Contingency table involving small numbers and the χ^2 test. *Journal of the Royal Statistical Society* (Supplement), *1,* 217–235.

The relationship between motivational components and reading competency of Hungarian-speaking children in three countries

A secondary analysis of the PIRLS 2001 and 2006 data[1]

Éva D. Molnár
University of Szeged, Szeged, Hungary

László Székely
Szent István University, Gödöllő, Hungary

In the 2001 and 2006 Progress in Reading Literacy Study (PIRLS) assessments, the language of tuition of all or some of the students in three of the participating countries, namely, Hungary, Romania, and the Slovak Republic, was Hungarian. This present study drew on the PIRLS data from these countries in order to explore connections between motivational components of reading competency and the students' reading achievement on the PIRLS assessment instrument. The motivational components included attitudes toward reading and reading-related self-concept. The study also considered the factors that appeared to influence these components. Analysis involved construction of two hierarchical linear models for each country and data-collection time (i.e., 2001 and 2006). Because the educational systems of the three countries are similar, the study also compared the findings of the hierarchical linear modeling across the three countries.

---

1 The study was funded by the Developing Diagnostic Assessments Project of the School Renewal Operative Programme of the New Hungarian Development Plan (TÁMOP 3.1.9. – Diagnosztikus mérések fejlesztése).

INTRODUCTION

Hungary's participation, since 1991, in international large-scale assessments of students' reading achievement changed the research culture in Hungary. The results of studies conducted by the International Association for the Evaluation of Educational Achievement (IEA) and the Organisation for Economic Co-operation and Development (OECD) studies highlighted, for Hungary, the importance not only of regularly assessing this area of educational achievement but also of systematically studying students' acquisition of the basic skills of reading. The results, moreover, provided Hungary with a valuable new set of national reading-achievement benchmarks.

However, the international surveys presented an ambiguous picture of Hungarian students' achievement. The findings of iterations of the IEA Progress in International Reading Literacy Study (PIRLS) show that the reading literacy of Hungarian 10-year-olds is highly satisfactory (Balázsi, Balkányi, Felvégi, & Szabó, 2008). The OECD Programme for International Student Assessment (PISA) surveys, however, present a far less positive picture (OECD, 2004, 2007). It is important to note, at this point, that comparison of the findings of the two survey programs cannot be fully justified because they are based on different theoretical constructs and measure different age groups. Nevertheless, these seemingly conflicting results for Hungary deserve further consideration.

We took a step in this direction in the present study. Our aim was not to compare the PIRLS and PISA data but rather to conduct research that, in association with existing research and later studies, might contribute to explanations for the ostensible differences in reading achievement between the younger and older populations of Hungarian students. Our particular interest in this study centered on possible relationships between indices of students' motivation to read and students' reading competency. To this end, we conducted two detailed analyses. The first examined the relationship between students' attitudes toward reading and students' reading competency. The second addressed the relationship between students' self-reported perceptions of their reading ability and students' reading competency. Because an important issue in reading research concerns the question of what factors influence the development of attitudes toward reading and reading-related self-concept, we considered several of the background details, such as home environment, typically collected from students participating in international studies of educational achievement. The data that we used for our analyses came from the PIRLS databases for 2001 and 2006 and included the results for the Hungarian-speaking Grade 4 populations of Hungary, the Slovak Republic, and Romania. The five-year span between the two assessments allowed us to compare, across time, the relationships between the two motivational indices and reading achievement for students who spoke Hungarian but studied in different schools systems and in different countries.[1]

---

1 Native speakers of Hungarian live not only in Hungary but also in several neighboring countries, including the Slovak Republic and Romania. Both of these countries have large numbers of people who are native (generally monolingual) speakers of Hungarian.

BACKGROUND CONSIDERATIONS

Understandings of Reading Acquisition and Their Relevance to Assessments of Reading Competency

Analysis directed at understanding influences on reading competence has been a central concern of theorists and researchers for many years. According to Cs. Czachesz (2005), research on the attainment of reading skills has been influenced, over time, by five theoretical frameworks—empirical-behaviorist, psycholinguistic and sociolinguistic, cognitive psychological, constructivist, and motivated learning. These paradigms have taken us from understanding reading as a simple decoding skill to understanding it as a complex functional skill, acquisition of which is influenced by such contexts as the reader's social environment, previous knowledge, personal interpretation, and personal interests and attitudes (Nagy, 2006).

International large-scale assessments of reading, such as PIRLS and PISA, address three main areas of interest:

1. Reading skills, assessed through tasks that require students to engage in specific processes—retrieve information, form a broad general understanding, develop an interpretation, reflect and evaluate (OECD, 2000, 2006);

2. Reading competence, assessed through students' ability to engage with and comprehend different types of text, such as narrative, document, and explanatory (PIRLS), and different forms of text, such as continuous and non-continuous (PISA); and

3. The sociocultural and socioeconomic contexts within which reading takes place (PIRLS, PISA).

Drawing on contemporary research, the research teams responsible for designing PIRLS and PISA developed the following conceptions of reading literacy. In PIRLS,

> reading literacy is defined as the ability to understand and use those written language forms required by society and/or valued by the individual. Young readers can construct meaning from a variety of texts. They read to learn, to participate in communities of readers in school and everyday life, and for enjoyment. (Mullis, Kennedy, Martin, & Sainsbury, 2006, p. 3)

In PISA, reading literacy is defined as "understanding, using, and reflecting on written texts, in order to achieve one's goals, to develop one's knowledge and potential, and to participate in society" (OECD, 2003, p. 108). Both definitions emphasize the ability to use reading as a tool to achieve certain goals, but because the two surveys assess different age groups, the definitions are operationalized slightly differently.

PIRLS concentrates more on students' ability to function appropriately in the typical environment in which they read, whereas PISA focuses more on students acquiring reading literacy in order to benefit society. Nonetheless, both definitions relate reading literacy to everyday functioning. This form of literacy is, therefore, not simply about the ability to decode certain texts; it is also about learners using, in everyday situations, their reading skills and the information that they have acquired through reading.

The first IEA assessment of reading in which Hungary participated (the Study of Reading Comprehension 1968–1972) focused on the behavioral aspects of reading, namely, decoding and reproduction. The tasks used to assess these competencies measured reading comprehension, reading speed, and vocabulary (Cs. Czachesz, 2001). The results of this assessment, conducted with students in Grade 4, influenced how reading is taught in Hungary. The second IEA assessment, modified by the experience of the first assessment, defined reading not merely as decoding, but also as a process involving functionality. This second assessment, again involving Grade 4 students, was thus augmented by a new domain of competence, that of understanding charts and diagrams, a skill which reflects a general ability to cope with everyday tasks (Cs. Czachesz, 2001). The results of both assessments showed that, by the end of Grade 4, 10-year-old Hungarian students were, in general, competent readers who had acquired the basic skills of reading.

The third and fourth assessments—PIRLS 2001 and PIRLS 2006—also focused on the reading competence of Grade 4 students. The texts used in this study included ones concerned with reading for literary experience and texts concerned with reading to acquire and use information (Mihály, 2003). Four basic processes were distinguished—*focus on and retrieve explicitly stated information, make straightforward inferences, interpret and integrate ideas and information*, and *examine and evaluate content, language, and textual elements* (Mullis, Martin, & Gonzalez, 2004).

The acquisition of reading competence does not happen independently of characteristics unique to the learner. Variables related to motivational aspects such as attitudes toward learning and school as well as personal goals and self-concept appear to be associated with students' reading skills and engagement. For example, students who express positive attitudes toward reading—who say they like to read and who consider themselves to be good readers—read more often for recreational purposes and choose a wider variety of texts to read than do students who do not express such attitudes (Mullis, Martin, González, & Kennedy, 2003).

The more recent international assessments of reading literacy have evaluated students' acquisition of basic skills within the context of students' learning motives and learning strategies because of the assumption that effective skill development is associated with positive learning characteristics (see, for example, Haahr, Nielsen, Hansen, & Jakobsen, 2005). The PIRLS iterations of 2001 and 2006 considered the motivational components associated with students' attitudes toward reading and students' self-rating (self-concept) of their reading skills. The PISA 2000 and 2003 assessments considered four motivational characteristics—intrinsic motivation, extrinsic motivation, sense of belonging to school, and attitudes toward learning. PIRLS 2006 and PISA 2000 and 2003 also considered reading efficacy, that is, students' confidence in their ability to engage effectively with texts.

Multivariate analyses of data from these studies suggest that approximately 10% of the variance in reading results can be explained by students' attitudes toward reading (Haahr et al., 2005). However, according to Haahr et al. (2005), positive attitudes are neither sufficient nor necessary for good results. The authors observed that students in both Finland and Japan achieved, on average, good reading-competency results in PIRLS and PISA despite gaining relatively low scores on the attitudinal scale.

In Hungary, both the international and the national publications on PIRLS reported little association between reading ability and attitudes. Even students with low scores on the attitude index achieved relatively high scores on the reading ability test (see Balázsi et al., 2008). Self-concept, however, showed a relationship with reading ability. Students who gained high scores on the self-concept index scored significantly higher on the reading test than did students with low scores on the self-concept index. Despite achieving higher overall scores on the PIRLS reading assessment test in 2006 than in 2001, the Hungarian students were more likely to appear in the low self-concept category in 2006 than they were in 2001. Thus, more students in 2006 than in 2001 said that they could not read well (Balázsi et al., 2008).

The Hungarian-Speaking Students Assessed in PIRLS 2001 and 2006

In 2001, a group of 35 countries took part in PIRLS (Mullis et al., 2003); in 2006, 40 countries did so (Mullis, Martin, Kennedy, & Foy, 2007). All three countries that are the focus of our present study participated in both assessments, allowing us to compare the data we examined not only across time but also cross-culturally. Table 1 presents a summary of the size of the populations for which data were collected in both years.

The education systems of the three countries are very similar in the initial stages, that is, up to approximately Grade 4. There are no crucial differences between the system of majority and minority education[2] in the Slovak Republic and Romania, although there are some differences in the curricula for the two areas of this system. All three countries have decentralized education systems, which means that schools can decide what to include in their curricula and how to run their schools, as long as

Table 1: The PIRLS 2001 and 2006 selected samples in the three countries

Country/ language of test	Year	Number of schools	Number of classes	Number of students	Total weight
Hungary/Hungarian	2001	216	216	4,666	117,238
	2006	149	196	4,068	104,649
Romania/Hungarian	2001	4	4	127	7,379
	2006	10	12	185	6,861
Slovak R./Hungarian	2001	12	12	170	4,167
	2006	22	31	566	3,674

Note: The numbers of schools and classes were equal in 2001 because only one class per sampled school was chosen during the selection procedure. The total weight shows the number of students represented by the selected sample.

---

2 The term "minority education" refers to educational provision for students from an ethnic grouping that speaks a language (e.g., Romanian) other than Hungarian. "Majority education" refers to education for students whose first language is the language used by the majority of the population (in the case of our study, Hungarian).

they heed the central government's national directives and standards for education. In Romania, the government introduced a curriculum framework for primary schools at the beginning of the 1998/99 school year, and implemented revisions to it in 2001 and 2003. Each country must use one of the reading-curriculum textbooks approved by the Ministry of Education. There are only two such books in the Slovak Republic, but many options in the other two countries. The number of reading classes per week varies between seven and nine, depending on grade level. The structure of preservice and inservice teacher training is similar in all three countries.

Since 2004, teachers in Hungary have been required to conduct an analytical written assessment of their students' reading achievement at the end of each of the first three grades of school and at the end of the first semester of the fourth school year. In the Slovak Republic, teachers conduct an oral assessment of their students' reading ability at the end of the first grade (see Felvégi & Ostorics, 2007; Lukackova & Obrancova, 2007; Noveanu & Sarivan, 2007). The populations of students included in this present study for Romania and the Slovak Republic all completed the tests in Hungarian.

METHOD

Variables Considered

As we noted earlier, the PIRLS 2001 and 2006 surveys took into account students' attitudes toward reading in order to obtain data that might help explain students' reading literacy scores. In PIRLS, attitudes encompassed the following categories: "student's attitudes toward reading," "student's self-concept regarding his/her reading ability," "student's attitudes toward school," and "student's reports of problematic behavior by other students at school." Our study focused on the first two categories only—student's attitudes toward reading, and student's self-concept regarding his/ her reading ability. We considered both as "motivation to learn" variables.

Attitudes toward reading were measured in PIRLS with the following statements: "I read only if I have to," "I like talking about books with other people," "I would be happy if someone gave me a book as a present," "I think reading is boring," "I need to read well for my future," and "I enjoy reading." Students responded to each statement by marking their preference on a four-point Likert scale: disagree a lot = 1, disagree a little = 2, agree a little = 3, and agree a lot = 4. Because some statements were negative in meaning, coding was reversed for these statements. A cumulative "attitudes toward reading" index was developed from the students' averaged scores on these items. The index had three categories: high (values between 3 and 4 on the Likert scale), medium (values between 2 and 3), and low (values between 1 and 2). Students in the high category agreed with most of the statements.

A four-point Likert scale was also used in the student questionnaire with respect to students' self-concept of their reading ability. The 2001 iteration of PIRLS contained the following statements: "Reading is very easy for me," "I do not read as well as other students in my class," "When I am reading by myself, I understand almost everything I read," and "Reading aloud is very hard for me." In 2006, the fourth question was modified to read: "I read slower than other students in my class." In 2001, the third statement was not included in the self-concept index, which again comprised the average of students' scores. In 2006, all four statements were taken into account during development of the index. In both years, the index had three categories of self-concept—high, medium, and low. Students with a high index considered themselves to be good readers and trusted in their ability to understand what they read. As was the case with the attitude-toward-reading items, reverse coding was used for self-concept items that were negative in orientation.

Analyses

When analyzing PIRLS data, one has to take into account sampling error and the fact that the students' results were weighted. To obtain descriptive statistics and correlation coefficients between two variables, we used the IEA International Database Analyzer (IEA, 2005), which is a free-to-download plug-in for SPSS.

Also, because the PIRLS data are nested, we used hierarchical linear modeling (HLM; see, for example, Raudenbush & Bryk, 2002) to ascertain associations between learning motives and reading literacy. We used two 2-level HLM models, in which individuals were placed on the first level, and classes/schools were placed on the second level. In an effort to determine what association, if any, school and class had with students' reading performance, we constructed our first model as a one-way analysis of variance (ANOVA) with random effects, and reading achievement as the dependent variable. Our second model was a random-coefficient HLM in which attitude and self-concept indices were the Level 1 predictors and reading achievement was the dependent variable. Both predictors were centered around their group means. The results from the first model allowed us to calculate the proportions of variance in reading achievement scores explained by these indices. The HLM software that we used during our analyses was developed by Raudenbush, Bryk, Cheong, Congdon, and du Toit (2004).

RESULTS AND INTERPRETATIONS

Comparison Between Countries and Across Time of Reading Achievement

Table 2 provides the mean reading achievement scores and their standard errors for the students in each country who participated in the two PIRLS assessments. The table also states the language(s) in which the reading assessment was presented in each country.

It is important, when considering the information in Table 2, to note that the achievement scores are not equal to the means of the students' raw test scores. In order to obtain these, and thereby set the scale for international comparison, the PIRLS research team used item response theory (IRT) techniques to analyze the students' reading achievement. The responses were then subjected to a conditioning process, which provided the probability distribution of the achievement of each

Table 2: Reading achievement of students in the three countries on the PIRLS 2001 and 2006 assessments, by language of test

Country	Language of test	2001			2006		
		Number of students	Mean	s. e.	Number of students	Mean	s. e.
Hungary	Hungarian	4,666	543.23	2.20	4,068	550.89	2.98
Romania	Romanian	3,498	511.06	4.68	4,088	488.49	5.09
	Hungarian	127	535.98	9.41	185	516.99	9.16
	Romania jointly	3,625	511.71	4.59	4,273	489.47	5.01
Slovak Republic	Slovakian	3,640	516.06	2.97	4,814	532.26	2.91
	Hungarian	170	550.76	8.59	566	511.63	7.64
	Slovak R. jointly	3,810	518.09	2.85	5,380	530.81	2.75

student, given student responses and background data. These posterior distributions of achievement led to drawing a sample of five elements (plausible values), which, as a set, represented the expected proficiency and the uncertainty associated with the measure (see also von Davier, Gonzalez, & Mislevy, 2009).

The IRT analysis allowed the definition of a common scale of reading achievement across the countries, which was then transformed to have 500 points as the international average (the PIRLS average) and 100 points as the standard deviation. Application of this rescaling transformation to the set of plausible values for a student's or a country's average score allows one to establish a student's or a country's level of achievement. The benefit of the conditioning model is that it improves the reliability of the achievement measurement (for details, see Martin, Mullis, & Kennedy, 2007; Mullis et al., 2007) while preserving (through the use of plausible values) an accurate measure of the remaining uncertainty.

The 500 points average established in 2001 changed in 2006 because of the participation of additional countries. However, the original PIRLS average was kept to 500, while the international average was established as 492, thus allowing the results for individual countries to be compared to both averages.

To determine whether a country achieved above the PIRLS average, the international average, or another reference score at the 95% confidence level, it is necessary to calculate the confidence intervals for each country's average score. The lower boundary of a confidence interval equals the mean score minus 1.96 times the standard error; the upper boundary is the mean score plus 1.96 times the standard error. If 500 falls within a country's confidence interval, then that country's mean score is not statistically different from the 500-point score. However, if the lower boundary of the confidence interval of that country's mean score is greater than 500, then its achievement is significantly higher than the international average. Its achievement is lower if the upper boundary is less than 500. In order to compare the average achievement of students of two countries, or of students from the same country at different occasions, independent samples t-tests can be applied.

All three countries that we considered achieved significantly above the PIRLS-average (500 point) in the 2001 PIRLS assessment. In the Slovak Republic, the Hungarian-speaking students gained significantly higher test scores (t = -2.86, p = .004) than the students of the majority population in the country, that is, the Slovakian-speaking students. In Romania, the difference in scores between the achievement of the Hungarian-speaking students and the Romanian-speaking students was not statistically significant (t = -0.87, p = .384).

In 2006, however, students in Romania (including those in the Hungarian-speaking subsample) scored significantly lower than they had in 2001 (t = 3.21, p = .001). Although the students in the Slovak Republic achieved a higher mean reading score in 2006 than in 2001, there was a significant decline in the performance of the Hungarian subsample (t = 3.76, p = .000). In 2006, Hungarians from Hungary significantly outperformed the Hungarian-speaking minorities in the neighboring countries (t = 2.86, p = .004 and t = 2.46, p = .014), but there were no significant differences between the achievement of the Hungarian minorities in the Slovak Republic (M = 511.63, t = -0.39, p = .696) and Romania (M = 516.99). Note that because the numbers of students in the Romanian-Hungarian and Slovakian-Hungarian subsamples were relatively small, the standard errors of their mean scores tended to be somewhat higher than the mean scores for all participating students in those countries.

As mentioned earlier, we used a one-way ANOVA with random effects to gain some idea of the degree of association between schools and reading performance. (Note that the within- school variance obtained from this model was necessary for further calculations.) Table 3 shows that, except in Romania in 2001, all between-school differences were significant. The exception may be due to the small number of schools in that specific sample. Overall, across the two time periods, the within-school differences were always higher than the between-school differences for all three subsamples.

Table 4 provides a summary of the findings of our analysis of reading achievement data for 2006. We were not able to consider class-level data for 2001 because each school that participated in the PIRLS assessment of that year was represented by one class only. As is evident from Table 4, all between-class variances were significant, and the within-class differences were larger again than those values for each subsample in each country.

Table 5 presents the results of our calculation of the between-class correlation coefficients, which is the proportion of the variance between groups and the total variance (Raudenbush & Bryk, 2002), for both the school level and the class level at the two data-collection times. The highest variance occurred in the Hungarian-speaking subsample in the Slovak Republic. Here, the between-school and within-school variances accounted for between 35 and 40% of the total variance in reading achievement; the proportion at the class level was even greater, at 43%. The smallest school-level and class-level differences to emerge were those for the Hungarian-speaking Romanian subsample. In Hungary, the school-level variance of 25% was

Table 3: Differences in reading achievement of students in the three countries on the PIRLS 2001 and 2006 assessments, by country and school level

Country/ language of test	Year	Fixed effect			Random effect				
		Coeff.	s. e.	Between sch. τ_{00}	Within sch. σ^2	df	χ^2	p
Hungary/Hungarian	2001	543.41	2.69	902.27	3272.53	215	1377.39	0.000
	2006	547.35	3.60	1242.86	3667.73	148	1426.69	0.000
Romania/Hungarian	2001	540.20	5.06	1.00	5332.63	3	1.39	> 0.5
	2006	522.08	12.66	548.19	4572.61	9	28.05	0.001
Slovak R./Hungarian	2001	538.05	20.39	2872.80	4325.06	11	63.60	0.000
	2006	502.44	13.42	2510.31	4636.46	21	226.77	0.000

Table 4: Differences in reading achievement of students in the three countries on the PIRLS 2006 assessment, by country and class level

Country/ language of test	Year	Fixed effect			Random effect				
		Coeff.	s. e.	Between class τ_{00}	Within class σ^2	df	χ^2	p
Hungary/Hungarian	2006	547.73	3.36	1400.86	3538.74	195	1661.7	0.000
Romania/Hungarian	2006	522.48	11.96	615.36	4449.56	11	34.83	0.000
Slovak R./Hungarian	2006	503.95	12.22	3013.02	4057.09	30	335.52	0.000

Table 5: Intra-class correlation values, by school level and class level

Country/language of test	Year	Intra-class correlation School level	Intra-class correlation Class level
Hungary/Hungarian	2001	0.22	–
	2006	0.25	0.28
Romania/Hungarian	2001	0.00	–
	2006	0.11	0.12
Slovak R./Hungarian	2001	0.40	–
	2006	0.35	0.43

marginally lower than the 28% of the respective class level. The high school- and class-level variances in reading achievement in the Hungarian subsample in the Slovak Republic may have been partly due to the very low numbers of students in the subsamples.

The Relationship Between Reading Literacy Achievement and Learning Motives

Table 6 presents the means and standard errors on the attitude and self-concept indices for the three countries at the two data-collection points. Here we can see that, of the subsamples of participating Hungarian-speaking students, the Romanian subsample held the most positive attitudes in both 2001 and 2006. Across the subsamples, attitudes toward reading and self-concept barely changed between 2001 and 2006; the differences were too slight to be statistically significant.

Table 6: Attitudes toward reading and reading-related self-concept indices for 2001 and 2006

Country/language of test	Attitude index				Self-concept index			
	2001		2006		2001		2006	
	Mean	s. e.	Mean	s. e.	Mean	s. e.	Mean	s. e.
Hungary/Hungarian	3.00	0.02	2.98	0.02	3.04	0.02	3.03	0.02
Romania/Hungarian	3.22	0.06	3.08	0.10	2.93	0.23	2.82	0.06
Slovak R./Hungarian	3.15	0.08	2.97	0.07	2.93	0.05	3.04	0.04

The next two tables present the reading achievement scores for the three index groups (high, medium, low) for attitudes toward reading (Table 7) and reading self-concept (Table 8). For both indices, no substantial differences could be observed between 2001 and 2006 in any of the countries represented. Students who gained the higher scores on the attitude index tended to achieve higher reading achievement scores, but those whose scores placed them low on the index also achieved relatively high scores. The pattern of achievement scores on the self-concept index was a little more complex than the pattern for the attitude index. We can see, in Table 8, that the highest reading achievement scores were obtained by those students with high self-concept scores and the lowest achievement scores were obtained by those students with low self-concept scores. In Hungary, those students with lower self-concept scores, that is, the students who did not consider themselves good readers, gained scores below the international mean scores for 2001 and 2006. In 2001, all Hungarian-speaking Romanians, irrespective of their self-concept index, outperformed the international mean. In 2006, the average achievement score of the Hungarian-speaking students in the Slovak Republic who had a medium self-concept was below the international mean of 492 score points.

Table 7: Differences in reading achievement of students in the three countries on the PIRLS 2001 and 2006 assessments, by attitudes-toward-reading index categories

Country/language of test	Category	2001			2006		
		% of students	Mean	s. e.	% of students	Mean	s. e.
Hungary	Low	9.22	522.93	4.18	10.60	531.03	3.09
	Medium	37.64	526.48	2.32	37.78	533.23	4.18
	High	47.81	565.08	2.64	49.02	571.25	2.91
Romania/Hungarian	Low	0			4.21	459.18	25.51
	Medium	37.39	521.58	16.55	33.90	497.61	17.79
	High	55.67	550.62	7.92	49.95	541.18	7.72
Slovak R./Hungarian	Low	1.97	504.57	77.71	10.04	485.72	17.26
	Medium	44.20	546.91	13.75	37.29	493.35	11.77
	High	52.89	556.84	10.38	47.88	535.42	8.64

Note: Students who did not answer one or more of the five questions were excluded from the analysis.

Table 8: Differences in reading achievement of students in the three countries on the PIRLS 2001 and 2006 assessments, by self-concept index categories

Country/language of test	Category	2001			2006		
		% of students	Mean	s. e.	% of students	Mean	s. e.
Hungary/ Hungarian	Low	6.90	485.45	5.13	4.00	497.43	7.20
	Medium	43.64	525.12	2.37	49.29	531.41	3.33
	High	45.59	572.94	2.12	44.46	579.50	2.69
Romania/ Hungarian	Low	5.24	542.16	106.24	9.53	450.53	15.33
	Medium	57.70	527.69	19.18	54.79	509.57	9.89
	High	35.74	553.15	9.30	34.00	551.30	11.57
Slovak R. /Hungarian	Low	10.32	469.99	28.53	3.86	423.01	28.51
	Medium	45.07	545.76	9.55	44.50	486.99	7.36
	High	38.92	570.05	10.03	47.60	546.91	8.64

Note: Students who did not answer one or more of the three (2001) or four (2006) questions were excluded from the analysis.

Table 9 presents the correlations between the attitude index and reading achievement and between the self-concept index and reading achievement. We used Fisher's z transformation to determine the significance of these relationships. In each subsample, reading-related self-concept showed a statistically stronger correlation with reading achievement than attitudes toward reading. This finding led us to the tentative conclusion that, at the age of 10, Hungarian-speaking children's perception of their own reading competence is more closely associated with reading achievement than with whether or not they like reading.

Table 9: Correlations between the attitudes-toward-reading and self-concept indices and reading achievement

Country/language of test	Attitude index				Self-concept index			
	2001		2006		2001		2006	
	Corr.	s. e.	Corr.	s. e.	Corr.	s. e.	Corr.	s. e.
Hungary	0.31	0.02	0.27	0.02	0.47	0.01	0.42	0.02
Romania/Hungarian	0.28	0.18	0.28	0.12	0.31	0.18	0.42	0.08
Slovak R./Hungarian	0.13	0.13	0.28	0.07	0.32	0.11	0.50	0.05

Note: All values significant at the $p \leq .05$ level.

On observing the individual subsamples more closely, we found that while the correlation coefficients significantly decreased between 2001 and 2006 in Hungary, the correlation coefficients for the Hungarian subsample in the Slovak Republic were higher in the 2006 study than in the 2001 assessment. In Romania, the change in the correlation coefficients between attitudes toward reading and achievement was not significant. The highest correlation observed for the Hungarian subsample of the Slovak Republic was between reading-related self-concept and reading achievement ($r = .50$) in 2006.

This finding is particularly interesting given that the reading achievement of the students in this subsample was lower in 2006 than in 2001 (see Table 2). The fact that the decline in reading achievement was paralleled by a strengthening of the relationship between self-concept and reading achievement warrants further investigation.

To examine the extent to which the two motivation indices explained reading achievement at the school level, we calculated Level 1 variances from the one-way ANOVA with random effects (see σ^2 in Table 3) and the random-coefficient HLM with the two indices as Level 1 predictors. Because of the amount of data in the results of the six regression analyses, we present in this paper only the Level 1 variances (σ^2(Random)) needed to calculate the proportion of variance explained at Level 1. A summary of the results of this analysis appears in Table 10.

Table 10: Explanatory power of the combined attitudes toward reading and self-concept indices

Country/ language of test	Year	σ^2(Random)	Dependent variable: reading; independent variable: attitude and self-concept indices
			Variance explained
Hungary	2001	2440.04	0.25
	2006	2899.49	0.21
Romania/Hungarian	2001	4066.40	0.24
	2006	3407.39	0.25
Slovak R. /Hungarian	2001	3214.57	0.26
	2006	3068.13	0.34

As can be seen in the table, the combined indices explained 21% to 34% of the variance in reading achievement. In Hungary and in Romania, there were no substantial differences between the 2001 and the 2006 data; approximately 25% of the reading achievement was explained by the combined attitude/self-concept index in these countries. However, in the Slovak Republic, the explained variance was considerably higher (34%) in 2006 than in 2001. On the basis of these results, we drew these conclusions: in the Slovak Republic, more than 30% of the differences in reading achievement could be explained by attitudes and self-concept; in Hungary and Romania, the explanatory power of these two factors was at least 10% lower than the explanatory power of these two factors in the Slovak Republic.

Factors Influencing Learning Motives

Table 11 shows correlations between the index of home educational resources,[3] which was reversely coded, and the attitudes and self-concept indices. Overall, the correlation coefficients indicated a significantly positive, albeit weak, relationship between home educational resources and the reading-related self-concept of Hungarian-speaking students in all three countries, and across both PIRLS assessment cycles. The strongest correlations between self-concept and home educational resources were those for the Hungarian-speaking students in the Slovak Republic and Romania who participated in the PIRLS 2006 survey. The data for Hungary showed no significant changes between the PIRLS 2001 and 2006 assessments.

The correlations between the other background factors and reading achievement that we examined (e.g., early reading activities in the home, engagement in the reading activities outside school, reading magazines, parents' reading habits) were insufficiently strong to warrant presenting them here. We also observed no significant differences between the subsamples.

Table 11: Correlations between attitudes toward reading and self-concept indices and index of home educational resources

Country/language of test	Attitude index				Self-concept index			
	2001		2006		2001		2006	
	Corr.	s. e.	Corr.	s. e.	Corr.	s. e.	Corr.	s. e.
Hungary	0.16	0.02	0.18	0.02	0.19	0.02	0.19	0.02
Romania/Hungarian	0.20	0.02	-0.20	0.10	0.14	0.11	0.30	0.15
Slovak R./Hungarian	0.12	0.06	0.21	0.07	0.11	0.05	0.29	0.07

Note: All values significant at the $p \leq .05$ level.

SUMMARY AND CONCLUSIONS

In our study, we analyzed and compared Hungarian-speaking students' reading achievement data from PIRLS 2001 and 2006 for Hungary, the Slovak Republic, and Romania. We examined the relationships between reading achievement and motivational components (attitudes toward reading and reading-related self-concept) and reading achievement, and we compared these relationships across subsamples and between the two PIRLS data-collection points (2001 and 2006).

Our findings need to be interpreted cautiously given that our analyses were characterized by the limitations of cross-sectional studies and given that we were not able to draw basic causal inferences. As such, our results should be treated as merely indicative; they should not be used for drawing long-term conclusions about students' reading achievement in the three countries and factors potentially influencing that achievement.

The Hungarian students living in Hungary who participated in PIRLS achieved significantly higher reading scores in the 2006 study than in the 2001 study. In contrast, the reading achievement scores of the Hungarian-speaking students in the Slovak Republic and Romania dropped significantly between the two time periods. Reading achievement differences appeared mostly within schools and classes; thus, individual differences in achievement were larger between students and were independent of

---

3 This index was based on students' responses to two questions about home educational resources—number of books in the home, and educational aids in the home (computer, study desk/table for own use, books of one's own, access to a daily newspaper), and on parents' responses to two questions—number of children's books in the home, and parents' educational attainment (refer Balázsi et al., 2008, p. 44).

the students' schools. This tendency was observed in all three subsamples. This was a surprising result for Hungary, because the PISA study indicated that differences across schools in Hungary were the highest of any of the participating countries, possibly because of the high degree of selectivity into the differentiated secondary schools of the Hungarian education system (OECD, 2004). It appears, though, albeit on the basis of data from the two different programs of assessment (PISA and PIRLS), that these between-school differences hold for secondary schools, but not for primary schools.

Although the education systems in the three countries are similar in terms of majority and minority educational provision, and although nothing of significance occurred that might have influenced the results of the 2001 and 2006 assessments, our analyses of the data from both assessments for the three countries under consideration highlighted contradictory outcomes. The reading performance of students in Hungary improved noticeably between the two periods, but the performance of the minority Hungarian-speaking students in Romania, as well as of the Romanian students, in general, deteriorated markedly. The performance of the students overall in the Slovak Republic also improved significantly between 2001 and 2006, but the performance, on average, of the minority Hungarian-speaking students in that country deteriorated considerably.

As for the relationships between the attitudes-toward-reading and self-concept indices and reading achievement, we found that reading-related self-concept was more closely associated than attitudes with achievement in each country. This finding led us to the tentative conclusion that students' perceptions of their own reading competence is a more reliable predictor of students' reading achievement than is liking or not liking reading.

We used two HLM models to determine correlations between reading competency and motives. The results of our one-way ANOVA with random effects regarding the differences between schools, classes, and individual students were compatible with the results of a Hungarian assessment of reading competency of fourth graders (Csapó, Székely, & Tóth, 2009). PISA results, however, show that differences between schools were highest in Hungary, which, as previously mentioned, has a particularly strong system of school selectivity at the secondary level (OECD, 2004, 2007). The differences between PIRLS and PISA can be explained by the different assessment frameworks used in the two programs of assessment, as well as by the sample selection processes employed in the two studies.

Our second model was a two-level random-coefficient hierarchical linear model in which the attitudes and self-concept indices served as Level 1 predictors. The explanatory potential of the two indices regarding variance in reading achievement was the same for all subsamples of students, except for the Slovakian subsample of 2006, where it was higher and reached a level of about 35% to 40%. The reason for this difference in results cannot be explained by the variables we used; the reason may relate to a specific process associated with education policy.

We found only weak correlations between the motivational variables (attitudes toward reading, reading-related self-concept) and the student background factors (encompassed in the index of home educational resources) that supposedly influence the former. The number of books in the home, having a study desk or table for one's own use, having access to a daily newspaper, and parents' educational qualifications had minor, but consistently positive, associations across all subsamples and both assessment cycles with how much the students liked reading and their perceptions of their own reading competence. Low correlations between the attitudes and the self-concept indices and the various student background variables that we considered thus offered low explanatory potential. However, because the economic backgrounds of the three countries involved are similar, we were not surprised by this finding.

In conclusion, we could find no essential differences between the subsamples with respect to the studied factors. Although significant differences between the countries could be identified for certain factors, no country could be singled out as showing a pattern diverging from the other countries in either a positive or a negative direction.

References

Balázsi, I., Balkányi, P., Felvégi, E., & Szabó, V. (2008). *PIRLS 2006 summary report on the reading literacy of 10-year-old students in Hungary*. Budapest, Hungary: Hungarian Educational Authority.

Cs. Czachesz, E. (2001). Ki tud olvasni? Nemzetközi összehasonlító vizsgálatok és magyar eredményeik [Who can read? International comparative assessments and Hungarian results]. *Iskolakultúra, 11*, 21–30.

Cs. Czachesz, E. (2005). Változó perspektívák az olvasási képesség pedagógiai értelmezésében: Út a készségtől a motivált jelentéskonstrukcióig [Changing perspectives in the pedagogical interpretation of reading skills]. *Iskolakultúra, 15*, 44–52.

Csapó, B., Székely, L., & Tóth, E. (2009). *Az iskolai különbségek változása egy longitudinális vizsgálat adatai alapján* [Variations of school differences based on a longitudinal assessment], in press.

Felvégi, E., & Ostorics, L. (2007). Hungary. In A. M. Kennedy, I. V. S. Mullis, M. O. Martin, & K. L. Trong (Eds.), *PIRLS 2006 encyclopedia* (pp. 165–172). Chestnut Hill, MA: Boston College.

Haahr, J. H., Nielsen, T. K., Hansen, M. E., & Jakobsen, S. T. (2005). *Explaining student performance: Evidence from the international PISA, TIMSS and PIRLS surveys*. Aarhus, Denmark: Danish Technological Institute.

International Association for the Evaluation of Educational Achievement (IEA). (2005). *IEA International Database Analyzer* (IEA IDB Analyzer). Retrieved from http://www.iea.nl/iea_studies_datasets.html

Lukackova, Z., & Obrancova, E. (2007). The Slovak Republic. In A. M. Kennedy, I. V. S. Mullis, M. O. Martin, & K. L. Trong (Eds.), *PIRLS 2006 encyclopedia* (pp. 363–372). Chestnut Hill, MA: Boston College.

Martin, M. O., Mullis, I. V. S., & Kennedy, A. M. (2007). *PIRLS 2006 technical report.* Chestnut Hill, MA: Boston College.

Mihály, I. (2003). Nemzetközi olvasásvizsgálat: PIRLS 2001 [International reading assessment: PIRLS 2001]. *Új Pedagógiai Szemle, 53,* 201–211.

Mullis, I. V. S., Kennedy A. M., Martin, M. O., & Sainsbury M. (2006). *Assessment framework and specifications.* Chestnut Hill, MA: Boston College.

Mullis, I. V. S., Martin, M. O., & Gonzalez, E. J. (2004). *International achievement in the processes of reading comprehension: Results from PIRLS 2001 in 35 countries.* Chestnut Hill, MA: Boston College.

Mullis, I. V. S., Martin, M. O., González, E. J., & Kennedy, A. M. (2003). *PIRLS 2001 international report: IEA's study of reading literacy achievement in primary schools in 35 countries.* Chestnut Hill, MA: Boston College.

Mullis, I. V. S., Martin, M. O., Kennedy, A. M., & Foy, P. (2007). *PIRLS 2006 international report.* Chestnut Hill, MA: Boston College.

Nagy, J. (2006). Olvasástanítás: A megoldás stratégiai kérdései [Teaching reading: Solutions to strategic issues]. In J. Krisztián (Ed.), *Az olvasási képesség fejlődése és fejlesztése* [Development and improvement of reading skills]. Budapest, Hungary: Dinasztia Tankönyvkiadó.

Noveanu, G. N., & Sarivan, L. (2007). Romania. In A. M. Kennedy, I. V. S. Mullis, M. O. Martin, & K. L. Trong (Eds.), *PIRLS 2006 encyclopedia* (pp. 317–326). Chestnut Hill, MA: Boston College.

Organisation for Economic Co-operation and Development (OECD). (2000). *Measuring student knowledge and skills: The PISA 2000 assessment of reading, mathematical and scientific literacy.* Paris, France: Author.

Organisation for Economic Co-operation and Development (OECD). (2003). *The PISA 2003 assessment framework: Mathematics, reading, science and problem-solving knowledge and skills.* Paris, France: Author.

Organisation for Economic Co-operation and Development (OECD). (2004). *Learning for tomorrow's world: First results from PISA 2003.* Paris, France: Author.

Organisation for Economic Co-operation and Development (OECD). (2006). *Assessing scientific, reading and mathematical literacy: A framework for PISA 2006.* Paris, France: Author.

Organisation for Economic Co-operation and Development (OECD). (2007). *PISA 2006: Science competencies for tomorrow's world: Executive summary.* Paris, France: Author.

Raudenbush, S. W., & Bryk, A. S. (2002). *Hierarchical linear models: Applications and data analysis methods* (2nd ed.). Thousand Oaks, CA: Sage.

Raudenbush, S. W., Bryk, A. S., Cheong, Y. F., Congdon, R., & du Toit, M. (2004). *HLM 6: Hierarchical linear and nonlinear modeling.* Lincolnwood, IL: Scientific Software International.

von Davier, M., Gonzalez, E., & Mislevy, R. (2009). What are plausible values and why are they useful? *IERI Monograph Series: Issues and Methodologies in Large-Scale Assessments*, *2*, 9–36.

Principles of multiple matrix booklet designs and parameter recovery in large-scale assessments

Eugenio Gonzalez
Educational Testing Service, Princeton, NJ, USA[1]
Leslie Rutkowski
Indiana University, Bloomington, IN, USA[2]

Large-scale assessments usually set out to cover an extensive content domain. Because of this, and to avoid overburdening students and schools, assessments are designed in such a way that each student is administered only a fraction of all the available items in the assessment. These designs are referred to as matrix sampling or multiple matrix sampling. This approach to test design and administration allows one to estimate sufficiently precise proficiency distributions of the target population and sub-populations and a complete coverage of the assessment framework, while reducing individual examinee burden and testing time at the school. Many of the choices and trade-offs in designing a multiple matrix sampled assessment are discussed and several example designs are described. A simulation study illustrates the impact that sparseness strategies can have on person and item parameter recovery. Implications for test design are discussed.

1 The opinions expressed herein are those of the author and do not necessarily represent those of Educational Testing Service.

2 The authors thank Andreas Oranje, Matthias von Davier, Rebecca Zwick, and an anonymous reviewer for suggestions and for comments on previous versions of this paper.

INTRODUCTION

Large-scale assessment (LSA) programs are charged with measuring what members of a given population know and can do in a given content domain or whether those members have acquired the skills necessary for performing future life activities. The breadth of topics measured by these programs is such that a large number of contents and skills are assessed. A number of national and international large-scale assessment programs exist. Each has its own focus and underlying philosophy. For example, the Trends in International Mathematics and Science Study (TIMSS) assesses mathematics and science knowledge and skills acquired by fourth and eighth graders (Mullis et al., 2005; Neidorf & Garden, 2004); the Programme for International Student Assessment (PISA) seeks to measure mathematics, scientific, and reading literacy of examinees who are 15 years of age (OECD, 2006); and the Progress in International Reading Literacy Study (PIRLS) aims to measure the reading literacy of fourth graders, an age when children are expected to make the transition from learning to read to reading to learn (Mullis, Kennedy, Martin, & Sainsbury, 2006). National large-scale assessment programs also aim to measure knowledge and skills of examinees of different ages and grade levels. For example, in the United States, the National Assessment of Educational Progress (NAEP) (National Center for Educational Statistics, 2010) assesses students at Grades 4, 8, and 12 in a number of content areas.

Because of the ambitious scope of these large-scale assessment programs, each assessment is designed in such a way that each student is administered only a fraction of all the available items in that assessment. In other words, each student is administered a particular combination of test items, thus ensuring sufficient content coverage across the population while reducing the assessment burden for any one student. The term multiple matrix sampling (Shoemaker, 1973), or, in older literature, item-sampling (Lord, 1962), arises from the practice of sampling both examinees and items; that is, giving samples of items to samples of examinees. Table 1 provides an example of multiple matrix sampling. In this example, each subject is administered a set of four of the six available items, and each item is administered to eight of the 12 examinees. Students 1 and 7 are each administered Items 1 through 4, Students 2 and 8 are each administered Items 2 through 5, and so on. Students 1 and 7 and Students 2 and 8, for example, may also be administered Items 2 through 4.

Matrix sampling of items is thus used in large-scale assessments to accommodate a broad coverage of the content domain, thereby ensuring that items are administered to a sufficient number of students without necessitating excessive testing time for any one individual student. Matrix sampling of items also allows us to estimate proficiency distributions of the population, while reducing individual examinee burden and testing time at the school, and representing the assessment framework satisfactorily. As is the case in most large-scale assessments, individual measurement precision is sacrificed in the interest of increased content coverage. This emphasis, or set of priorities, makes the booklet designs used in large-scale assessments rarely optimal for individual reporting, yet useful for group-level reporting. For operational expediency, large-scale assessment items are assigned to blocks that are then combined into forms

Table 1: Multiple matrix sampling

Subject	Set	Item 1	Item 2	Item 3	Item 4	Item 5	Item 6
1	1	x	x	x	x		
2	2		x	x	x	x	
3	3			x	x	x	x
4	4	x			x	x	x
5	5	x	x			x	x
6	6	x	x	x			x
7	1	x	x	x	x		
8	2		x	x	x	x	
9	3			x	x	x	x
10	4	x			x	x	x
11	5	x	x			x	x
12	6	x	x	x			x

according to a particular design or specification. This approach differs from other matrix sampling approaches where items are sampled randomly from the universe of possible items (see, for example, Barcikowski, 1972; Scheetz & Forsyth, 1977; Gressard & Loyd, 1991).

While mathematical optimization routines exist for optimizing booklet designs subject to a number of constraints (e.g., van der Linden & Carlson, 1999; van der Linden, Veldkamp, & Carlson, 2004), our focus in this article is not only on the practical issues that researchers need to consider when selecting a particular multiple matrix sampling design but also on the consequences of that process for the estimation of the population and item parameters. This paper contains two related sections. In the first, we briefly review the history, theory, and implementation of booklet designs. A substantial portion of this discussion includes details on current uses of matrix sampling in large-scale assessments (e.g., TIMSS, PIRLS, and PISA), the advantages and disadvantages of using multiple-matrix-sample booklet designs, and practical guidelines on selecting a particular booklet design. In the second section, we conduct an empirical investigation of the degree to which population and item parameters are recovered as a function of matrix sparseness and sample size during use of an incomplete booklet design. To explore this issue, we simulate data under different booklet designs. We then generate simulated responses to these booklet designs, assuming that a two-parameter logistic item response theory (IRT) model is sufficiently robust to assess the recovery of population and item parameters under different booklet designs.

THE ORIGINS OF MULTIPLE-MATRIX-SAMPLE BOOKLET DESIGN

Traditional approaches to sampling generally relied on sampling examinees from the population; however, a number of initial investigations (Johnson & Lord, 1958; Lord, 1962; Pugh, 1971) suggested that item sampling, in which small subsets of the total available items are administered in groups to the entire population, or multiple matrix sampling, could be an efficient and cost-effective way of assessing examinees and populations. Early work in the field of multiple matrix sampling, also referred to as item-examinee sampling and item sampling (Shoemaker, 1973), showed that, in many circumstances, this method is a reasonable (and sometimes advantageous) way to estimate group means (Gressard & Loyd, 1991; Johnson & Lord, 1958; Plumlee, 1964) and standard deviations (Gressard & Loyd, 1991; Pugh, 1971). Lord (1962) used empirical data to show that item sampling with replacement, where the entire normed population responds to small groups of possibly overlapping test items, is an effective means of recovering the known population norm values. Results from a study that mailed full and item-sampled questionnaires to a random sample of principals showed significantly higher response rates for the item-sampled questionnaires (Munger & Loyd, 1988).

A number of early empirical studies sampled items at random for assignment to subtests, or *forms* in large-scale assessment terminology (e.g., Lord, 1962; Plumlee, 1964; Shoemaker, 1970a, 1970b). During the same period, researchers used stratification techniques to assign items to subtests based on item difficulty (Kleinke, 1972; Scheetz & Forsyth, 1977) or item discrimination (Myerberg, 1975; Scheetz & Forsyth, 1977). Lord (1965) suggested that balanced incomplete block (BIB) designs might be advantageous for multiple-matrix sampling, because they fulfill the conditions that every item block appears an equal number of times in all block positions. This balancing of positions by means of BIB and variants of this design is a commonly used tool in experimental design (Nair, 1943; Yates, 1939). Knapp (1968) subsequently incorporated Lord's suggestion and found that a BIB design was an extremely efficient means of estimating the mean, variance, and reliability coefficient of several assessments. The BIB design was eventually, and successfully, implemented in the 1983/1984 NAEP assessment (Beaton, 1987; Beaton & Zwick, 1992; Johnson, 1992).

Many of the early studies depended on percent-correct methods for estimating test scores on multiple matrix sampled assessments (c.f., Johnson & Lord, 1958; Lord, 1962; Plumlee, 1964; Pugh, 1971). The rise of item response theory (IRT) methods in educational assessment facilitated the integration of multiple matrix sampling schemes (Bock, Mislevy, & Woodson, 1982). In this context, Mislevy (1983, 1984), Mislevy and Sheehan (1987), Reiser (1983), and others developed group-level models that estimated the underlying latent traits measured by assessments that followed a multiple matrix booklet design.

The dominant approach, applied to NAEP since 1983/1984 (Beaton, 1987) and clearly laid out in Mislevy (1991), uses a population model to integrate the advantages of multiple matrix sampling with IRT models. The approach is a latent regression IRT model. It integrates an IRT-based measurement model with a population model that utilizes covariates of proficiency. The latent regression model is utilized to estimate posterior distributions of examinee proficiency, given item responses and covariates. This posterior distribution, which draws on Rubin's (1976, 1978, 1987) multiple imputation technique, is used as the basis upon which to impute a set of plausible values for each examinee and each of the subscales.

Definition of Key Terms

Before proceeding further, we define some concepts in order to facilitate subsequent discussions. To understand the implementation of booklet designs, it is useful to clarify what is operationally understood by items, units, blocks or clusters, forms, and (ultimately) the assessment.

- *Items:* Items are the most basic unit of an assessment. Usually, an item is an individual task administered to a respondent, and it receives a score. Scores can be assigned automatically by machine or computer, or by people who examine the response and determine the best score based on the scoring rubric for the item. In general, when there is a single test form, scored item responses are summed for each examinee to compute a total score on a given test. Alternatively, methods that make assumptions about a latent trait (e.g., modern test theory methods) can be used to generate individual or group test scores. In a modern test theory framework, the score for each examinee is based on estimated item parameters. Even though observed correct scores can be used (after adjusting for form differences) to report results across multiple forms, modern test theory methods such as item response theory (IRT) are particularly useful when the assessment is composed of multiple forms. They are useful because they allow a formal evaluation of how well the different test forms can be aligned along a common scale.

    Items are generally of three kinds—multiple-choice, open-ended or constructed response, and performance. Multiple-choice items typically ask an examinee to read a given problem statement (usually referred to as the *stem*) and to select an answer from a fixed set of possible answers (usually referred to as the response *options*). The same item followed by the same response options, but in a different sequence, should generally be treated as a different item, unless there is evidence indicating that the order of the options does not affect the overall performance on the item. Open-ended or constructed-response items usually present a problem, and the examinee is expected to provide an answer in a specified format (e.g., essay or short-answer). Performance items pose a problem or question, and the examinee is asked to perform a task or demonstrate a skill (e.g., nursing students asked to measure a patient's blood pressure).

- *Units:* These consist of a common stem or stimulus that is followed by several items. An individual item is a special case of a unit. Examples of units include a reading assessment text followed by a series of items, all of which relate to the text. These types of units are common in PIRLS. Units are also regularly used in PISA. Depending on the assessment purpose, the units can be of different lengths and have varying numbers of items; however, what defines a unit is a set of items with a common stimulus. As with the multiple-choice items, the same stimulus followed by the same items, but in a different order, should be treated as different units, unless there is sufficient evidence to indicate that the order of the items does not affect the overall performance on the unit.

- *Blocks or clusters:* A block or cluster is a set of items, units, or some combination of the two, that is presented to examinees. In its simplest form, a block could contain just one item or one unit. Items (or units) are generally grouped into blocks to facilitate the assignment of items across different forms and to easily control content representation of the areas assessed across the forms. Grouping items into blocks helps maintain the context in which sets of items occur. The item context is a nuisance variable that has been shown to affect examinee performance. As an example of how organizing items into blocks helps, let us assume that we want to administer 10 items from a pool of 1,000 mathematics items—all multiple-choice with five response options—and let us assume that, of the 10 items we want, two items come from one of five mathematics subdomains. If we randomly pick 10 items from the entire pool, it is possible, although unlikely, that we could pick 10 items from only one or two of the subdomains, or 10 items with the correct answer being "A" or "B." Instead, we could organize the 1,000 items into 200 blocks of five items each. Here, each block would have one item from each of the subdomains, and each of the five response options would be used. Of course, we would not advertise that each of the five response options is used in every block, and this particular constraint might be difficult to implement. However, the test developer should certainly try to avoid undesirable and detectable patterns.

When assembling blocks of items, the order in which the items are placed within the blocks could have an effect on the difficulty of the items. Although commonly used scaling models assume local independence of the items, local dependencies may be found. Verifying that the local independence assumption is not violated, as well the absence of position effects within or across blocks, is crucial. Analytic procedures rely on the assumption that the same item presented in two or more different positions can be treated as statistically equivalent instances of the same item.

- *Forms:* A test form is the actual set of items, in a specific sequence, that is administered to examinees. These items are organized in blocks, so technically a form is a set of blocks organized in a particular sequence. The same items administered in two different sequences are considered to be different forms. The term booklet is used to refer to the paper-and-pencil version of a form, whereas the term *form* covers paper-and-pencil administration as well as computer-based administration. The key consideration is that a different set of items or units, or the same set of items or units in a different sequence, is treated as a different form of the assessment and that evidence is gathered to show that the results on these items in the different forms are comparable.

- *Sessions:* The session is the particular time period during which a form, or part of it, is administered. Depending on its length, a form can be administered in one or more sessions. Most, but not all, large-scale assessments administer booklets in two sequential but distinct sessions. Each of the sessions is separately timed, and examinees are assigned a specific section of the form during each session.

- *Assessments:* The assessment constitutes the entirety of the item pool that is administered. Depending on the item pool and the purpose and duration of the program, the assessment could span multiple blocks, and multiple forms across administration cycles. Consider, for example, the PISA 2003 mathematics assessment. In this case, the total item pool consists of those items and units administered during the 2003 application. The PISA mathematics assessment item pool, however, would include all of the items and units administered across all four assessment cycles (2000, 2003, 2006, and 2009).

The concepts above can be represented as follows:

$$(\text{Assessment}_a (\text{Form}_f (\text{Block}_b (\text{Unit}_u (\text{Item}_i))))).$$

In the case of some large-scale assessments, where the same assessment is administered in different languages, we would have the following:

$$(\text{Assessment}_a (\text{Language}_l (\text{Form}_f (\text{Block}_b (\text{Unit}_u (\text{Item}_i)))))).$$

Item$_i$ is thus nested within *Unit$_u$*, which is nested within *Block$_b$*, and so on. In its simplest form, an assessment can be constructed with just one form composed of one block that consists of one unit comprised of one item—a one-item assessment.

Booklet designs

The booklet design is the set of rules that we use to assign items to respondents. The set of rules could be as simple as assigning to every respondent all the items in the assessment in the same format and sequence. It is also possible to construct a sophisticated design that allows one to decide, during administration of the assessment, which item to administer next. This is the case in computer adaptive testing (CAT). Paper-based booklet designs require that these governing rules be defined prior to printing the forms. Computer-based assessments are more flexible with respect to design choices because algorithms can be used to decide—even as the assessment is being administered—which specific items to administer next.

An example

Most large-scale educational assessments (e.g., TIMSS, PIRLS, and NAEP) measure a defined set of skills within a representative sample of the population of interest. The goal of these assessments is to describe groups within the population with respect to broadly defined areas of school- or work-relevant skills. A commonality of these assessments is that individual scores are not assigned to examinees. Although this feature might be seen as a limitation, it actually allows for more flexibility in the choice of design.

Take the example of TIMSS 2007, which included in its Grade 8 mathematics assessment content domain number, *algebra*, *geometry*, and *data and chance*. Across these wide content domains, examinees were expected to draw on the cognitive domains of *knowing*, *applying*, and *reasoning* (Mullis et al., 2005). This approach brought the total number of reporting scales to eight (seven overlapping subscales plus overall mathematics). Reporting in this fashion implies that an ample number of items in each of the reporting sub-domains is administered across the population, such that sufficiently precise estimates of proficiency distributions are possible.

In total, the TIMSS 2007 mathematics assessment consisted of 215 items, a number that made it impossible to test all examinees on every item. (Estimates for completing one item ranged from one minute for the multiple-choice items, to three to four minutes for the open-ended items.) Instead, the 215 items were distributed across 14 mathematics blocks; each examinee received two of these. This design ensured linking across booklets because each block (and therefore each item) appeared in two different booklets. Booklets were then administered to randomly equivalent samples of examinees, such that the total assessment material was divided into more reasonable 90-minute periods of testing time for each examinee. With this design, examinees received just a small subset of the total available items.[2] (For complete details on the TIMSS 2007 booklet design, see Olson, Martin, & Mullis, 2008.)

While a multiple matrix booklet design ensures coverage of a broad content domain in a reasonable amount of time, it poses challenges associated with putting the items onto a common scale, estimating examinee proficiency, and ultimately obtaining population estimates. Advanced statistical techniques are available to estimate the distribution of proficiencies in populations and subpopulations of examinees. Mislevy (1991), Mislevy, Beaton, Kaplan, and Sheehan (1992), and Mislevy, Johnson, and Muraki (1992) describe these methods. Description and discussion of more recent developments can be found in von Davier, Sinharay, Oranje, and Beaton (2006) as well as in Adams and Wu (2007).

Selecting a booklet design
Selecting a suitable booklet design for the reporting needs of the assessment program requires careful consideration of many factors and an analysis of the advantages and disadvantages of the different options that are available and possible. The exact booklet design is a response to the specific needs of the assessment program, and a booklet design that is suitable for one program might not be suitable for another. Note that we qualify the design chosen as "suitable" rather than as "right" or "correct." We do this because the booklet design will only be "right" or "correct" to the extent that it is able to address all the needs of the assessment program. As we will see, the "right" booklet design will always be a result of numerous compromises based on a multitude of factors, some of which we mention below.

---

2 We note here that when blocks are rotated across the different booklets, an assumption is made that the examinee will have time to reach all the items in the book, and that fatigue or other effects that may affect performance will not have set in.

The guiding factor in developing and choosing a booklet design is the purpose of the assessment. A critical question that needs to be asked during the development process is if the assessment is intended for selection, assigning grades, diagnosis, or for describing a population? When the assessment is designed for the purpose of individual or group decision-making, more measurement precision is necessary, which means that more items generally need to be included in the particular forms administered. In general, the booklet design should allow for the administration of a sufficient number of items on the domain of interest to ensure that the desired statistical precision requirement is met; however, in this regard, there are no absolutes. If the purpose of the assessments is to make decisions about individuals, as in admission tests, it is critical to ensure that individuals are measured with a high level of precision. This precision should, to the extent possible, be relatively uniform across the individuals, particularly around the points in the proficiency continuum where decisions will be made. However, if the purpose of an assessment is to describe skills of subgroups of interest, less precision is necessary at an individual level; sufficient precision must nevertheless be achieved at the subgroup level.

Once the purpose of the assessment is decided, a natural next choice is to consider how broad a domain we want to measure. For example, a Grade 8 student's assessment could include only content covered during Grade 8 or content covered up to and including material covered in Grade 8. A third option could include an assessment that measures content necessary to advance to Grade 9. Deciding on the assessment breadth also gives an idea of the breadth of the content that would need to be included in the assessment. In addition, it is important to consider the number of reporting domains and subdomains. For example, it may be desirable to report only overall mathematics achievement or, additionally, achievement in algebra, geometry, and numbers. The types of knowledge and skills assessed also help one make decisions about how many items are necessary to reliably measure the domains of interest. For example, reading assessments at lower grades usually consist of a one- to three-page text followed by a set of items referring to the text. Because of the time needed to read the text, it is not possible to administer, to any one individual, the numbers of items that can typically be administered during a mathematics or science test. The nature of a writing assessment usually limits the number of writing tasks to two or three during one session. Depending on the area assessed, the booklet design might accommodate more or fewer items.

The number of reporting scales is another important consideration in the booklet design. In general, a positive relationship exists between the number of reporting scales and the number of items that need to be included in the assessment (Embretson & Reise, 2000). As a general rule, and depending on the characteristics of the test items (mainly discrimination and difficulty), it is advisable to include 20 to 30 items per subscale in any given administration of a survey assessment (von Davier, Gonzalez, & Mislevy, 2009). But this choice ultimately depends on the content that needs to be covered as part of the domain. The content coverage requirement and measurement precision will provide the general guidelines for determining the optimal number of items per domain.

The topics in the domain of interest should be proportionately represented in the assessment. However, the number of items necessary is inversely related to their quality, as measured by the amount of information they provide. Nonetheless, it is important to consider that adding low discriminating items or off-target items does not make for better measurement, and that too few items, even if on target and discriminating, are unlikely to capture, in a useful way, the breadth of the domain measured. When there are five subscales, for example, using a rule of 20 to 30 items per subscale leads to an assessment of about 100 to 150 items. Clearly, these numbers represent too many items to administer to any single student within a reasonable period of time, assuming we want to avoid a speeded assessment.

Once we have determined how many items are necessary to cover the domain of interest, our next considerations are the time available to administer the tests, and the time necessary to complete the tasks in the assessment. We need to know not only how much time is available but how many items can reasonably be administered and answered during a given time period. Piloting the items will provide a good estimate of how much time is needed to answer the questions in the assessment. Items with a heavy reading load generally take longer, and younger examinees generally take longer because of the reading involved. Older examinees tend to be faster readers, and can also maintain their focus and attention for longer periods of time. Consequently, it is reasonable to test adults for longer periods.

Among the other matters that need to be considered when determining a suitable booklet design is how much time is available to administer the tests. In international studies such as TIMSS and PIRLS, participation in large-scale assessments does not carry high-stakes consequences for examinees or schools, and participation is voluntary. An overly time-consuming assessment will only discourage participation, and will be seen more as a disruption to the school day rather than as an opportunity to learn what examinees know and can do. Another time consideration is the length of the school's class and recess periods, which often need to be observed to minimize disruptions and distractions during test administration. Many schools around the world organize their day in 45- to 60-minute periods, with longer periods necessitating a break at some point. It is because of period lengths that assessments such as NAEP use 50 minutes of testing time. Other assessments, such as PIRLS, administer the booklets for Grade 4 in two 40-minute sessions with a 5- to 10-minute break in between. TIMSS uses two 45-minute sessions for Grade 8, with one 5- to 10-minute break in between. PISA, administered to 15-year-olds, uses two 60-minute sessions, with a 5- to 10-minute break in between.

It is also important to consider, with respect to the number of reporting scales in the assessment, how the actual results will be reported. For instance, will a unidimensional skill variable be reported in the assessment or will there be multiple proficiency variables, one for each of the subscales? As a general rule, the greater the number of variables that are reported, the greater the number of items needed to reliably estimate these scores across the population.

An additional and related consideration is whether results are reported as simple scale scores or as attainment of educational standards in the form of cut-scores or benchmarks in the achievement distribution. It is important, when reporting whether examinees have reached a particular point in the distribution, to make sure that the number and the quality of items administered across the population allow us to make such inferences with respect to the domain. A form generated dynamically and based on examinee responses to the items administered initially will allow us to effectively tailor an assessment to the level at which the examinee is ultimately classified, provided appropriate content-control algorithms are used. However, a static form administered to an examinee will need to measure, with an acceptable level of precision, different points in the distribution to make it possible to infer whether or not the examinee has met or surpassed such points in the distribution.

One last consideration is the number of times that the assessment will be administered. Assessments that are administered only once often require a simpler booklet design, whereas ongoing cyclical assessment programs require careful consideration of issues related to item-release policies, linking scores from one administration to the next and across all administrations, renewal of the framework, refreshment of the item pool, introduction of new components in the assessment, and last, but not least, risk of disclosure of the items and test security. The greater the number of administrations planned for an assessment, the greater the need for carefully considering all the issues mentioned above so that proper linking of the results from the administrations can take place, and so that adequate inference can be made from the assessment results.

Deciding on a booklet design depends on the answer to the questions posed above, and perhaps to some others that are unique to the particular assessment programs. Except for simple cases, no single booklet design will fit all programs, or will fit any one program. The design is always a compromise between what is desired and what is possible, given the specific circumstances and resources available. In a recent article, Frey, Hartig, and Rupp (2009) discuss in more detail many of the constraints that need to be considered when choosing a design.

Examples of booklet designs

Although booklet designs are specific to the assessment, we can classify them for explanatory purposes, and to elucidate a number of advantages and disadvantages of each kind.

In general, we can classify booklet designs into two overarching categories—*complete* and *incomplete* designs. In *complete* matrix booklet designs, all the forms contain all the items, and therefore all examinees are administered all items in the assessment. *Incomplete* matrix booklet designs are characterized by a design in which any one form has only a subset of the items, and any one examinee is administered only a subset of the total number of items. Even though a complete matrix booklet design requires all examinees to take all the items, the existence of multiple forms can rotate the position of the blocks within the forms. Reasons for this practice include controlling for position effects within the booklet or form, and preventing examinees from copying one another's responses during test administration.

A *balanced* booklet design is one in which each block of items is rotated to appear an equal number of times in each position within the forms across the entire booklet design. This feature is a desirable one if an order effect is suspected (i.e., the order of the items has an influence on examinees' responses to the items). A *balanced* booklet design controls for such an effect.

Tables 2 and 3 show examples of complete and incomplete matrix booklet designs, respectively, for a three-block assessment. In each table, the top set of rows shows an unbalanced booklet design, whereas the bottom set of rows shows a balanced booklet design. Under the incomplete booklet design, each form consists of only two blocks, or two-thirds of the assessment. This allows for a one-third reduction in test time or for the inclusion of 50% more items in the same amount of time as the complete booklet design. However, note that the first incomplete booklet design shown in Table 3 does not include a form in which Blocks A and C are administered together. As a consequence, we cannot directly compute the correlation between the items from these two blocks—an important aspect that many multivariate methods rely on and something the balanced booklet design shown will allow. An added complication might arise if Block B occurs in all forms. Because Blocks A and C occur in only one of the two forms, the precision of the parameter estimates for A and C will be less than that for Block B.

Table 2: Example of complete matrix booklet designs

Form	Blocks		
1	A	B	C
Form	Blocks		
2	A	B	C
3	B	C	A
4	C	A	B

Table 3: Example of incomplete matrix booklet designs

Form	Blocks	
1	A	B
2	B	C
Form	Blocks	
3	A	B
4	B	C
5	C	A

Incomplete booklet designs can also be generated dynamically, as is the case with some computer-delivered tests. Table 4 shows three booklet designs, each with different numbers of blocks. In this example, an examinee would be first administered an "average" block and, based on his or her performance on this block, would then be presented with an easier or more difficult block. Imagine a very able examinee who excels at an average block. The next block administered would be a "difficult" block. If the examinee performed poorly on this block, a somewhat less difficult block would be administered.

Table 4: Example of dynamic incomplete matrix booklet designs

Very easy	Easy	Somewhat easy	Average	Somewhat difficult	Difficult	Very difficult
A	B	C	D	E	F	G
A B	C D	E F	G H	I J	K L	M N
A B C	D E F	G H I	J K L	M N O	P Q R	S T U

When such an assessment is implemented, it is important that the screening block is of very high reliability to ensure the examinee is not routed to blocks that are too easy or too difficult. Including several blocks at each level also allows booklet designers to broaden the coverage of the domain. This practice minimizes exposure of items and prevents subsequent examinees from being administered the same sequence of items during an administration, thus lessening opportunities for cheating.

One booklet design that has many desirable characteristics is the 7-block Youden squares design, originally used in experimental biological research designs (Preece, 1990). This design is often referred to as the BIB7 design. Table 5 shows this design, which was first used in an educational assessment context in NAEP. Extensions of this design can also be found in assessments such as TIMSS and PISA. The design consists of seven blocks and seven forms, with each form containing three blocks. Each block appears once in each position in the design, and each block also appears once with each of the other blocks. Despite the desirable characteristics of the BIB7 design, the fact that there is an odd number of blocks for each form makes it unsuitable for administration in assessment situations involving two sessions with a break in between. Depending on the number of items within the blocks, and the time needed to answer them, this design is better suited for assessments conducted over one or three sessions.

Table 5: Balanced incomplete 7-block design (BIB7 or Youden squares design)

Form	Block		
1	A	B	D
2	B	C	E
3	C	D	F
4	D	E	G
5	E	F	A
6	F	G	B
7	G	A	C

The designs shown above illustrate just some of the possibilities available, and many of them can and often need to be extended over time. Table 6 shows a BIB7 design extended over four years of an annually administered assessment. In this design, one of the forms is released to the public every year. The released blocks are then replaced the next year. In the table, the released blocks are underlined, and the new blocks appear in bold. Note that as the assessment progresses from year to year, the item pool is renewed with new blocks and items. Year 4 of the assessment includes one block from Year 1 (G1), one from Year 2 (A2), two from Year 3 (B3 and E3), and three blocks from Year 4 (C4, D4, and F4). After the release of Form 4 in Year 4, the Year 1 items will no longer appear in the design.

Table 6: Balanced incomplete 7-block design over four years

Form	Year 1			Year 2			Year 3			Year 4		
1	_A1_	_B1_	_D1_	A2	B2	D2	A2	B3	D2	A2	B3	**D4**
2	B1	C1	E1	_B2_	_C1_	_E1_	B3	C3	E3	B3	**C4**	E3
3	C1	D1	F1	C1	D2	F1	_C3_	_D2_	_F1_	**C4**	D4	F4
4	D1	E1	G1	D2	E1	G1	D2	E3	G1	_D4_	_E3_	_G1_
5	E1	F1	A1	E1	F1	A2	E3	F1	A2	E3	**F4**	A2
6	F1	G1	B1	F1	G1	**B2**	F1	G1	**B3**	**F4**	G1	B3
7	G1	A1	C1	G1	**A2**	C1	G1	A2	**C3**	G1	A2	**C4**

AN EXAMINATION OF PARAMETER RECOVERY USING DIFFERENT BOOKLET DESIGNS

Analytical Approach

We used the above examples of different booklet designs to examine how these designs influence the recovery of the parameters that were used to generate the data. In particular, we used a simulated dataset to investigate how well we could recover the generating parameters for the population and the items, and to determine the effect of these designs on reporting group-level results. Knowing the generating values is useful when comparing estimates that try to recapture these values.

For our analysis, we generated mathematics proficiency-skill levels for 4,000 cases crossed with two known background characteristics—school type with Levels A and B, and socioeconomic status (SES), also with two levels, high (H) and low (L). This approach resulted in four (2x2) distinct groups, each with 1,000 cases. We simulated the average difference in mathematics skills between School Types A and B to be 0.000, and we set the average difference based on parental SES to 1.414. The average ability level was +0.707 for the SES H group, and -0.707 for the SES L group. Let us for now ignore considerations as to whether these assumptions about school and SES differences are particularly realistic or unrealistic, especially given that these variables may show different effects in different populations.

Table 7 presents the means and standard deviations that we used to generate the response data. We set the standard deviation within each of these groups to 0.707, which yielded a variance within each of the four groups of about 0.5 (or 0.707^2), and an overall variance and standard deviation of 1.000. The data that we used in this analysis were the same as those that von Davier et al. (2009) used in their analysis.

Table 7: Means and standard deviations (in parenthesis) used to generate the simulated dataset

		School					
		A		B		Total	
SES	L	-0.707	(0.707)	-0.707	(0.707)	-0.707	(0.707)
	H	+0.707	(0.707)	+0.707	(0.707)	+0.707	(0.707)
	Total	0.000	(1.000)	0.000	(1.000)	0.000	(1.000)

We simulated the responses of all examinees to a pool of 56 items, assuming a two-parameter logistic response model (2-PL). The 2-PL describes the probability of a correct response to an item as a function of the person's ability, and the discrimination and difficulty parameter of the item. In the 2-PL IRT model, the probability of a correct response is given by:

$$P(x_i=1 \mid \theta_k, a_i, b_i) = \frac{1}{1 + \exp^{(-1.7\, a_i\, (\theta_k - b_i))}}$$

where

x_i is the response to item i, and 1 if correct and 0 if incorrect;

θ_k is the proficiency of an examinee on scale k;

a_i is the slope parameter or discrimination of item i; and

b_i is the location parameter or difficulty of item i.

Item difficulties were distributed uniformly between -1.0 and +1.0. Item discriminations ranged between 0.5 and 1.5. No correlation was built in between difficulty and discrimination, and the items were randomly assigned to each block.

We simulated the responses to the items under four different conditions:

1. All examinees were administered the 56 items.

2. Items were randomly assigned to one of seven blocks, labeled A, B, C, D, E, F, and G. Based on the form booklet design, every examinee was administered three blocks (24 items in total) in the assessment pool. The design organized the blocks according to the BIB7 design described earlier. The resulting forms were (ABD), (BCE), (CDF), (DEG), (EFA), (FGB), and (GAC).

3. Every examinee responded to two blocks (16 items in total) in the assessment pool; the blocks used were the same as those composed for (2). The blocks were organized into seven pairs as follows: (AB), (BC), (CD), (DE), (EF), (FG), and (GA).

4. Items were randomly assigned to one of 14 blocks, named A through N. Every examinee responded to two of these blocks (eight items in total) in the assessment

pool. These blocks were organized into 14 pairs as follows: (AB), (BC), (CD), (DE), (EF), (FG), (GH), (HI), (IJ), (JK), (KL), (LM), (MN), and (NA).

No block order effects were introduced into the simulation. The item parameters used to generate the data thus stayed the same for the items, even when administered in different block positions.

We next calibrated the items with PARSCALE Version 4.1 (Muraki & Bock, 1997), using marginal maximum likelihood estimation procedures. We used EAP (expected a posteriori) estimators to compute the reliability estimates for each examinee, and we then compared the results for each of the four conditions in terms of their ability to recover the generating parameters. Because EAP scores are point estimates, aggregating EAP scores leads to underestimation of the variance of the population. We compared achievement means and standard deviations overall and by subgroups. We also computed correlations between the estimates and the generating parameters, and constructed plots to display graphically the differences and the effects of the different designs.

Results

We present the results in two sections. In the first, we present the comparison between the generating ability and the EAP estimates obtained from the analysis under each of the four conditions. In the second section, we present the comparisons between the generating item parameters and the estimates of the item parameters. In total, we conducted 100 simulations. The results presented in the tables that follow are the average results for the simulations.

Comparing person ability estimates

Table 8 presents the number of cases within each simulation group, defined by the number of items administered to the examinees, the average true and estimated person ability of these cases, and their corresponding standard deviations. Tables 9 and 10 present the same results, but broken down by the two background variables used to generate the simulated data. We note again that because we simulated no school effect, the overall means by school are the same. We did, however, simulate a SES effect, such that those in the group SES Type H were more able than those in SES Type L.

Table 8: Means and standard deviations overall

Number of items	N	Average true score	Average EAP score	Standard deviation of true ability	Standard deviation of EAP estimate
8 items	4,000	-0.010	0.007	0.994	0.872
16 items	4,000	-0.010	0.010	0.994	0.933
24 items	4,000	-0.010	0.012	0.994	0.956
56 items	4,000	-0.010	0.015	0.994	0.984

Table 9: Means and standard deviations, by school

Number of items	School	N	Average true score	Average EAP score	Standard deviation of true ability	Standard deviation of EAP estimate
8 items	A	2,000	-0.027	-0.006	0.980	0.868
16 items	A	2,000	-0.027	-0.004	0.980	0.925
24 items	A	2,000	-0.027	-0.002	0.980	0.947
56 items	A	2,000	-0.027	-0.002	0.980	0.972
8 items	B	2,000	0.007	0.020	1.008	0.876
16 items	B	2,000	0.007	0.024	1.008	0.940
24 items	B	2,000	0.007	0.025	1.008	0.965
56 items	B	2,000	0.007	0.031	1.008	0.995

Table 10: Means and standard deviations, by SES

Number of items	SES	N	Average true score	Average EAP score	Standard deviation of true ability	Standard deviation of EAP estimate
8 items	H	2,000	0.686	0.559	0.721	0.674
16 items	H	2,000	0.686	0.632	0.721	0.669
24 items	H	2,000	0.686	0.659	0.721	0.708
56 items	H	2,000	0.686	0.694	0.721	0.720
8 items	L	2,000	-0.706	-0.545	0.698	0.676
16 items	L	2,000	-0.706	-0.611	0.698	0.691
24 items	L	2,000	-0.706	-0.636	0.698	0.699
56 items	L	2,000	-0.706	-0.664	0.698	0.703

In general, Tables 9 and 10 show that the EAP estimate of the mean overall and by school, where there were no simulated group differences, matched the overall true mean of the simulated data. However, one noticeable difference between the EAP scores and the generating abilities was that as the number of items decreased, so too did the variability of the estimated posterior means of abilities. The latter reached only 0.87 when eight items were administered, whereas the standard deviation for the generating abilities was 0.994, overall. We observed similar differences when we broke down the results by school type. When we inspected the results by SES, we noticed not only that the variability decreased, as it did overall and by school type, but also that the means for these two groups and, as a consequence, the differences between these two groups, diminished. The reason behind this effect is explained in von Davier et al. (2009).

In Table 11, we present the student-level correlation between the generated simulated scores and the ability estimates. Consistent with the previous results, the reduction in variation as the number of items administered decreased paralleled a decrease in the correlation between these variables. (These values are also a measure of the reliability of the measurement.)

Table 11: Correlations between "true" and estimated ability

Number of items	Correlation
8 items	0.869
16 items	0.925
24 items	0.946
56 items	0.974

Figure 1 presents the plots of the ability estimates obtained from the simulations under the two extreme conditions (8 items and 56 items per person), plotted against the true ability used to generate the data. The plots include the regression line and 95%-confidence intervals for the data. These plots provide further evidence that as the number of items administered increased, so too did the correspondence between the estimated ability and the true ability of the subjects. Figure 1 allows us to observe graphically what the previous tables illustrated numerically: as the number of items increased, the variability of the scores also increased, approaching the true variability of ability, while the distribution of true scores at any one point on the continuum of the estimated abilities diminished, indicating better precision of the estimates.

Figure 2 shows the plots of the standard errors of the EAP scores, again from one simulation, plotted against the EAP estimate, under the two extreme conditions. As we expected, the estimates toward the extreme of the distribution, where measurement was *less* precise, had larger standard errors, while the estimates toward the center of the distribution, where measurement was *more* precise, tended to be smaller. The higher precision toward the center of the distribution occurred because the difficulties of the item parameters used in this simulation ranged between -1.0 and +1.0, resulting in more precise measurement in this area of the distribution. Also worth noting in these plots is the pattern that we expected: as the number of items increased, the error of the estimates decreased. But notice also that the decrease or increase in the average error is not proportional to the change in the number of items. For example, the average error at the center of the distribution ranges from 0.40 to 0.50 when 8 items are administered, whereas it is about 0.18 when all 56 items are administered.

The last set of results comparing person ability estimates, perhaps the set that should raise more concerns among those interested in estimating group differences using matrix booklet designs, is shown in Figures 3 through 6. Again, remember that in our simulation we introduced a SES effect, but there were no differences between school types. In these figures, we plotted the true and estimated average difference between examinees from each of these groups (School A and B or SES types L and H), at each percent-correct score (of the total items) in the distribution. (We use the percent-correct metric in these plots because it better illustrates our point.) Note that in Figures 3 and 4 there are virtually no differences by school type in the theta metric, except in the extremes. These differences were eliminated in the EAP metric. Thus, examinees at any percent-correct point of performance along the distribution received about the same estimated score regardless of the type of school they were attending (Figure 4); this is what we would expect, given the true scores (Figure 3).

Figure 1: Plots of "true" ability against estimated ability, by numbers of items administered

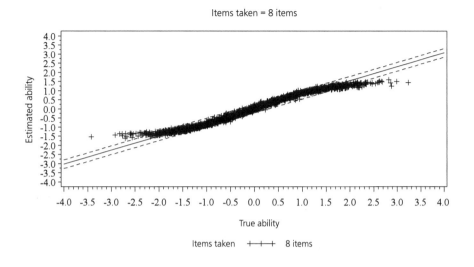

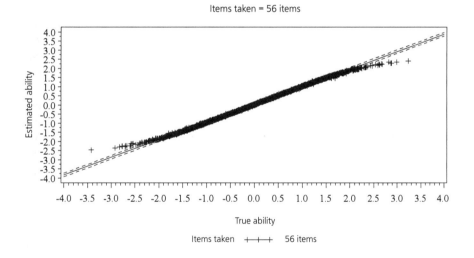

Figure 2: Plots of estimated ability against the standard error of the estimate, by numbers of items administered

Items taken = 8 items

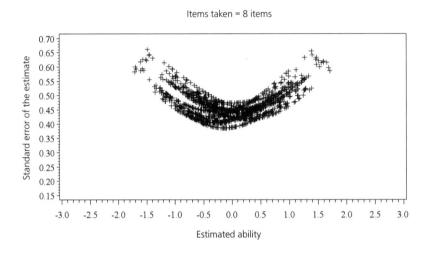

Items taken = 56 items

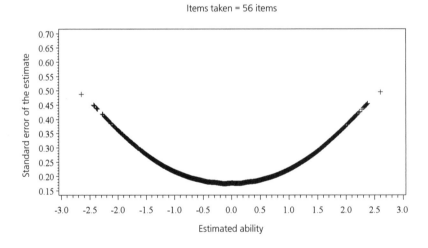

Figure 3: Plot of true (theta) average differences between examinees from Schools A and B, by percent correct

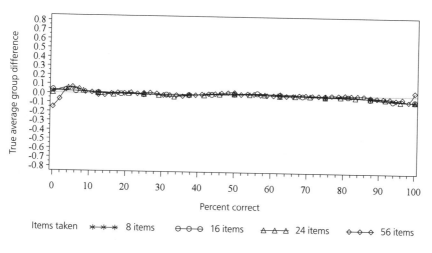

Figure 4: Plot of estimated (EAP) average differences between examinees from Schools A and B, by percent correct

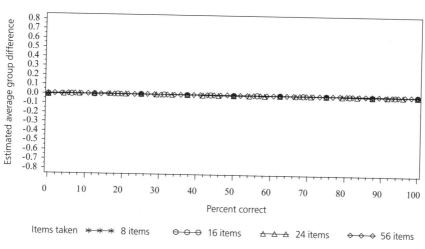

However, when we look at these results by SES type in Figures 5 and 6, we notice that although examinees who obtained the same percent-correct score (as is clear from the true scores in Figure 6) had, on average, different true abilities, depending on their SES type, these differences did not show up in the EAP scores. In other words, real group differences were underestimated, and the degree to which these differences were underestimated increased noticeably as the number of items administered decreased.

How one can properly estimate these differences is beyond the scope of this paper, but it is the subject of the paper by von Davier et al. (2009). Of concern to us in this paper is the fact that, as the number of items decreased, our estimates of a person's ability became less reliable, and we underestimated group differences in the population, when these existed. These findings likely lead the reader to ask, "How many items are necessary?" The answer is, "It depends"—on the number of items needed to sufficiently cover the domain of interest and on the quality of the items. We can only say for certain that there was a meaningful relationship between the number of items and estimate precision. For individual score reporting, the 24 and 56 items seemed to yield sufficient reliability. Note that even in the 16-item case, we estimated a reliability of above .9. However, in real applications, this estimate might not be as easy to achieve. Simulated data are far cleaner in the sense that these simulated examinees produce responses that follow the model perfectly.

Comparing item parameter estimates

When reviewing the results of the item parameter estimates, keep in mind that because of the rotation of each block within each design, the items were administered to samples of varying sizes. When all 56 items were administered to all examinees, each item was attempted by the total sample of 4,000 people. With a 24-item administration, each block appeared in three of seven total books. As such, each item had about 1,700 responses under this design. In the designs with 16 and 8 items, each item had just 1,150 and 570 examinee responses per item, respectively. To maintain consistency with the previous section, we present the results for the item parameter recovery by number of items administered to an individual.

Tables 12 and 13 present descriptive statistics for the difficulty and discrimination parameters. While the estimates did not exactly match the true parameters, we found no particular pattern in the data. In fact, we can see from the tables that even when the examinee sample size was reduced to 570, as was the case when each individual was administered only eight items, the distribution of the estimated item difficulties and discrimination was, on average, fairly close to the true difficulty and discriminations. Table 14 provides further evidence of this finding. Here, we can observe that the correlation between the estimated parameters and the true parameters, particularly the difficulty parameters, was close to 1.0. This correspondence was also true of the discrimination parameter; however, the correlation decreased slightly as the number of respondents decreased.

Figure 5: Plot of true (theta) average differences between examinees from SES L and H, by percent correct

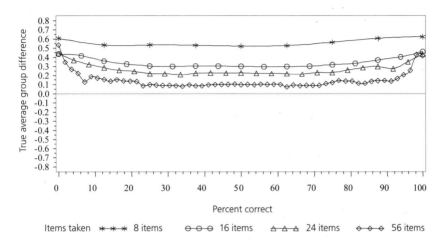

Figure 6: Plot of estimated (EAP) average differences between examinees from SES L and H, by percent correct

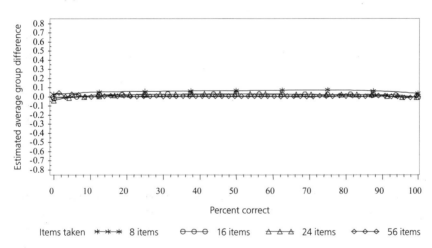

Table 12: Descriptive statistics of item difficulty parameter estimates, by number of items administered

Number of items	Average true difficulty	Average estimated difficulty	Standard deviation of true difficulty	Standard deviation of estimated difficulty
8 items	-0.064	-0.032	0.529	0.531
16 items	-0.064	-0.024	0.529	0.549
24 items	-0.064	-0.034	0.529	0.516
56 items	-0.064	-0.040	0.529	0.536

Table 13: Descriptive statistics of item difficulty parameter estimates, by number of items administered

Number of items	Average true discrimination	Average estimated discrimination	Standard deviation of true discrimination	Standard deviation of estimated discrimination
8 items	0.929	0.951	0.249	0.260
16 items	0.929	0.927	0.249	0.264
24 items	0.929	0.939	0.249	0.266
56 items	0.929	0.931	0.249	0.253

Table 14: Correlations between item parameter estimates and true parameters

Number of items	Correlation of difficulty	Correlation of discrimination
8 items	0.983	0.936
16 items	0.994	0.966
24 items	0.996	0.972
56 items	0.999	0.992

Figures 7 and 8 support the previous findings with respect to the fairly close match between the difficulty estimates and the true difficulties, regardless of the condition. To save space, we present only the plots for when students were administered 8 and 56 items. The plots of conditions in between simply showed a continuation of the observed pattern.

Figure 7 presents the plots of the estimated item difficulties with the true item difficulties, along with the linear regression line and the 95% confidence interval. Here, and again as we expected, as the number of respondents to the items increased, so too did the precision with which the item difficulties were estimated. In Figure 8, which plots the difficulty estimates against the error of the estimates, we can observe the expected pattern of a slight U-shaped spread, indicating that the difficulty estimates for the more difficult and easier items were not as precise as the estimates of the items toward the middle of the continuum—the area containing most of the distribution of respondents. Nonetheless, as the number of people responding to the items increased, the precision increased, particularly at the extremes of the distribution.

Figure 9 shows the plots of the discrimination parameter estimates against the true discrimination parameters, and Figure 10 illustrates the plots of the discrimination parameter estimates against the error of the estimate. As with the difficulty parameter, we can see that the estimates were well matched to the distribution of true parameters, and that this match improved as the number of items administered to any one individual—and, as a consequence, the number of respondents per item—increased. A pattern different from that observed with the difficulty estimates is the positive and linear relationship between the item discrimination estimate and the error of the estimate. However, this relationship weakened as the number of respondents per item increased. This was because more information from responses was available for use in the estimation of the discrimination parameter.

Figure 7: Plots of difficulty estimates against "true" difficulty, by number of items administered

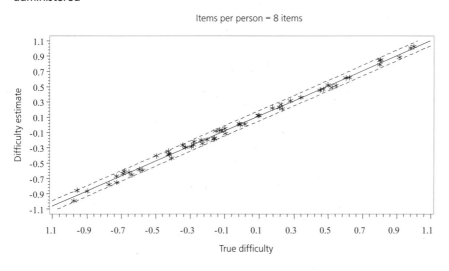

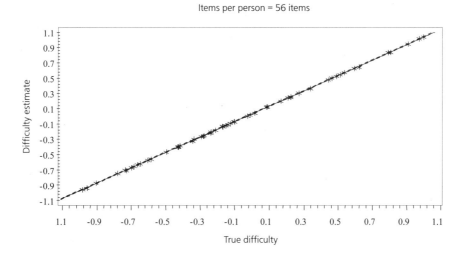

Figure 8: Plots of estimated difficulty against the standard error of the estimate, by number of items administered

Items per person = 8 items

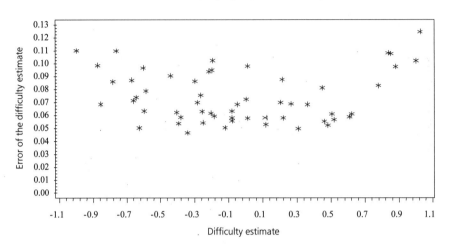

Difficulty estimate

Items per person = 56 items

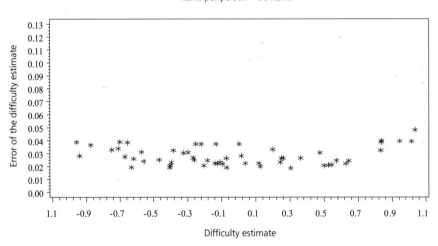

Difficulty estimate

Figure 9: Plots of discrimination estimates against "true" discrimination, by number of items administered

Items per person = 8 items

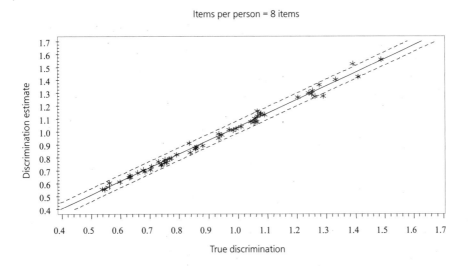

Items per person = 56 items

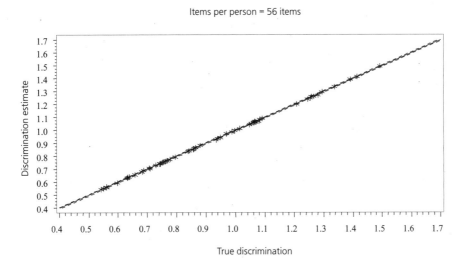

Figure 10: Plots of estimated discrimination against the standard error of the estimate, by numbers of items administered

Items per person = 8 items

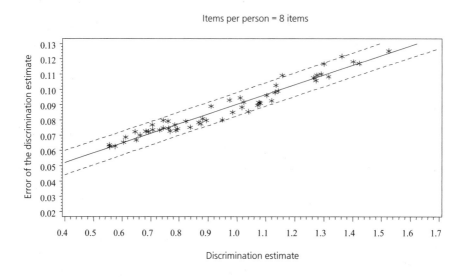

Items per person = 56 items

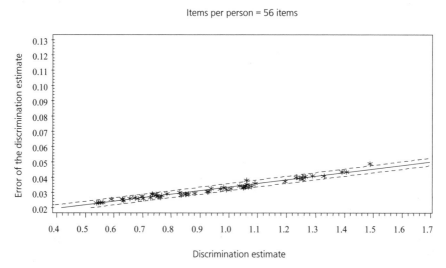

CONCLUSIONS AND RECOMMENDATIONS

In this article, we have discussed issues that test developers and other interested parties need to consider when developing a booklet design. Underlying all of the issues that we have mentioned is the purpose and use that will be made of the assessment results, the breadth of the content that is intended to be covered, the time available for administering the assessment, and the precision of the resulting estimates that is expected or tolerable. We also presented a few examples of multiple matrix sampling booklet designs and discussed their advantages and disadvantages. Finally, we used simulated data to describe the effects of a few different simulated designs on the parameter estimates obtained.

In general, we hope that readers understand that choosing one design over another is a decision based on trade-offs. More precision is obtained with more items, but these do require more response time per examinee and more time and expense in terms of item development. Fewer items administered per person results in less precise estimates; however, respondent burden is reduced. In the end, test developers and psychometricians need to come together to explore the consequences of the different options and to develop a design that ensures proper coverage of the domain assessed and proper coverage of the population assessed. They also need, throughout this process, to ensure that the levels of precision achieved are acceptable with respect to the reporting purpose. Using simulated data or using item and examinee samples from real data collected in previous assessments will help answer some of these questions.

In discussing the results presented in this paper, we should point out that they are based on simulated data with specific characteristics, and therefore in some sense are relatively clean compared to what can be expected from real data stemming from operational data collection. It is likely, therefore, that different results would be obtained if real assessment data were used. For example, in the simulations, we used a well-targeted set of items, with difficulties well within the range of the abilities of the respondents. These items, moreover, were administered to random samples of respondents, with abilities normally distributed around the area where items provide more information.

We did not include, in our simulations, conditions such as order effects, skewed score distributions of students, and mismatch of the test information such as curve to the ability of the population of interest, or other effects that might have adversely influenced the results if a model had been used that did not take these into account. Different and perhaps unexpected results might be obtained by simulating (among other conditions) sets of items that poorly measure the ability levels of the population, by simulating items administered to distributions that are skewed, and by simulating situations where there are numerous missing data due to non-response rather than missing by design. Those wanting to investigate the effects or consequences of the different designs should conduct similar simulations with empirically obtained item parameters and ability distribution characteristics.

References

Adams, R. J., & Wu, M. L. (2007). The mixed-coefficients multinomial logit model. A generalized form of the Rasch model. In M. von Davier & C. H. Carstensen (Eds.), *Multivariate and mixture distribution Rasch models: Extensions and applications* (pp. 55–76). New York: Springer.

Barcikowski, R. (1972). A Monte Carlo study of item sampling (versus traditional sampling) for norm construction. *Journal of Educational Measurement*, 9(3), 209–214.

Beaton, A. E. (1987). *Implementing the new design: The NAEP 1983/1984 technical report*. Princeton, NJ: Educational Testing Service, National Assessment of Educational Progress.

Beaton, A. E., & Zwick, R. (1992). Overview of the National Assessment of Educational Progress. *Journal of Educational Statistics*, 17(2), 95–109.

Bock, R. D., Mislevy, R. J., & Woodson, C. (1982). The next stage in educational assessment. *Educational Researcher*, 11(3), 4–11.

Embretson, S., & Reise, S. (2000). *Item response theory for psychologists*. Mahwah, NJ: Lawrence Erlbaum.

Frey, A., Hartig, J., & Rupp, A. (2009). An NCME instructional module on booklet designs in large scale assessments of student achievement: Theory and practice. *Educational Measurement: Issues and Practice*, 28(3), pp. 39–53.

Gressard, R., & Loyd, B. (1991). A comparison of item sampling plans in the application of multiple matrix sampling. *Journal of Educational Measurement*, 28(2), 119–130.

Johnson, E. J. (1992). The design of the National Assessment of Educational Progress. *Journal of Educational Measurement*, 29(2), 95–110.

Johnson, M., & Lord, F. (1958). An empirical study of the stability of a group mean in relation to the distribution of test items among students. *Educational and Psychological Measurement*, 18(2), 325–329.

Kleinke, D. (1972). *The accuracy of estimated total test statistics*. Washington, DC: National Center for Educational Research and Development. (ERIC Document Reproduction Service No. ED064356)

Knapp, T. (1968). An application of balanced incomplete block design to the estimation of test norms. *Educational and Psychological Measurement*, 28, 265–272.

Lord, F. (1962). Estimating norms by item-sampling. *Educational and Psychological Measurement*, 22(2), 259–267.

Lord, F. (1965). *Item sampling in test theory and in research design* (ETS Research Bulletin No. RB-65-22). Princeton, NJ: Educational Testing Service.

Mislevy, R. J. (1983). Item response models for grouped data. *Journal of Educational and Behavioral Statistics*, 8(4), 271–288.

Mislevy, R. J. (1984). Estimating latent distributions. *Psychometrika*, 49, 359–381.

Mislevy, R. J. (1991). Randomization-based inference about latent variables from complex samples. *Psychometrika*, 56, 177–196.

Mislevy, R. J., Beaton, A. E., Kaplan, B., & Sheehan, K. M. (1992). Estimating population characteristics from sparse matrix samples of item responses. *Journal of Educational Measurement*, *29*(2), 133–161.

Mislevy, R. J., Johnson, E. G., & Muraki, E. (1992). Scaling procedures in NAEP. *Journal of Educational Statistics*, *(17)2*, 131–154.

Mislevy, R. J., & Sheehan, K. M. (1987). Marginal estimation procedures. In A. E. Beaton (Ed.), *The NAEP 1983–84 technical report* (No. 15-TR-20). Princeton, NJ: Educational Testing Service, National Assessment of Educational Progress.

Mullis, I., Kennedy, A., Martin, M., & Sainsbury, M. (2006). *PIRLS assessment framework and specifications*. Chestnut Hill, MA: Boston College.

Mullis, I., Martin, M., Ruddock, G., O'Sullivan, C., Arora, A., & Erberber, E. (2005). *TIMSS 2007 assessment frameworks*. Chestnut Hill, MA: Boston College.

Munger, G., & Loyd, B. (1988). The use of multiple matrix sampling for survey research. *Journal of Experimental Education*, *56*(4), 187–191.

Muraki, E., & Bock, R. D. (1997). *PARSCALE: IRT item analysis and test scoring for rating scale data* [computer software]. Chicago, IL: Scientific Software.

Myerberg, N. J. (1975, April). *The effect of item stratification in multiple-matrix sampling*. Paper presented at the annual meeting of the American Educational Research Association, Washington, DC.

Nair, K. R. (1943). Certain inequality relations among the combinatorial parameters of balanced incomplete block designs. *Sankhyā*, *6*, 255–259.

National Center for Educational Statistics. (2010). *About NAEP*. Retrieved from http://nces.ed.gov/nationsreportcard/about/

Neidorf, T., & Garden, R. (2004). Developing the TIMSS 2003 mathematics and science assessments and scoring guides. In M. O. Martin, I. V. S. Mullis, & S. J. Chrostowski (Eds.), *TIMSS 2003 technical report* (pp. 23–66). Chestnut Hill, MA: Boston College.

Olson, J., Martin, M., & Mullis, I. (Eds.). (2008). *TIMSS 2007 technical report*. Chestnut Hill, MA: Boston College.

Organisation for Economic Co-operation and Development (OECD). (2006). *Assessing scientific, mathematical, and reading literacy: A framework for PISA 2006*. Paris: Author.

Plumlee, L. (1964). Estimating means and standard deviations from partial data: An empirical check on Lord's sampling technique. *Educational and Psychological Measurement*, *14*(3), 623–630.

Preece, D. A. (1990). Fifty years of Youden squares: A review. *Bulletin of the Institute of Mathematics and Its Applications*, *26*, 65–75.

Pugh, R. (1971). Empirical evidence on the application of Lord's sampling technique to Likert items. *Journal of Experimental Education*, *39*(3), 54–56.

Reiser, M. (1983). An item response model for the estimation of demographic effects. *Journal of Educational Statistics*, *8*(3), 165–186.

Rubin, D. (1976). Inference and missing data. *Biometrika*, *63*, 581–592.

Rubin, D. (1978). Multiple imputations in sample surveys: A phenomenological Bayesian approach to nonresponse. *Proceedings of the Section on Survey Research Methods, American Statistical Association* (pp. 20–34). Alexandria, VA: American Statistical Association.

Rubin, D. (1987). *Multiple imputation for nonresponse in sample surveys*. New York: Wiley.

Scheetz, J., & Forsyth, R. (1977, April). *A comparison of simple random sampling versus stratification for allocating items to subtests in multiple matrix sampling*. Paper presented at the annual meeting of the National Council on Measurement in Education, New York.

Shoemaker, D. M. (1970a). Allocation of items and examinees in estimating a norm distribution by item sampling. *Journal of Educational Measurement*, *7*(2), 123–128.

Shoemaker, D. M. (1970b). Item-examinee sampling procedures and associated standard errors in estimating test parameters. *Journal of Educational Measurement*, *7*(4), 255–262.

Shoemaker, D. M. (1973). *Principles and procedures of multiple matrix sampling*. Cambridge, MA: Ballinger Publishing Company.

van der Linden, W. & Carlson, J. (1999). *Calculating balanced incomplete block design for educational assessments*. Paper presented at the National Assessment Governing Board Achievement Levels Workshop, Boulder, CO.

van der Linden, W., Veldkamp, B., & Carlson, J. (2004). Optimizing balanced incomplete block designs for educational assessments. *Applied Psychological Measurement*, *28*, 317–331.

von Davier, M., Gonzalez, E., & Mislevy, R. (2009). Plausible values: What are they and why do we need them? *IERI Monograph Series: Issues and Methodologies in Large-Scale Assessments*, *2*, 9–36.

von Davier, M. Sinharay, S., Oranje, A., & Beaton, A. (2006). Statistical procedures used in the National Assessment of Educational Progress (NAEP): Recent developments and future directions. In C. R. Rao & S. Sinharay (Eds.), *Handbook of statistics: Vol. 26. Psychometrics* (pp. 1039–1055). Amsterdam, The Netherlands: Elsevier.

Yates, F. (1939). The recovery of inter-block information in variety trials arranged in three-dimensional lattices. *Annals of Eugenics*, *9*, 126–156.

A blind item-review process as a method to investigate invalid moderators of item difficulty in translated assessment items

Enis Dogan
American Institutes for Research, Washington DC, United States
Ruhan Circi
Bogazici University, Istanbul, Turkey

The purpose of this study was to explore the utility of a blind item-review process as a method for investigating whether test items designed for cross-cultural use include invalid moderators of difficulty. An invalid moderator of difficulty is an item characteristic that affects students' ability to demonstrate their true competence. The item review process suggested here was applied to the Third International Mathematics and Science Study-Repeat (TIMSS-R) eighth-grade science items translated from English into Turkish. First, an item review tool featuring 13 statements was developed. Each statement targeted a specific invalid moderator of difficulty. A sample of 100 Turkish teachers rated an intermixed pool of TIMSS-R and "local" science items (items developed originally in Turkish) on each statement. The teachers did not know the source of the items. Mean teacher ratings of the TIMSS-R and the local items were computed and compared. TIMSS-R items had significantly lower ratings on all 13 statements. Mean teacher ratings on five of the 13 statements correlated significantly with the differences between p-values for the Turkish sample and the average p-values for the international cohort.

INTRODUCTION

We conducted this study in order to determine if a blind item-review process provided a method for investigating whether test items designed for cross-cultural use include invalid moderators of difficulty. An invalid moderator of difficulty is an item characteristic that affects students' ability to demonstrate their true competence. Invalid moderators of difficulty can potentially lead to construct-irrelevant variance in test scores. Invalid moderators emerge when an item has unnecessarily complex language (for a given grade or age level) and unfamiliar graphs, charts, and tables (i.e., material that is not commonly used in classrooms at a given grade level). Other problematic features include unfamiliar technical terms (e.g., scientific and mathematical terms that have not been introduced in the classrooms), words, and phrases. The context in which the item is posed can also be an invalid moderator, depending on the learning experiences of the target student population. In this study, we used Third International Mathematics and Science Study-Repeat (TIMSS-R) eighth-grade science items translated from English into Turkish in order to explore the utility of our item review process.

TIMSS and the Validity of International Assessments

The Trends in International Mathematics and Science Study (TIMSS) is one of the world's most comprehensive international comparative studies of educational achievement. Designed to assess and compare the mathematics and science achievement of students from different countries, the study also allows for cross-national comparisons of educational background variables. TIMSS has been administered every four years thus far—in 1995, 1999, 2003, and 2007.

TIMSS-R was conducted under the auspices of the International Association for the Evaluation of Educational Achievement and included 38 countries. It assessed the mathematics and science achievement of Grade 8 students (ages 13 and 14) and was based on the mathematics and science curricula of the participating countries. Content areas included in the science assessment were earth science, life science, physics, chemistry, environmental and resource issues, scientific inquiry, and nature of science (Gonzalez & Miles, 2001). The science assessment included 146 items: 42 constructed-response (CR) and 104 multiple-choice (MC). All items used in TIMSS-R were first developed in English and then translated into 32 languages, including Turkish. TIMSS-R translation guidelines called for two independent translations of each test instrument from English to the target language. A translation review team compared the two translations to create the final version. O'Connor and Malak (2000) document and discuss the details of these processes.

International studies such as TIMSS are designed to provide data useful to educational policymakers. Multiple factors have the potential, however, to undermine the validity of the results obtained from international assessments. For example, Hambleton, Yu, and Slater (1999) argue that the alignment between the topics covered in international assessments and the national curriculum of each country can affect countries' performances. Different degrees of alignment can thus undermine the validity of comparisons made across countries. Ramseier (1999) also argues that close alignment between a national curriculum and an international assessment indicates the relevance of comparisons of achievement for that country.

As Pollitt and Ahmed (2001) argue, if the items used in international assessments, such as TIMSS, do not measure the intended constructs (e.g., science or mathematics), the results regarding the relative performance of the participating countries cannot be valid. Pollitt and Ahmed also point out that unless the cognitive processes invoked in students' minds match the ones intended by the item writers, the items lose their validity. The two authors explain that the level of familiarity students have with the context of the items (the story around which the problem is constructed) is a key factor in students' understanding of the tasks that these items require. For example, a mathematics item that discusses subway stations might not be familiar to students living in areas without a subway system.

TIMSS recognizes that it is important when "comparing student achievement across countries ... that the comparisons be as fair as possible" (Mullis et al., 2000, p. 379). Because of concerns about the relationship between assessment results and curriculum-to-assessment alignment, TIMSS conducted a test-curriculum matching analysis (TCMA). The national research coordinator (NRC) from each participating country was asked to choose someone who was familiar with the mathematics and science curricula of the grade tested to determine the extent to which the tests were relevant to those curricula. During this process, the rater deemed an item appropriate if it was in the intended curriculum for more than 50% of the students. The details of this process can be found in Mullis et al. (2000). A group of Turkish experts concluded that over 95% of all science items in TIMSS-R fit the intended national curriculum for Turkey.

Despite this close alignment, Turkey ranked 34th out of the 38 participating countries in terms of TIMSS-R science achievement. We can offer a number of potential explanations for the relatively poor performance of Turkish students on the TIMSS-R science assessment besides the obvious one that the achievement of Turkish students after eight years of formal education is low. For example, Turkish students might have been less motivated to complete a low-stakes assessment, such as TIMSS-R, compared to the high-stakes assessments to which they are accustomed. It is also possible that both low motivation and poor performance resulted from the differences between the enacted curriculum to which the Turkish students were exposed and the content of the TIMSS-R science assessment. This conjecture, however, does not readily accord with the Turkish experts' opinion that 95% of the TIMSS-R items were covered in the national curriculum.

These possible explanations for Turkey's poor performance on TIMSS-R also apply to the other participating countries. For instance, TIMSS-R was a low-stakes assessment for all students participating in the study. Also, differences between what TIMSS-R measured and what was taught in the classrooms existed for all countries because the curricula of each differed.

Translation/Adaptation of Achievement Tests and Invalid Moderators of Item Difficulty

A major challenge in TIMSS-R is that the assessment is developed in English and translated and administered in different languages to students with different learning experiences. A substantial body of literature illustrates how the difficulty and meaning of test items can be affected when they are administered in different languages to students with different learning experiences (Abedi, 2006; Abedi & Gandara, 2006; Ercikan, Gierl, McCreith, Puhan, & Koh, 2004; Gierl & Khaliq, 2001; Hambleton, 2005; Sireci, Patsula, & Hambleton, 2005; Solano-Flores, Contreras-Nino, & Backhoff, 2006; Solano-Flores & Trumbull, 2003; van de Vijver & Poortinga, 2005).

Several researchers (e.g., Allalouf, Hambleton, & Sireci, 1999; Gierl & Khaliq, 2001) have used differential item functioning (DIF) analyses to identify translated/adapted test items that exhibit different psychometric features for different groups of students taking the test in different languages. After identifying DIF items, the analyst's next step is to examine the items in order to uncover the sources of DIF. Our approach was different. We decided not to examine items known to display DIF because we considered that these *post hoc* comparisons could bias experts' judgment of what might be wrong with a given item. We hypothesized that certain characteristics of the translated TIMSS-R science items contributed to the poor performance of Turkish students. We called such characteristics "invalid moderators of difficulty." An invalid moderator of difficulty is an item characteristic that affects students' ability to demonstrate their true competence (Leong, 2006).

In his 2006 article, Leong discusses factors that affect the difficulty of test items. He introduces an item difficulty framework that includes content difficulty, stimulus difficulty, task difficulty, and expected response difficulty. Leong defines content difficulty as the difficulty of the subject matter assessed: "In the assessment of knowledge, the difficulty of a test item resides in the various elements of knowledge such as facts, concepts, principles and procedures" (p. 3). The content difficulty level has three categories—basic (very familiar to the learner), appropriate (central to the core curriculum), and advanced (something the learner may not have had the opportunity to learn). He argues that content difficulty increases as more knowledge elements are involved in an assessment.

Stimulus difficulty is related to understanding the words, phrases, and representations (e.g., diagrams, tables) used in an item. Test items containing words and phrases that require only simple and straightforward comprehension are usually easier than those that require careful or technical comprehension. Task difficulty refers to the complexity of the process involved in producing an answer or formulating a solution. Generally, items that include more than one step to reach the solution are classified as harder items than those that do not require this step. The level of guidance provided in the items and the complexity of the cognitive processes also affect the difficulty of a task.

Expected response difficulty is reflected in the scoring rubrics. The level of detail in an expected response to the item determines the response difficulty level. In Leong's (2006) framework, this aspect of difficulty applies to CR items only, and is most likely to occur when examinees are unclear about the demand of a response and do not produce an answer that is sufficient to earn marks that reflect their abilities. Leong discusses moderators of difficulty that prevent a valid measurement of the construct of interest. Moderators can prevent examiners from assessing students' knowledge in terms of the intended construct, because, as we noted earlier, test-takers who are faced with invalid moderators might not be able to demonstrate their true ability or competence.

Note that Leong's classification in itself does not say anything about the use of more or fewer difficult items for comparisons across countries. While the measurement accuracy may decrease with increasing difference between item pool difficulty and population ability, modern psychometric methods, such as the ones used in TIMSS, help prevent bias in those situations.

To make a moderator an *invalid* moderator, there needs to be construct-irrelevant variance that affects a subgroup or all of the population. In addition to determining the level of task difficulty, stimulus difficulty, and expected response difficulty, the analyst needs to assess whether these factors are affecting one or more subgroups in ways that differ from the ways affecting other subgroups. For example, if a physics item requires familiarity with subway maps in addition to content knowledge about classical mechanics, as taught in physics, these features would constitute invalid moderators. If the knowledge required in classical mechanics is simply higher than what is typically taught in a certain country, but nevertheless aligns with the curriculum, as agreed by the experts judging the TIMSS item, this feature might make the item too difficult for certain populations, but it would not involve invalid moderators of difficulty. This consideration would remain true as long as the probability of a correct response to the item increases with nothing other than physics-related skills and knowledge; in other words, knowledge and skills about things other than physics would not be required.

METHOD

We developed an item review tool, written in Turkish and based on the literature mentioned above and Leong's (2006) framework of moderators of item difficulty. The tool featured, along with Leong's moderators, descriptors that brought the total number of statements to 13. We then asked a sample of 100 school teachers to use these statements to rate, on a Likert scale, a set of 100 science items. We did not tell the teachers the source of the items.

As we describe below, 10 teachers rated each item. Fifty of these items were translated (i.e., items from TIMSS-R) and the rest were "local" items (items developed originally in Turkish to assess Turkish students). Thirteen of the 50 TIMSS-R items were CR items. Local items were either from a pool of items from the 1999 national test for eighth-graders[1] or they were items that teachers developed for formative classroom assessments. The national test, developed by the Turkish Ministry of Education, contained 24 items, all of which were MC. Of the remaining 25 classroom assessment items, six were CR and 19 were MC.

We assembled the local and the TIMSS-R items into blocks of five items, resulting in 10 blocks of local items and 10 blocks of TIMSS-R items. We then arranged these blocks in 100 booklets, each of which included one local block and one TIMSS-R block. We randomly assigned blocks to booklets in a way that ensured that each of the 100 test items was rated by 10 teachers. (During this assignment step, we kept in place the constraint mentioned above, that is, each booklet to contain one local block and one TIMSS-R block.) Because each teacher received one booklet and rated only 10 items, the teachers were not overburdened. We asked the teachers to rate items according to the 13 statements in the item review tool. Some of the statements applied to MC items only.

The Raters

We recruited the 100 participating teachers through an email posted on a number of professional list-servers on internet. Participation was voluntary, and the teachers were not offered any incentive to participate. All teachers with at least two years of teaching experience at the sixth-, seventh-, or eighth-grade within the boundaries of Istanbul[2] at the time of the study (2008) were eligible to participate. We invited teachers to participate in a study to evaluate the quality and the appropriateness of science test items. We did not mention TIMSS during the recruitment and the data-collection phases. Nor did we mention that some of the items had been translated. Our aim, in this regard, was to keep the review process blind by ensuring that the teachers did not have the opportunity to detect hints from the items suggesting that they had been translated.

Seventy percent of the 100 teachers who agreed to participate were female. Thirty-one percent taught at public schools. The rest were teachers from various private schools. The median age of the participating teachers was 31. The median number of years of teaching experience was six.

Instrument

Table 1 sets out the wording of the item review tool in English. Table 2 provides the original version, written in Turkish. As noted above, we based the statements largely on Leong's (2006) taxonomy of invalid moderators of item difficulty. We asked the teachers to rate each of the test items on a Likert scale, where 1 indicated *strongly agree* and 5 indicated *strongly disagree*, and we instructed them to think about a typical student in their classroom while rating the items. In keeping with Leong's taxonomy, we divided the survey questions into four clusters: content (C), stimuli (S), task (T), and expected response (R) difficulty. Not all statements were applicable to all science items reviewed by the teachers. T2 and R2 applied to MC items only.

---

1 The national test determines students' access to high school.

2 This restriction was put in place to minimize the cost of conducting the study. Note, however, that roughly 15% of all students and 13% of all teachers in Turkey reside in Istanbul.

Table 1: Item review tool: A survey of difficulty factors and additional invalid moderators of item difficulty

Carefully read this science question. Think about how your students might approach this question. Think about the challenges they might face in understanding or solving this question. Now, rate this question on each of the following statements.

C1: The item includes concepts unfamiliar to students.
S1: There is inaccuracy or inconsistency in the information given in the item.
S2: There is insufficient information in the item to reach a clear answer.
S3: There is uncommon vocabulary in the item.
S4: There are grammatical errors in the item that can lead to misunderstanding.
S5: There are unfamiliar representations (diagrams, graphs, tables, pictures) in the item.
S6: The item includes unfamiliar terminology.
T1: There are unfamiliar sentence structures used in the item.
T2: Alternatives contain concepts unfamiliar to students.
T3: The problem is presented in an unfamiliar context.
T4: The stem of the item is misleading to the students.
R1: The item has a number of plausible correct answers.
R2: Alternatives are insufficient to reach the correct answer.

Note: C = Content difficulty, S = Stimulus difficulty, T = Task difficulty, R = Expected response difficulty.

Table 2: The original version of the item review tool in Turkish

Önünüzdeki fen bilgisi sorusunu dikkatlice okuyun. Öğrencilerinizin bu soruya nasıl yaklaşacağını düşünün. Soru çözmede yada anlamada karşılaşabilecekleri zorlukları düşünün. Simdi, bu soruyu asağıdaki önermeler için değerlendirin.

  1: Soru öğrenciler için tanıdık olmayan kavramlar içermekte.
  2: Soruda verilen bilgilerde tutarsızlık var.
  3: Soruda doğru yanıta ulaşmak icin yetersiz bilgi verilmiş.
  4: Soruda öğrenciler için tanıdık olmayan kelimeler kullanılmış.
  5: Soruda yanlış anlamaya sebep olabilecek dilbilgisi hatası var.
  6: Soruda verilen kaynaklar (diyagram, grafik, resim) ögrencilerin sık karşılaşmadığı türden.
  7: Soru öğrenciler için tanıdık olmayan terminoloji içermekte.
  8: Sorudaki kullanılan kelime dizilimi öğrencilerin aşina olmadığı türden.
  9: Cevap şıkları öğrencilerin alışık olmadıkları kavramlar içermekte.
 10: Sorunun içeriği (bağlam) öğrencinin ilgi kurabileceği türden değil.
 11: Soru cümlesi öğrencilerileri yanlış yönlendirecek tarzda.
 12: Sorunun birçok alternatif doğru cevabı var.
 13: Cevap şıkları öğrencilerin doğru yanıtı bulmaları için yetersiz.

Analysis

Our first step was to compute, for each science item rated in the study, the mean ratings and the associated variance (across raters) for all 13 statements in the item review tool. We recorded items with mean ratings lower than 3 for any of the 13 statements and labeled these as items with "poor" mean ratings. We then used a hierarchical linear modeling (HLM) approach to compare the items from different sources (i.e., TIMSS-R or local) according to their mean ratings on all 13 statements. Here, we treated the items as nested under teachers, an acknowledgment that ratings from different teachers on the same item constitute dependent observations.

RESULTS

Mean Ratings and Variation Across Ratings

We computed the mean rating and the associated variance (across 10 raters) for each item on the item review tool. Table 3 displays the range and the average value of these means and variances for each statement across all 100 items rated. The average mean ratings ranged from 3.67 (C1: unfamiliar concepts) to 4.03 (R2: insufficient alternatives). The average variance associated with these means ranged from 0.10 (T4: misleading stem) to 0.28 (T1: unfamiliar sentence structures). Note that lower variances indicate higher agreement among raters.

Table 3 also displays the range of the means and variances. For all 13 statements, the minimum value of the variance of ratings (across the 10 raters) was 0.00, indicating that there was at least one item where all raters gave the same rating. The actual number of items where there was a perfect agreement across all 10 raters ranged from 37 items for C1 (unfamiliar concepts) to 53 items for S4 (grammatical errors).

Table 3: The range and the average of means and variances of ratings on each of the 13 statements in the item review tool across the 100 items rated

	Mean			Variance		
	Min	*Max*	*Average*	*Min*	*Max*	*Average*
C1: unfamiliar concepts	1.00	4.50	3.67	0.00	1.21	0.27
S1: inaccurate/inconsistent information	1.40	4.90	3.93	0.00	1.11	0.15
S2: insufficient information	1.50	5.00	3.93	0.00	1.07	0.16
S3: uncommon vocabulary	2.00	5.00	3.88	0.00	1.07	0.15
S4: grammatical errors	1.30	5.00	3.94	0.00	0.99	0.11
S5: unfamiliar representations	2.00	4.70	3.86	0.00	1.11	0.23
S6: unfamiliar terminology	2.00	4.70	3.83	0.00	1.11	0.19
T1: unfamiliar sentence structures	2.10	4.80	3.80	0.00	1.11	0.28
T2: alternatives with unfamiliar concepts	1.40	5.00	3.89	0.00	1.07	0.16
T3: unfamiliar context	2.10	4.80	3.91	0.00	1.11	0.19
T4: misleading stem	2.10	5.00	3.99	0.00	0.77	0.10
R1: multiple plausible correct answers	2.00	5.00	3.89	0.00	1.11	0.22
R2: insufficient alternatives	2.30	5.00	4.03	0.00	1.11	0.11

Items With Poor Ratings

As we noted earlier, we regarded items with mean ratings (across raters) lower than 3 on the Likert scale as having poor mean rating. According to this criterion, 32 of the 100 items had poor mean ratings on one or more of the 13 dimensions in the item review tool. These items, 32 of which were TIMSS-R items, are listed with the corresponding mean ratings in Table 4.

Table 4 also displays the number of dimensions on which each of these items had poor mean ratings. The three local items, one a national test (NT) item and two classroom assessment (CA) items, had poor mean ratings on the same statement: C1 (unfamiliar concepts). Seven TIMSS items had poor mean ratings on four or more statements. One of these TIMSS items (Item 41 in Table 4) had poor mean ratings on seven of the 13 dimensions: C1 (unfamiliar concepts), S3 (uncommon vocabulary), S4 (grammatical errors), S6 (unfamiliar terminology), T2 (alternatives with unfamiliar concepts), T3 (unfamiliar context), and T4 (insufficient alternatives).

Table 4 furthermore shows the number of items with poor mean ratings for each of the 13 dimensions. S3 (uncommon vocabulary), S6 (unfamiliar terminology), and T1 (unfamiliar sentence structures) had the highest number of items with poor mean ratings. S3 (uncommon vocabulary) had 10, S6 (unfamiliar terminology) had 11, and T1 (unfamiliar sentence structures) had eight such items, all of which were from the TIMSS-R item pool.

Comparison of TIMSS and Local Items

After computing the mean ratings across raters on all 100 items for each of the 13 statements in the item review tool, we plotted the ratings according to item source (see Figure 1). As is evident from Figure 1, the mean ratings of the TIMSS-R items were lower than the mean ratings of the NT and CA items. However, the mean ratings of the NT and the CA items did not differ on any of the 13 statements. We accordingly combined these two types of items as "local items" in the next phase of analysis.

In order to test the significance of these differences, we conducted an HLM analysis in which we treated items as nested under teachers. We formulized the HLM model as follows:

Level 1: $Y_{ij} = \beta_{0j} + \beta_{1j} (Local) + \varepsilon_{ij}$
Level 2: $\beta_{0j} = \gamma_{00} + u_{0j}$
$\qquad \beta_{1j} = \gamma_{10}$

where Y_{ij} is the jth teacher's rating for item i and Local is a dummy variable that is 0 for TIMSS-R items and 1 for local items. We ran the model separately for each statement in the item review tool.

This approach accommodated the dependency among the teacher ratings for the same science item being rated. The analysis took into account the variance between teachers (raters). We then computed, within the same framework, the generalizability (G) coefficients, and partitioned the variance in ratings across the two levels (i.e., items and raters).

Table 4: Items with poor mean ratings by source, type, and total number of items with poor mean ratings on each of the 13 statements in the item review tool

Item	Source	Type	Number of poor ratings*	Mean teacher ratings												
				C1	S1	S2	S3	S4	S5	S6	T1	T2	T3	T4	R1	R2
Item 41	TIMSS	MC	7	1.4			2.3	1.3		2.8		1.4	2.6	2.9		
Item 6	TIMSS	MC	6		2.3	2.6	2.2	2.2	2.6		2.5					
Item 17	TIMSS	MC	5		2.5		2.8		2.0	2.0			2.1			
Item 38	TIMSS	MC	5				2.6			2.4		2.3			2.5	2.3
Item 8	TIMSS	MC	4		2.8			2.4	2.3	2.4						
Item 11	TIMSS	MC	4					2.9	2.6	2.7					2.0	
Item 56	TIMSS	CR	4			2.2	2.3			2.8			2.4			
Item 15	TIMSS	MC	3			2.7	2.4			2.6						
Item 31	TIMSS	MC	3					2.5			2.8				2.9	
Item 46	TIMSS	MC	3				2.2			2.2		1.9				
Item 4	TIMSS	MC	2				2.4				2.1					
Item 36	TIMSS	MC	2		1.4	1.5										
Item 45	TIMSS	MC	2							2.8		1.7				
Item 54	TIMSS	MC	2								2.8	2.1				
Item 57	TIMSS	MC	2							2.6		2.4				
Item 59	TIMSS	CR	2					2.5			2.7					
Item 76	TIMSS	CR	2				2.7			2.8						
Item 10	TIMSS	MC	1				2.0									
Item 19	TIMSS	MC	1		2.9											
Item 21	TIMSS	MC	1								2.2					
Item 25	TIMSS	MC	1	1.6												
Item 26	TIMSS	MC	1										2.8			

Table 4: Items with poor mean ratings by source, type, and total number of items with poor mean ratings on each of the 13 statements in the item review tool (contd.)

Item	Source	Type	Number of poor ratings*	Mean teacher ratings												
				C1	S1	S2	S3	S4	S5	S6	T1	T2	T3	T4	R1	R2
Item 39	CA	MC	1	1.6												
Item 61	TIMSS	MC	1								2.8					
Item 70	TIMSS	MC	1												2.3	
Item 73	CA	MC	1	1.0												
Item 82	NT	MC	1	1.2												
Item 84	TIMSS	MC	1			2.8										
Item 20	TIMSS	CR	1												2.4	
Item 40	TIMSS	CR	1								2.5					
Item 50	TIMSS	CR	1						2.9							
Item 68	TIMSS	CR	1											2.2		
Number of items with poor mean ratings				5	5	5	10	6	5	11	8	6	4	2	5	1

Notes:
* A poor item is defined as one with a mean rating lower than 3.
Only items with a mean rating lower than 3 are listed in the table.

Figure 1: Mean ratings on each of the 13 statements in the item review tool according to item source

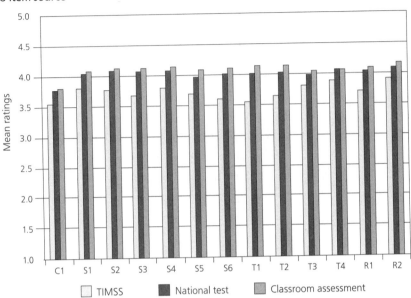

Note: Lower ratings indicate unfavorable ratings.

C1: unfamiliar concepts
S1: inaccurate or inconsistent information
S2: insufficient information
S3: uncommon vocabulary
S4: grammatical errors
S5: unfamiliar representations
S6: unfamiliar terminology

T1: unfamiliar sentence structures
T2: alternatives with unfamiliar concepts
T3: unfamiliar context
T4: misleading stem
R1: multiple plausible correct answers
R2: insufficient alternatives

The G coefficients ranged from .88 to .96 for the 13 statements in the item review tool, indicating that only a small portion of the variance in ratings was due to teachers. Table 5 presents a summary of the results of the HLM analyses. The table also depicts the differences between mean ratings (across raters and items). All comparisons were statistically significant. TIMSS-R items had significantly lower ratings on all 13 statements, indicating that the raters judged these items as more problematic than the local items on all dimensions.

Teacher Ratings and Item Difficulty

After observing that teachers rated the TIMSS-R items less favorably than the other items, we investigated whether these ratings were associated with the relative difficulty of TIMSS-R items for the Turkish sample compared to the international sample. We explored the relationship between the mean ratings on 13 survey questions and the difference between the percentage of correct values for the international and Turkish samples (p_{INT-TR}) for the TIMSS-R items. This correlation was across items, not raters; that is, it was based on the ratings across items on 13 statements and the percentage correct for each of these items.

Table 5: Mean ratings of TIMSS-R and local items on each statement in the item review tool and the results of significance test comparing these means

	TIMSS-R items		Local items		Mean comparisons with HLM			
	Mean	SD	Mean	SD	γ_{01}	SE	t	p
C1: unfamiliar concepts	3.53	0.73	3.79	0.73	0.25	0.03	8.23	0.00
S1: inaccurate/inconsistent information	3.80	0.55	4.05	0.25	0.25	0.03	9.88	0.00
S2: insufficient information	3.76	0.61	4.10	0.20	0.35	0.04	9.25	0.00
S3: uncommon vocabulary	3.67	0.70	4.09	0.21	0.42	0.04	10.63	0.00
S4: grammatical errors	3.79	0.64	4.10	0.18	0.31	0.04	8.98	0.00
S5: unfamiliar representations	3.68	0.54	4.03	0.28	0.34	0.04	8.72	0.00
S6: unfamiliar terminology	3.60	0.64	4.06	0.25	0.45	0.04	11.43	0.00
T1: unfamiliar sentence structures	3.54	0.61	4.06	0.22	0.52	0.04	12.22	0.00
T2: alternatives with unfamiliar concepts	3.64	0.83	4.07	0.22	0.38	0.04	9.16	0.00
T3: unfamiliar context	3.80	0.50	4.01	0.27	0.21	0.04	5.73	0.00
T4: misleading stem	3.92	0.41	4.06	0.15	0.15	0.03	5.44	0.00
R1: multiple plausible correct answers	3.70	0.59	4.08	0.30	0.37	0.04	9.06	0.00
R2: insufficient alternatives	3.91	0.42	4.12	0.24	0.19	0.03	7.05	0.00

Ratings on five survey items (S3, S4, S6, T3, and R1) correlated significantly ($p < .05$) with p_{INT-TR}. The correlation coefficients were -.46 (S4: grammatical errors); -.39 (R1: multiple plausible correct answers); -.37 (T3: unfamiliar context); -.33 (S6: unfamiliar terminology); and -.31 (S3: uncommon vocabulary). The negative but not strong significant correlation coefficients indicate an association between unfavorable ratings on these five statements and the Turkish students finding it relatively difficult to answer these TIMSS-R items correctly. The issue here is that, of these five statements, two (T3, S6) can be viewed as difficulty factors, which are, by themselves, not necessarily invalid moderators. A third statement (S3) could be viewed as a difficulty factor as well as an invalid moderator because of contextualized items that tap into construct-irrelevant sources of variance. Difficulty in correctly answering the remaining two items (S4, R1) could be due to factors associated with the translation or adaptation of them.

DISCUSSION AND CONCLUSIONS

An increasing number of countries are interested in participating in international assessments so that they can better understand the achievement of their student populations and assess the outcomes of their educational provision in relation to inputs, such as curricular materials and teacher training (Kellaghan & Greaney, 2001). However, the validity of the results of international assessments depends on the quality of the test translation and adaptation process.

In order to address this matter (among others), the International Test Commission adopted guidelines for translating and adapting tests for cross-cultural use (Hambleton, 2005). Two of these guidelines (p. 26) are especially relevant for international assessments such as TIMSS:

D1: Test developers/publishers should ensure that the adaptation process takes full account of linguistic, psychological, and cultural differences in the intended populations.

D3: Test developers/publishers should provide evidence that item content and stimulus materials (e.g., any passages) are familiar to all intended populations of interest.

We undertook our study to illustrate the utility of a blind item-review process designed to provide information, assuming the above guidelines were followed, about whether the translation/adaptation of test items used in an international assessments was done correctly. The item review process that we used in our study allowed for the detection of invalid moderators of difficulty in translated/adapted items designed for cross-cultural use. Such moderators can stem from differences in linguistic background and from content and stimulus familiarity, along with other factors.

Our study did, however, have several limitations. First, the apparent lack of literature on invalid moderators of difficulty means that our conceptual framework and item review tool need further evaluation. Second, the released TIMSS-R items that we used in the study were not necessarily representative of the larger pool of TIMSS-R science items in terms of content, cognitive demand, and linguistic features. Moreover, the content and the item-type distribution of the TIMSS-R and local items were not identical. Third, the raters in this study were mostly teachers from private schools in Istanbul. This group of teachers was not a representative sample of science teachers in Turkey, and the method we used to recruit them was not an ideal way to obtain a representative sample. Fourth, the limited burden that could be put on the science teachers who volunteered to participate also limited the number of ratings that could be required from each of them, which limited the data base for the study. More data points would have been valuable. Fifth, we based our item review tool largely on work conducted by Leong (2006).

These limitations need to be addressed in future studies designed to build on the blind item-review process and to improve the use of this process. Future studies also need to examine the dimensionality of this survey tool. And the tool itself could be improved by incorporating the work of others in the field. Abedi and Gandara (2006), Ercikan et al. (2004), and Hambleton, Merenda, and Spielberger (2005) are excellent such sources.

With refined items, and possibly a revised rating scale, the item review tool and the associated blind item-review process suggested here could serve as a valuable tool for practitioners and researchers alike who are interested in better translation and adaptation procedures for items used in international assessments. Such procedures would result in more valid items, free of invalid moderators of difficulty, which in turn would generate more valid results.

References

Abedi, J. (2006). Psychometric issues in the ELL assessment and special education eligibility. *Teachers College Record*, *108*(11), 2282–2303.

Abedi, J., & Gandara, P. (2006). Performance of English language learners as a subgroup in large-scale assessment: Interaction of research and policy. *Educational Measurement: Issues and Practices*, *26*(5), 36–46.

Allalouf, A., Hambleton, R. K., & Sireci, S. (1999). Identifying the causes of DIF in translated verbal items. *Journal of Educational Measurement*, *36*(3), 185–198.

Ercikan, K., Gierl, M. J., McCreith, T., Puhan, G., & Koh, K. (2004). Comparability of bilingual versions of assessments: Sources of incomparability of English and French versions of Canada's national achievement tests. *Applied Measurement in Education*, *17*, 301–321.

Gierl, M., & Khaliq, S. N. (2001). Identifying sources of differential item and bundle functioning on translated achievement tests: A confirmatory analysis. *Journal of Educational Measurement*, *38*(2), 164–187.

Gonzalez, E. J., & Miles, J. A. (2001). *TIMSS-R user guide for the international database*. Chestnut Hill, MA: Boston College.

Hambleton, R. K. (2005). Issues, designs, and technical guidelines for adapting tests into multiple languages and cultures. In R. Hambleton, P. Merenda, & C. Spielberger (Eds.), *Adapting educational and psychological tests for cross-cultural assessment* (pp. 3–38). Hillsdale, NJ: Lawrence Erlbaum.

Hambleton, R. K., Merenda, P., & Spielberger, C. (Eds.). (2005). *Adapting educational and psychological tests in cross-cultural assessment*. Hillsdale, NJ: Lawrence Erlbaum.

Hambleton, R. K., Yu, J., & Slater, S. C. (1999). Field-test of the ITC guidelines for adapting psychological tests. *European Journal of Psychological Assessment*, *15*(3), 270–276.

Kellaghan, T., & Greaney, V. (2001). The globalisation of assessment in the 20th century. *Assessment in Education*, *8*(1), 87–102.

Leong S. C. (2006, May). *On varying the difficulty of test items*. Paper presented at the annual meeting of the International Association for Educational Assessment, Singapore. Retrieved from http://www.iaea2006.seab.gov.sg/conference/download/papers/On%20varying%20the%20difficulty%20of%20test%20items.pdf

Mullis, I. V. S., Martin, M. O., Gonzalez E. J., Gregory K. D., Smith T. A., Chrostowski, S. J., ... O'Connor, M. K. (2000). *TIMSS-R: International science report*. Chestnut Hill, MA: Boston College.

O'Connor, K. M., & Malak, B. (2000). Translation and cultural adaptation of the TIMSS instruments. In M. O. Martin, K. D. Gregory, & S. E. Stemler (Eds.), *TIMSS 1999 technical report* (pp. 89–100). Chestnut Hill, MA: Boston College.

Pollitt, A., & Ahmed, A. (2001). *Science or reading? How students think when answering TIMSS questions*. Paper presented at the annual meeting of the International Association for Educational Assessment, Rio de Janeiro, Brazil.

Ramseier, E. (1999). Task difficulty and curricular priorities in science: Analysis of typical features of the Swiss performance in TIMSS-R. *Educational Research and Evaluation*, 5(2), 105–126.

Sireci, S., Patsula, L., & Hambleton, R. (2005). Statistical methods for identifying flaws in the test adaptation process. In R. Hambleton, P. Merenda, & C. Spielberger (Eds.), *Adapting educational and psychological tests for cross-cultural assessment* (pp. 93–116). Hillsdale, NJ: Lawrence Erlbaum.

Solano-Flores, G., Contreras-Nino, L. A., & Backhoff, E. (2006). Test translations and adaptation: Lessons learned and recommendations for countries participating in TIMSS, PISA, and other international comparisons. *REDIE: Electronic Journal of Educational Research*, 8(2).

Solano-Flores, G., & Trumbull, E. (2003). Examining language in context: The need for new research and practice paradigms in the testing of English-language learners. *Educational Researcher*, 32(2), 3–13.

van de Vijver, F., & Poortinga, Y. K. (2005). Conceptual and methodological issues in adapting tests. In R. Hambleton, P. Merenda, & C. Spielberger (Eds.), *Adapting educational and psychological tests for cross-cultural assessment* (pp. 39–61). Hillsdale, NJ: Lawrence Erlbaum.

INFORMATION FOR CONTRIBUTORS

Content

IERI Monograph Series: Issues and Methodologies in Large-Scale Assessments is a joint publication between the International Association for the Evaluation of Educational Achievement (IEA) and Educational Testing Service (ETS). The goal of the publication is to contribute to the science of large-scale assessments so that the best available information is provided to policy-makers and researchers from around the world. Papers accepted for this publication are those that focus on improving the science of large-scale assessments and that make use of data collected by programs such as IEA-TIMSS, IEA-PIRLS, IEA-Civics, IEA-SITES, U.S.-NAEP, OECD-PISA, OECD-PIAAC, IALS, ALL, etc.

If you have questions or concerns about whether your paper adheres to the purpose of the series, please contact us at IERInstitute@iea-dpc.de.

Style

The style guide for all IERI publications is the *Publication Manual of the American Psychological Association* (5th ed., 2001). Manuscripts should be typed on letter or A4 format, upper and lower case, double spaced in its entirety, with one-inch margins on all sides. The type size should be 12 point. Subheads should be at reasonable intervals to break the monotony of lengthy text. Pages should be numbered consecutively at the bottom of the page, beginning with the page after the title page. Mathematical symbols and Greek letters should be clearly marked to indicate italics, boldface, superscript, and subscript.

Please submit all manuscripts electronically, preferably in MS-Word format and with figures and tables in editable form (e.g., Word, Excel) to the editorial team at IERInstitute@iea-dpc.de and attach the Manuscript Submission Form, which can be obtained from the IERI website: www.ierinstitute.org. For specific questions or inquiries, send emails to editors at the same address. Only electronic submissions are accepted.

Author Identification

The complete title of the article and the name of the author(s) should be typed only on the submission form to ensure anonymity in the review process. The pages of the paper should have no author names, but may carry a short title at the top. Information in the text or references that would identify the author should be deleted from the manuscript (e.g., text citations of "my previous work," especially when accompanied by a self-citation; a preponderance of the author's own work in the reference list). These may be reinserted in the final draft. The author (whether first-named or co-author) who will be handling the correspondence with the editor and working with the publications people should submit complete contact information, including a full mailing address, telephone number, and email addresses.

Review Process

Papers will be acknowledged by the managing editor upon receipt. After a preliminary internal editorial review by IERI staff, articles will be sent to two external reviewers who have expertise in the subject of the manuscript. The review process takes anywhere from three to six months. You should expect to hear from the editor within that time regarding the status of your manuscript. IERI uses a blind review system, which means the identity of the authors is not revealed to the reviewers. In order to be published as part of the monograph series, the work will undergo and receive favorable technical, substantive, and editorial review.

Originality of Manuscript and Copyright

Manuscripts are accepted for consideration with the understanding that they are original material and are not under consideration for publication elsewhere.

To protect the works of authors and the institute, we copyright all of our publications. Rights and permissions regarding the uses of IERI-copyrighted materials are handled by the IERI executive board. Authors who wish to use material, such as figures or tables, for which they do not own the copyright must obtain written permission from IERI and submit it to IERI with their manuscripts.

Comments and Grievances

The Publications Committee welcomes comments and suggestions from authors. Please send these to the committee at IERInstitute@iea-dpc.de.

The right-of-reply policy encourages comments on articles recently published in an IERI publication. Such comments are subject to editorial review and decision. If the comment is accepted for publication, the editor will inform the author of the original article. If the author submits a reply to the comment, the reply is also subject to editorial review and decision.

If you think that your manuscript is not reviewed in a careful or timely manner and in accordance with standard practices, please call the matter to the attention of the institute's executive board.

Publication Schedule

There is one publication per year. This publication will consist of five to seven research papers. Manuscripts will be reviewed and processed as soon as they are received and will be published in the next available monograph series. In the event that, in a single year, there are more than seven accepted manuscripts, the editorial committee determines whether the manuscript(s) will be published the next year or in an additional monograph in the same year. Manuscripts are accepted any time of the year.